MODERNISM, ROMANCE AND THE *FIN DE SIÈCLE*

*Popular Fiction and
British Culture, 1880-1914*

In this book Nicholas Daly explores the popular fiction of the 'romance revival' of the late Victorian and Edwardian years, focusing on the work of such authors as Bram Stoker, H. Rider Haggard and Arthur Conan Doyle. Rather than treating these stories as Victorian Gothic, Daly locates them as part of a 'popular modernism'. Drawing on recent work in cultural studies, this book shows how the vampires, mummies and treasures hunts of these adventure narratives provided a form of narrative theory of cultural change, at a time when Britain was trying to accommodate the 'new imperialism', the rise of professionalism and the expansion of consumerist culture. Daly argues that the presence of a genre such as romance within modernism should force a questioning of the usual distinction between high and popular culture.

NICHOLAS DALY lectures in the Department of English, Trinity College, Dublin. He has published essays on popular fiction in such journals as *Novel, Literature and History, Texas Studies in Literature and Language* and *ELH*.

MODERNISM, ROMANCE AND THE *FIN DE SIÈCLE*

Popular Fiction and British Culture, 1880-1914

NICHOLAS DALY

CAMBRIDGE
UNIVERSITY PRESS

PUBLISHED BY THE PRESS SYNDICATE OF THE UNIVERSITY OF CAMBRIDGE
The Pitt Building, Trumpington Street, Cambridge, United Kingdom

CAMBRIDGE UNIVERSITY PRESS
The Edinburgh Building, Cambridge CB2 2RU, UK   http://www.cup.cam.ac.uk
40 West 20th Street, New York NY 10011-4211, USA   http://www.cup.org
10 Stamford Road, Oakleigh, Melbourne 3166, Australia

First published 1999

Printed in the United Kingdom at the University Press, Cambridge

Typeset in Baskerville 11/12.5pt [VN]

A catalogue record for this book is available from the British Library

Library of Congress cataloguing in publication data

Daly, Nicholas.
Modernism, romance, and the fin de siècle: popular fiction and
British culture / Nicholas Daly.
p.   cm.
Includes index.
ISBN 0 521 64103 9 (hardback)
1. English fiction – 19th century – History and criticism.
2. Popular literature – Great Britain – History and criticism.
3. English fiction – 20th century – History and criticism.
4. Literature and anthropology – Great Britain – History.
5. Adventure stories, English – History and criticism.
6. Gothic revival (Literature) – Great Britain.
7. Modernism (Literature) – Great Britain.
8. Culture in literature.   I. Title.
PR878.P68D35   1999
823'.809112 – dc21   98-55153 CIP

ISBN 0 521 64103 9 hardback

To the Dalys
and
Nicole Goldstein

Contents

Acknowledgements

In writing even such a slim volume as this I appear to have incurred too many debts to detail here. Among my principal creditors are those who supervised the doctoral dissertation on which this book is based: Nancy Armstrong, Neil Lazarus, Perry Curtis and Bill Keach. Less official support was lent in the same period by the Victorian Readers Group at Brown University, and by Jen Fleissner, Carolin and Hildegund Hah-nemann, Eric Slade, Garrett Sullivan, Len Tennenhouse, Cynthia Tolentino and Kristen Whissel. More recently, Claire Connolly, Ian Duncan, David Glover, Talia Schaffer and my colleagues at Trinity, especially Aileen Douglas, Nicholas Grene, Darryl Jones, Stuart Murray, and John Nash deserve thanks. I would like to thank Ray Ryan at Cambridge University Press for his help, and the press's anonymous readers for many helpful suggestions. Anne Fogarty, Pat Coughlan and Roger Henkle, who all made popular Victorian fiction seem like something worth studying, deserve a special mention, as do John Marx and Bob Scholes for some last-minute assistance. And for their unstinting support I would like to thank my family and Nicole Goldstein.

I am grateful to the Arts and Social Sciences Benefactions Fund at Trinity for enabling me to do additional research at the British Library.

An earlier version of chapter 1 appeared as 'Incorporated Bodies: *Dracula* and the Rise of Professionalism', *Texas Studies in Literature and Language* 39.2 (Summer 1997) 181–203. A shorter version of chapter 2 first appeared as 'Irish Roots: the Romance of History in Bram Stoker's *The Snake's Pass*', *Literature and History*, 3rd series 4.2 (Autumn 1995) 42–70. Chapter 3 first appeared as 'That Obscure Object of Desire: Victorian Commodity Culture and Fictions of the Mummy', *Novel: A Forum on Fiction* 28.1 (1994) 24–51. Copyright NOVEL Corp. © 1994. I thank the editors of these journals for their permission to reprint this material.

Introduction

We begin with a play and a party. In December 1899 *The Ghost*, a play by Henry James, Robert Barr, George Gissing, H. Rider Haggard, Joseph Conrad, H. B. Marriott-Watson, H. G. Wells, Edwin Pugh, A. E. W. Mason and Stephen Crane, had its first and last performance in a village schoolhouse in Sussex.[1] Besides the eponymous ghost, the *dramatis personae* seem uncannily familiar, including as they do a Dr Moreau, a Peter Quint and, with a nod to Gilbert and Sullivan, 'Three Little Maids from Rye'. To mark the arrival of the new century, Crane had invited a large party, including some of the authors of *The Ghost*, and other well-known men of letters, to spend Christmas and New Year's Eve with him and his wife at Brede Place, near Rye, a partly modernized medieval manor house. In his *Experiment in Autobiography* (1934), H. G. Wells tries to evoke the spirit of the occasion:

I remember very vividly a marvellous Christmas Party in which Jane and I participated. We were urged to come over and, in a postscript, to bring any bedding and blankets we could spare . . . We were given a room over the main gateway in which there was a portcullis and an owl's nest, but at least we got a room. Nobody else did – because although some thirty or forty invitations had been issued, there were not as a matter of fact more than three or four bedrooms available . . . Later on we realized that the sanitary equipment . . . dated from the seventeenth century . . . and such as there was indoors, was accessible only through the Girls Dormitory [sc. the nickname given to the large bedroom used by the women guests]. Consequently the wintry country-side next morning was dotted with wandering melancholy, preoccupied, men guests . . . I remember that party as an extraordinary lark – but shot, at the close, with red intimations of a coming tragedy . . . When we were not dancing or romping we were waxing the floor or rehearsing a play vamped up by A. E. W. Mason, Crane, myself and others.[2]

One of the festive highlights was the performance of this 'vamped up' play, a Gothic burlesque based on the story of an ancient giant who haunted Brede Place in halves, having been sawn in two by the men of

1

Kent and Sussex in former times. A. E. W. Mason had composed a rough outline, which Crane then circulated among his literary acquaintances, asking them to add a line or two. For instance, as Crane's biographer, R. W. Stallman, recounts, 'Joseph Conrad contributed one line to the play: "This is a jolly cold world", and George Gissing another: "He died of an indignity caught in running after his hat down Piccadilly".'[3] Wells recalled that 'it amused its authors and cast vastly [though] [w]hat the Brede people made of it is not on record'.[4] Only a few pages of this odd collaborative effort survive, Crane never intending the play to be performed again. The festivities themselves ended suddenly on a tragic note when Crane, who had tuberculosis, suffered a haemorrhage from which he was never fully to recover. Wells was called on to summon help: 'There was a bicycle in the place and my last clear memory of that fantastic Brede House party is riding out of the cold skirts of a wintry night into a drizzling dawn along a wet road to call up a doctor in Rye'.[5]

I have chosen to begin this study of late Victorian and Edwardian popular fiction and its relation to British culture with this amusing yet poignant literary episode because it shows the distinctness of this period in British cultural history in two ways. In the first place the party illustrates the emergent trends at the moment of what Andreas Huyssen has called the 'great divide' between elite and mass culture.[6] At first glance, the party at Brede Place appears to provide a tragicomic echo of a famous episode associated with the popular fiction of an earlier era: the party at the Villa Diodati near Geneva in 1816 at which Shelley, Mary Godwin, Lord Byron and John Polidori spun Gothic tales to pass the time, producing two of our most resonant literary figures – Victor Frankenstein's patchwork monster and the aristocratic vampire. While it is tempting to see Crane's party as a late Victorian Gothic counterpart to that original Gothic gathering, it is the *difference* between the popular adventure romances of the late nineteenth century, described by some recent critics as 'imperial Gothic', or 'urban Gothic', and that older Gothic fiction, that will provide one of the points of departure for this study. In its illustration of the gap between the literary culture of the Romantics and that of the late Victorians, Crane's party emblematizes that difference. The Brede Place episode does replay some of the themes of the Romantic original, but in a different key: despite the Gothic trappings and setting, it was very much 'nineteenth century up-to-date with a vengeance'.[7] For one thing, the performance of *The Ghost* smacks more of advertising than of spontaneous yuletide amusement. These were scarcely *private* theatricals: notices appeared in the *Daily Chronicle*, *The Manchester Guardian* and such local papers as the *South Eastern Advertiser* and the *Sussex Express*.[8] Likewise, the appearance of the play's title page in *The Academy*, a contemporary literary magazine, more suggests a carefully orchestrated publicity stunt than a simple *jeu d'esprit*. I do not mean to imply that what separates late Victorian fiction from the Gothic or Romantic fiction of Polidori or Mary Shellley is that one is the product of a commercial literary culture while the other is not. Obviously the Romantics were also part of a commercial literary culture – the attribution of one of the Villa Diodati stories, Polidori's 'The Vampyre', to the best-selling Byron was in itself a clever piece of marketing, for instance. Nevertheless, a system of publicity of the sort that Crane was exploiting in 1899 was predicated on a literary market of a much greater scale and complexity than that of 1816. The Brede Place episode, in other words, was oriented towards a nascent literary 'mass market', though this term is not altogether satisfactory, as we shall see. This transformation of the late Victorian literary market, memorably evoked in George Gissing's *New Grub Street* (1891), entailed, among other things, the disappearance of the three-decker novel, the waning of the power of the circulating libraries, and the appearance of a new strain of light periodical literature after the fashion of George Newnes's *Titbits*. More generally, the emergence of a literary mass market was, of course, part of the development of modern consumer culture in late nineteenth-century Britain. These nascent trends represent the context for Crane's play-cum-publicity stunt, and indeed for all of the texts I will be looking at in this study.

The second reason for my selection of the Brede Place episode as a curtain-raiser is that while it indicates the emergent mass-market tendencies of this literary culture, what was most 'modern' about it, it also very clearly shows some residual features that would soon vanish. Crane's theatrical New Year's house party represents one of the last appearances on the stage of history of a decidedly Victorian ensemble. What strikes us now as curious is the collocation of 'significant' writers (James, Conrad, perhaps Wells) with writers whom we associate with a very different brand of literature (Haggard, Mason, Barr). What, we might ask, are the authors of such proto-modernist works as *The Golden Bowl* and *Heart of Darkness* doing, collaborating and socializing with the writers of *King Solomon's Mines* and that archetypal imperial melodrama, *The Four Feathers*? We don't, however, have to resort to a theory of the special cultural space of parties to explain this conjunction of disparate talents. Rather we need to adjust our literary-historical perspective. For what we see now as a chasm between two distinct literary cultures, the great divide, was scarcely more than a crack in 1899. In many respects this was still a homogeneous literary culture. We can scarcely imagine Virginia Woolf and Edgar Wallace taking up the cudgels over the proper vocation of the novel twenty years later, but in the late nineteenth century it was possible for a champion of realism like Henry James and a defender of romance like R. L. Stevenson to do just that.[9] Authors whom we now see as 'serious' and those whose names we have all but wiped from the slate of literary history, or consigned to the nursery as writers of children's literature, debated the merits of their particular schools, but they did not see themselves as *radically* different in kind. They wrote for the same magazines, were published by the same houses, and, in the case of the men at least, sometimes belonged to the same clubs. The proto-modernist Henry James was a close friend of two of the most significant 'romancists': Robert Louis Stevenson and George Du Maurier. (In fact Du Maurier offered James the germ of the story that later became the best-selling *Trilby*, though James never used it.)[10] Joseph Conrad's work appeared in mainstream periodicals like *Blackwood's*, not in 'little magazines' of the kind that flourished when high modernism came into its own. Similarly, while one of the best-known *fin-de-siècle* periodicals, *The Yellow Book*, may look like a late Victorian anticipation of modernist literary reviews, its authors were far from constituting a 'movement' of the modernist sort, including as they did figures such as Baron Corvo and the young John Buchan as well as those more anxious to shine in the high aesthetic line. While the popular late Victorian adventure romance may look forward to the modern bestseller, then, it appeared in a literary market that was still comparatively undifferentiated. This would soon change.

THE ROMANCE AS POPULAR MODERNISM

To move from the curtain raiser to the main performance, in this study of late nineteenth-century and early twentieth-century popular fiction I will be arguing that this fiction in effect takes over from the domestic realist novel as the narrative flagship of middle-class Britain. Far from providing mere light entertainment, I will suggest that such popular fiction filled an important cultural role in turn-of-the-century Britain. This then, is an attempt at a cultural study rather than a strictly literary one, and, as will be evident, it owes more than a little to both the

American and British strains of cultural studies. I have described my focus as 'popular fiction', but the latter is a far from transparent term. The connection between the object of study and my cultural studies approach provides one way of thinking about this opacity. Indeed it would be possible to trace a pre-history of cultural studies by following the changing fortunes of the label 'popular' in twentieth-century literary and cultural theory.[11] Arguments over the term 'popular' have very much turned on the question of cultural function: if on the one hand the term 'popular' suggests some noxious pulp canned by the sinister 'culture industry' decried by Theodor Adorno and Max Horkheimer in their *Dialectic of Enlightenment*, on the other it may suggest the putative opposite of this, some residual, resistive core of working-class practice of the sort celebrated in the work of, say, E. P. Thompson. One aim of this study is to question the assumptions behind the former usage: far from being pure pulp fiction, I want to argue that the romance played an important part in British culture as a form of narrative theory of social change.[12] However, I am certainly not using the term 'popular' in the Thompsonian sense either, since what I am describing as popular fiction could perhaps be more accurately termed popular *middle-class* fiction, insofar as it was produced by, broadly speaking, middle-class writers for a middle-class reading public.

In the last fifteen years or so the Hobson's choice of Frankfurt School pessimism or 'folk' optimism has been superseded by a very different conceptual frame. As Tony Bennett points out, the impact of the work of Antonio Gramsci on British cultural studies has meant that popular culture is more often theorized as a field of struggle rather than any particular set of texts or practices.[13] More specifically, popular culture comes to be defined as the site where a dominant culture and a subordinated culture collide. For Stuart Hall, for example, 'what is essential to the definition of popular culture is the relations which define "popular culture" in a continuing tension (relationship, influence, antagonism) to the dominant culture'.[14] We cannot identify, therefore, a set of practices or texts that is always essentially popular, or oppositional; the dominant culture can assimilate the artifacts of an oppositional culture, and indeed, aspects of the dominant culture can be given an oppositional edge.[15] It follows that from this perspective there is no possibility of 'rescuing' some authentic, fully autonomous essence of the popular; rather the popular inhabits that grey area where the less powerful confront, adopt, adapt, or even reject the ideologies of a more powerful group.

This same emphasis on popular culture as a space of negotiation between terms rather than as a fixed set of texts, or images, or practices characterizes the rather different cultural studies approach of John Fiske. For Fiske:

> Popular culture is made by subordinated peoples in their own interests out of resources that also, contradictorily, serve the economic interests of the dominant . . . There is always an element of popular culture that lies outside social control, that escapes or opposes hegemonic force. Popular culture is always a culture of conflict. . . .[16]

For Fiske, therefore, 'there can be no popular dominant culture'.[17] While in part resembling Hall's description of popular culture as an arena of struggle for position between classes, Fiske's theorization of popular culture has more in common with Michel de Certeau's account of popular practice in *The Practice of Everyday Life*, where de Certeau describes the tricks, ruses and adaptive practices by which the subordinated resist the encroachments of the state, the ' "ways of operating" [that] constitute the innumerable practices by means of which users reappropriate the space organized by techniques of sociocultural production'.[18] To this extent Fiske's popular culture sometimes seems to shade into a resistive, authentic working-class culture, though like Hall, Fiske seems reluctant to identify popular culture exclusively with the working class (or indeed any class).

While extremely suggestive, none of these formulations exactly describes the way in which I wish to theorize the adventure fiction of late Victorian and Edwardian Britain. In fact what I want to argue for is something resembling that 'popular dominant culture' whose very existence Fiske denies. Writers like Stoker, Haggard or Du Maurier were not from a subordinate class, nor were they writing for such a class. To that extent they may appear to be part of that somewhat loosely defined dominant culture referred to by Hall and Fiske. But within that dominant culture they can scarcely be seen as representatives of 'high' or 'official' culture. The work that they produced would have been read by a broad section of the middle class, but it would probably have been thought of as 'light' literature rather than as anything more demanding or rewarding (the reception of R. L. Stevenson may be seen as a partial exception in this respect). John Frow has argued that in the late twentieth century the terms 'high' and 'low' no longer define different, class-linked, types of culture, but divisions within all cultural domains. That is to say both 'popular' (e.g. television) and 'highbrow' (e.g. opera) forms may be approached from the stance of the expert or that of the casual consumer. While middle-class culture at the end of the nineteenth century was more homogeneous than it is now, we can see that at both the level of production and consumption it was marked by some degree of aesthetic stratification. To this extent the phrase 'popular middle-class culture' does not seem to me to be oxymoronic. Thus while I shall continue to use the term 'popular', *faute de mieux*, to designate the texts under discussion, my use of the term does not exactly correspond to its use in the work of Hall or Fiske. If the late Victorian and Edwardian era can be analysed in terms of a jockeying for position between a dominant and a dominated culture, the texts I will be discussing here belong on the side of the dominant; I will not be reading them for the signs of subaltern 'resistance'.

It might seem more logical at this point to replace the term 'popular' with the less ambiguous 'middlebrow', but there are a number of other reasons for retaining the more ambiguous term. It is worth noting that Hall develops his definition of the popular as a relation rather than an essence in tandem with a discussion of British culture between the 1880s and the 1920s, which is at once the period of the romance revival and the period of the appearance of the modern 'culture industry'. Hall suggests that this is the moment when something resembling an autonomous working-class culture is reshaped by the expansion of the news media and other facets of the culture industry. The same, I would argue, is true of middle-class culture in this period. If the romance revival begins as part of a more or less identifiable popular middle-class culture, these origins do not determine its later fate; the iconic figures of the romance revival, such as Dracula, or the mummy, Dr Jekyll or indeed Dr Moreau, quickly find new roles within a popular culture less easily broken down in terms of its class address.[19]

In addition to shifts in the marketing and reception of traditional print media, there is a shift in the very modality of narrative. This was also the moment when the boundaries between middle-class and working-class culture were cut across by a powerful new medium: cinema. The narratives and figures of the popular middle-class fiction under consideration in this study gain a new currency when they become important components of that new medium as it enters its narrative fictional phase. Turn-of-the-century popular fiction, then, like the party at Brede Place, looks backwards to the nineteenth century as well as forwards to the more unstable terrain of present-day international popular culture.

Even in the 1880s just where the 'middle' might be was increasingly in doubt. The middle class expanded and changed in these years due to a number of factors. One of these was the increase in numbers engaged in white-collar, clerical occupations (attracting women as well as men). At the end of the nineteenth century, the novel continued to be a middle-class form, as it had largely been from its eighteeenth-century beginnings, but its middle-class readers were not in any simple sense the direct heirs to those who earlier embraced Richardson's *Pamela*, or even Eliot's *Middlemarch*. Late Victorian and Edwardian writers themselves considered this shift and its implications for cultural production: in *Howards End* (1910), for example, E. M. Forster dramatizes the expansion and internal stratification of the middle class through Leonard Bast, the lower-middle-class bibliophilic clerk, and his relationship with the comfortably intellectual and financially independent Schlegels. Bast's aspirations to the literary culture that the Schlegels take for granted comes to a tragic end when he dies beneath an overturned bookcase (Charles Wilcox, Margaret Schlegel's stepson, is more directly responsible for Bast's death, but the symbolism is hard to ignore).

The broadening definition of the term 'professional' is a more significant factor in the redefinition of the boundaries of the middle class. We will have cause to return to look at this factor in more detail, since the rise of an ethos of professionalism and expertise relates to the revival of romance in a very direct way. This connection shows up most clearly in the character repertoire of the romance, which not infrequently pits a team of men with particular skills – sometimes actual professionals – against some outside threat (*Dracula* is the most obvious example of this narrative pattern). I will be suggesting, in fact, that the romance, insofar as it can be linked to a specific class or class fraction, embodies the fantasies of this emerging professional group, whose power is based on their access to and control of certain forms of knowledge. If, as John Frow has argued, present-day cultural studies expresses the politics of a similar 'knowledge class', then my study of late Victorian culture may also be seen as a return to the 'primal scene' of cultural studies.[20]

This study follows the particular strand of *fin-de-siècle* popular fiction that contemporary critics styled the 'revival of romance'. This was the literary current that began to overwhelm the domestic novel in the 1880s, and it was initially most closely associated with R. L. Stevenson and H. Rider Haggard, whose *Treasure Island* (1883) and *King Solomon's Mines* (1885) did much to create the popular perception of a new direction in fiction. 'Romance', though, was also the genre in which

readers would have placed the work of Anthony Hope, Arthur Conan
Doyle, Bram Stoker, George Du Maurier and their many rivals for the
attention of the popular reading public.[21] While the phrase '*revival* of
romance' seems to suggest a return to earlier narrative forms, and a
hankering after some lost literary world, I will be arguing that the
'revived' romance was in fact a distinctively *modern* phenomenon, and
that it was shaped in the same historical mould as literary modernism. It
makes more sense, I will maintain, to shelf a narrative like *She* or *Dracula*
with the work of modernists like Joyce and Woolf than that of eight-
eenth- and early nineteenth-century practitioners of romance like Ann
Radcliffe, or Sir Walter Scott: the novels of Rider Haggard and Bram
Stoker no more represent a simple revival of older forms than does
Stephen Crane's Gothic play, in which the Ghost shares the stage with
Dr Moreau.

In arguing for the modernity of the romance revival, and for the
existence of a 'popular modernism', I am reworking the broader argument of Fredric Jameson's 1979 essay, 'Reification and Utopia in Mass
Culture', that 'both modernism and mass culture entertain relations of
repression with the fundamental social anxieties and concerns, hopes
and blind spots, ideological antinomies and fantasies of disaster, which
are their raw material'.[22] In effect I am extrapolating this argument back
to the moment when modernism and mass culture could begin to be
glimpsed as distinct phenomena, when the niche market in which both
take their place was emergent, not dominant. Indeed Jameson himself
moves in this direction in the final chapter of *The Political Unconscious*,
where he brings the formidable historicizing apparatus he develops in
that work to bear on the fiction of Joseph Conrad, who, as he points out,
seems to float 'somewhere in between Proust and Robert Louis Stevenson'.[23] The case of Conrad, Jameson suggests, should remind us that the
'breakdown of older realisms' leads not simply to modernism, but to
'two literary and cultural structures [viz. modernism and popular cul-
ture], dialectically interrelated and necessarily presupposing each other
for any adequate analysis'.[24]

In arguing for the kinship of modernism and mass culture Jameson is
at pains not to collapse the two. Crucial to his argument is the idea that
they handle their 'raw materials' in quite different ways, modernism
providing certain stylistic compensations for the loss of the ability to
map the historical totality, while mass culture operates in an essentially
narrative register, harmonizing perceived contradictions. The tendency
of the former, then, is towards the fetishism of style; that of the latter

towards allegories of resolution. If this division of cultural labour seems
at times a little too neat – for my purposes, at least, Jameson's analysis of
fiction in relation to modernity and reification seems itself to risk reifying
the fluid relationship between the romance and early modernism – it is a
salutary reminder that all modernisms, high or popular, are not the
same, with consequences for their reception.

For Jameson, that high modernism's inevitable tendency is toward
pure style is itself to be understood in terms of the rationalization of life
under industrial capitalism, and in particular the over-development of
certain human capacities (e.g. analysis, abstraction, quantification) and
the concomitant under-development of others (e.g. sight, taste). Freed
from a more integrated role in work, or research, the visual sense finds a
new autonomous role for itself in the arts, where Impressionism, for
example, 'offers the exercise of perception and the perceptual recom-
bination of sense data as an end in itself'.[25] But in turn such new
aesthetic pleasures can be seen to have a role in 'mak[ing] us increasingly at home in what would otherwise . . . be a distressingly alien reality.
Viewed in this way . . . modernism can be seen . . . as a final and
extremely specialized phase of that immense process . . . whereby the
inhabitants of older social formations are culturally and psychologically
retrained for life in the market system' (my emphasis).[26] As Jameson
himself acknowledges in the Conclusion to *The Political Unconscious*, such
historicizations may appear excessively functionalist. Nonetheless, for
my purposes, there is something extremely attractive in this attempt to
grasp modernism as a species of 'retraining', though I do not altogether
agree as to the variety of training that is involved. I would add two
further riders: firstly, to the effect that this retraining is achieved as much
by what I am calling 'popular modernism' as by its high cultural
analogues; and secondly that retraining may be something that subjects
embrace.

In defining the romance revival as a sibling of modernism rather than
as its unusually decrepit great uncle, I am also indebted to a number of
other critics who have begun to lay the groundwork for a broader
definition of modernism and modernity. Marshall Berman, for
example, usefully defines modernism as 'any attempt by modern men
and women to become subjects as well as objects of modernization, to
get a grip on the modern world and make themselves at home in it'.[27]
His list of modernists thus effortlessly accommodates Dickens, Marx
and Baudelaire as well as more obvious candidates like the Italian
Futurists, Joyce and Woolf. As part of this broadening of the scope of

modernism, Berman argues for the importance of 'modernism in the streets',[28] modernism conceived of as a form of popular practice.[29] If Andreas Huyssen in *After the Great Divide* has demonstrated how a certain strain of modernism attempts to define itself against a popular modernity projected outside its own frontiers, writers like Berman make it possible, and indeed necessary, to broaden our perspective on what counts as the experience of the modern. In the process he opens up a longer historical *durée* for modernism, and frees it from definition in terms of form only. While work of this sort leaves itself open to the accusation that it expands the range of meaning of modernism to the extent that the term becomes almost meaningless, it nevertheless provides a useful corrective to accounts of modernism, or indeed of popular fiction, that treat them as completely *sui generis*, and it suggests ways of tracing family resemblances across a range of literary expression.[30] Recent work like Ann Ardis's *New Women, New Novels: Feminism and Early Modernism*, or the essays collected by Maria DiBattista and Lucy McDiarmid in *High and Low Moderns: Literature and Culture, 1889-1939*, suggests that literary history is beginning to take account of the multiple affiliations of literary modernism. Certainly, the received wisdom that the only connection between modernism and popular culture is the tendency on the part of modernism 'to incorporate the ephemera of low culture to dramatize the differing, transcendent value of [its] own creations' has become very much open to question.[31]

That Berman's modernists include Baudelaire and Dostoevsky indicates another important aspect of this work of recontextualization, that is the degree to which it focuses on the nineteenth-century roots of twentieth-century culture. The pioneering figure in this archaeology of the twentieth century was, of course, Walter Benjamin, who traced the emergence of twentieth-century subjectivities among the streets, arcades and department stores of nineteenth-century Paris.[32] However, while largely agreeing with this view of the nineteenth century as a century of modernization, my study also draws on the work of those writers who have identified a cultural shift around the end of the nineteenth century and the beginning of the twentieth, in which the lineaments of a particular modern culture come more sharply into focus. Stuart Hall has referred to a 'profound transformation in the culture of the popular classes which occurs between the 1880s and the 1920s', but I would argue that the same is true for British culture *tout court*. His view that 'somewhere in this period lies the matrix of factors and problems from which *our* history – and our peculiar dilemmas – arise' is one that, *mutatis*

mutandis, I would share.[33] Important components of present-day international popular culture can indeed be traced back to the popular
fiction of the late nineteenth and early twentieth centuries: in that sense
it is 'our' culture, our history. While my focus here will be mainly on the
'revival of romance', then, this study is also an attempt to bring us closer
to a conception of the structure of feeling of a more broadly defined
modernity that would allow us to map the connections among certain
historical transformations, the popular fantasies and narratives that
accompanied them, and their high cultural analogues.[34]

There has been considerable critical reluctance to see the late Victorian romance as a modern form at all. Just as the critics of the 1880s
sought to assimilate the apparent novelty of the romance as a 'revival' of
an older literature, present-day critics have interpreted the romance as a
revenant, as the ghost of eighteenth-century Gothic fiction, rather than
as a new departure, labelling it as 'Victorian Gothic', 'imperial Gothic',
or even 'urban Gothic'.[35] Yet the term Gothic is not used by the critics of
the 1880s and 1890s with reference to the novels of Stevenson, Haggard,
Stoker and their peers. When did this gothicization of the romance
revival take place, and what difference has it made to our critical
understanding of *fin-de-siècle* popular fiction? To answer this question we
will have to make a short detour through the history of Gothic criticism.

THE CURRENCY OF GOTHIC

Gothic fiction may be considered for our purposes to have begun with
Horace Walpole's *The Castle of Otranto* in 1764, and to have enjoyed its
heyday from the 1790s to the 1820s.[36] As Terry Lovell has written,
Gothic in this period was not some minor subgenre escorting for a time
the realist novel on its inevitable rise, but rather the mainstream of
British fiction.[37] But while literary history has commemorated individual works by Ann Radcliffe (*The Mysteries of Udolpho, The Italian*),
Matthew Lewis (*The Monk*) and a few others, it has interred the vast
majority of Gothic novels without a marker. Certain problems attach to
the definition of the original Gothic school. It is not, in fact, all that easy
to distinguish such a Gothic school from contemporary fictional cur-
rents like the sentimental or Jacobin novel, or indeed the historical
romances associated with Sir Walter Scott. As Gary Kelly observes,
'sharp generic distinctions were not part of Romantic literary culture'.[38]
Contemporary accounts seem to indicate that, like sentimental fiction, a
prominent strand of Gothic dealt with 'virtue in distress', the trials of

vulnerable young heroines in an often violently patriarchal world, but that unlike the latter genre, its settings were historical, and more often continental than British. While some late Gothic tales – perhaps influenced by German Romanticism – like Mary Shelley's *Frankenstein*, or Polidori's 'The Vampyre', deal with what might be called monsters, such creatures are in fact pretty rare in British Gothic fiction. Much more to the fore are plots dealing with human protagonists in search of 'origins, identity, and family connections', as Ann B. Tracy puts it.[39] These are indeed very much the concerns of Walpole's seminal *The Castle of Otranto*, Clara Reeve's *The Old English Baron*, and the novels of Ann Radcliffe. The readership for this fiction (and for fiction in general, indeed) probably came for the most part from the gentry and the professional middle class.[40] In part, this was a consequence of economics: while subscription libraries placed expensive, multi-volume books in the hands of more people than could otherwise afford them, access to such novels was still relatively expensive, even if one had the leisure for it. Thus the readership for Gothic – except in its cheapest chapbook form – was still highly circumscribed, and these books could hardly be seen as 'popular' in the way the romances of the 1880s and 1890s would be. Certainly no Gothic novels are likely to have been read by as many readers as were the romances of a successful romancist like H. Rider Haggard. When W. T. Stead published *She* as the first book in his series of Penny Novels in 1903 – some fifteen years after its initial publication – he was still able quickly to sell more than half a million copies.[41]

What is so different about the popular fiction of the late nineteenth century? To take an obvious instance of a literary echo, isn't Castle Dracula the Castle of Udolpho displaced to eastern Europe? Isn't Jonathan Harker a direct literary descendant of Emily St Aubert? At some level, of course, it is, and he is. However, the level at which this is true is the strictly literary level rather than the more broadly cultural. It is possible, that is, to trace the origins of certain romance settings and certain romance characters (including monsters like the vampire) to the influence of the eighteenth-century Gothic novel, but this does not mean that these narrative features meant the same thing for Radcliffe's readers as they did for Stoker's. As Peter Bürger has asserted in the context of art history: 'whereas art forms owe their birth to a specific social context, they are not tied to the context of their origin or to a social situation which is analogous to it, for the truth is that they can take on different functions in varying social contexts'.[42] Literary echoes

cannot simply be viewed as evidence of cultural resemblances. Without
even taking account of such factors as differences in readership or the
shift from Radcliffe's four-volume 'Romance, Interspersed With Some
Pieces of Poetry' to Stoker's single-volume page-turner, we can see that
The Mysteries of Udolpho and *Dracula* offer very different cultural narratives. At the level of characterization, Jonathan Harker is not really a
hero in distress in the way that Emily St Aubert is a heroine in distress.
Descriptions of Jonathan's sensibility never threaten to halt the forward
motion of the plot, as is the case with Emily: most importantly for the
novel, he is a team-member more than an individual, and the project of
the novel, as I will show in chapter 1, is the installation of the team of
professional men as the rightful victors over such dangerous individual-
ists (coded as pre-modern anachronisms) as Count Dracula.

Nor does the politics of the body work in the same way in the two
texts; the superficial resemblance between the fascination with the
grotesque body in *Udolpho* and the lovingly detailed account of Lucy
Westenra's 'staking' in *Dracula* may distract us from important differences. Whereas the context for the earlier text, I would argue, is the
collision of pre-modern and modern modes of bodily representation, the
context for the other, as I will show, is the rise in the late nineteenth
century of a culture of experts, and the production across a wide range
of discourses of the woman's body and the domestic sphere as proper
objects of professional intervention. *Dracula* is not interested in the flesh
per se, but in its providing a field of activity for the expert's techniques,
vividly figured here in the master-discourse of medicine.

The popular fiction of the late nineteenth century was *not* identified as
Gothic by contemporary readers, and it took some time for critics to
forge a connection between the 'revival of Romance' and the Gothic
romance. In fact, the tendency among literary critics to extend the
application of the term Gothic from the late eighteenth to the late
nineteenth century is a recent one. The classic studies of Gothic fiction,
Montague Summers's *The Gothic Quest* (1938) and Devendra Varma's *The
Gothic Flame* (1957), make little attempt to construct such an over-arching
'Gothic tradition'. Edith Birkhead's *The Tale of Terror* (1921) does so only
by arguing for terror's universal literary appeal: 'the tale of terror
appeals to deeply rooted instincts, and belongs, therefore, to every age
and clime'.[43] But Birkhead's citation of 'deeply rooted instincts' reson-
ates with another important event in the history of Gothic criticism: the
adoption of Gothic by the surrealist André Breton, who saw Gothic as
an early attempt to channel unconscious thought processes into literary

creativity.[44] This post-Freudian connection between Gothic fiction and the unconscious anticipated the expansion of the critical application of the term Gothic from the 1960s on. Where Gothic had once been associated with a particular literary *period* (as a title like M. Lévy's *Le Roman 'gothique' anglais 1764–1824* suggests), it began to be used to describe a transhistorical *mode* of fiction. Vijay Mishra notes that 'The first major critic to use this strategy was Robert D. Hume, who in 1969 claimed that the term Gothic may be extended to include *Wuthering Heights, Moby Dick*, and Faulkner's *Sanctuary*.'[45] Critical works by Elizabeth MacAndrew (*The Gothic Tradition*), David Punter (*The Literature of Terror*), William Patrick Day (*In the Circles of Fear and Desire*), and more recently, Eve Kosofsky Sedgwick (*Between Men*) similarly mounted colonizing expeditions into literary history under the flag of the Gothic.[46] While these critics offer quite different accounts of what the Gothic really means, they are all eager to instate it as an important tradition rather than as a short interlude in the rise of the novel, and as a tradition with a particular relation to the psychological, often to the unconscious, Freudian or Lacanian.[47]

For my purposes what is most troubling is the influence this work has had on our vision of late nineteenth-century popular fiction, where the invention of a Gothic tradition has tended to short-circuit historical inquiry. In particular, the linkage of Gothic to the unconscious has entailed the assumption that the business of Gothic fiction is to explore the taboo areas of a particular culture, and to express – and sometimes recontain – the anxieties and crises produced when the walls around these taboo areas begin to crumble. It is this 'anxious' definition of the Gothic that has made the term most attractive to critics attempting to map the literary territory of the *fin de siècle*, itself often characterized as an age of anxiety and crisis. Thus Patrick Brantlinger, for example, argues in *Rule of Darkness* that mid-Victorian confidence in empire wanes at the *fin de siècle*, and he uses the term 'imperial Gothic' to describe the stories by Stoker, Kipling, Haggard and others that he sees as expressing this new anxiety of empire. Gothic is invoked here as the shadow cast by a more confident official culture. One problem with this argument, of course, is that those critics who specialize in the mainstream of Victorian letters are often keen to demonstrate how anxious even the official culture is. More importantly, though, it becomes difficult to imagine how the unprecedented imperial expansion and domestic state expansion of the late nineteenth century could have been sustained by such anxious cultural materials, an issue to which I will return in chapter 1.

If we want to establish the historical significance of the 'revival of Romance', with its own particular formal characteristics, readerly address, and embranglement in the historical and political, we will have to look a little closer at the grain of history, and we can only do so by putting aside the idea of a Gothic tradition. Literary echoes there may well be across the decades – Jonathan Harker's Transylvanian adventures certainly owe *something* to Emily St Aubert's sojourn in the Apennines – but to realize this does not bring us any closer to deciding what cultural work the two novels performed for their very different original readerships. Let us turn, then, to the issue of what the romance *did* mean for *fin-de-siècle* readers.

THE 'REVIVAL OF ROMANCE'

By the last quarter of the nineteenth century the novel had consolidated its position as the middle-class literary form par excellence. Contemporary critics took note: writing in 1892 Edmund Gosse remarked in mock-horror that 'Since the memorable year 1837 the novel has reigned in English literature; and its tyranny was never more irresistible than it is today'.[48] One sign of the novel's preeminence was the appearance of a substantial body of criticism dealing with what Henry James, in one essay, termed 'The Art of Fiction'. In these critical essays we begin to see the term 'romance' take shape as a critical term defined by its opposition to the 'plotless' American novels of Henry James and W. D. Howells, as well as to more home-grown varieties of realism. The new generic self-consciousness provided J. M. Barrie with a target for his comic sketch of 1890, 'Brought back from Elysium', in which the intrepid H. M. Stanley escorts the spirits of the novelists of the past, Fielding, Smollett, Scott, Dickens and Thackeray, to a meeting with five modern practitioners of the novel.[49] The entertainers of the past find themselves at rather a loss before their specialized and professionalized descendants:

ELSMERIAN: . . . You will be surprised to hear that fiction has become an art.
FIELDING: I am glad we came, though the [messenger] was perhaps a little peremptory. You are all novelists?
ROMANCIST: No, I am a Romancist, this gentleman is a Realist, that one is a stylist, and –
ELSMERIAN: We had better explain to you that the word novelist has gone out of fashion in our circles. We have left it behind us –
SIR WALTER [SCOTT]: I was always content with story-teller myself.

AMERICAN: Story-teller! All the stories have been told.

SIR WALTER (*wistfully*): How busy you must have been since my day.

ROMANCIST: We have, indeed, and not merely in writing stories – to use the language of the nursery. Now that fiction is an art, the work of its followers consists less in writing mere stories (to repeat a word that you will understand more readily than we) than in classifying ourselves and (when we have time for it) classifying you.[50]

But despite Barrie's comic proliferation of literary schools, the contro-versialists who filled the columns of the literary magazines of the time tended to declare themselves for one of the two main tendencies. While a plethora of overlapping terms develops, that is – romance sometimes appears as the 'novel of adventure' or the 'novel of incident', and realism expands to include Zola's naturalism as well as Henry James's studies of character – realism/romance seems to have provided the principal axis of difference. For example, George Saintsbury sees the two trends in English fiction to be the 'analytic novel' and the 'romance of adventure';[51] Hall Caine opposes realism and idealism, but then equates the latter with romance. Henry James alone affects to see no distinction between novel and romance, arguing that narrative interest can be developed as much by interior as exterior incident. Juxtaposing Edmond de Goncourt's *Chérie* and Stevenson's *Treasure Island*, he insists that 'the moral consciousness of a child is as much part of life as the islands of the Spanish Main' and possesses just as much 'story' poten-tial.[52] But James is very much outside the critical consensus, for whom Stevenson and de Goncourt are poles apart.

Realism was often represented as essentially a noxious weed of foreign growth, deriving from the school of Zola and the Goncourts, and imported into Britain by American expatriates like James and Howells; romance, on the other hand, often strived to establish links to Scott (though *not* to the Gothic romance of the eighteenth century), and to imagine a grand tradition of native British fiction. Stevenson was perceived by some to be a new Scott, and like his fellow-countryman was given credit for changing the course of the English novel. Writing in 1915, William L. Phelps described how 'when the giant Realism had got the spirit of English fiction safely locked into the dungeon, the young knightly figure of Stevenson arrived to release her'. His novels 'worked a revolution in English fiction' to such an extent that 1894, the year of his death, saw 'the beginning of a tidal wave of romanticism'.[53]

The romance as Stevenson theorizes it is an attempt to move away from the contemplative pleasures of contemporary realism in order to recapture the immersive reading experience of childhood. Rather than offering us an exercise in analysis, reading should offer us a thoroughgoing holiday from our own intellectual nature, from the very limits indeed of our own subjectivity: we should be 'rapt clean out of ourselves', and leave the book in a state in which we are 'incapable of sleep or of continuous thought'.[54] He regrets that at the time of writing English readers are too much given over to a species of domestic fiction that resounds with 'the clink of tea-spoons and the accents of the curate'.[55] Such novels without incident can never effect the escape from the limits of selfhood that Stevenson desires, since it is 'not character, but incident that woos us out of our reserve. Something happens, as we desire to have it happen to ourselves . . . Then we forget the characters; then we push the hero aside; then we plunge into the tale in our own person and battle in fresh experience; and then, and then only, do we say we have been reading a romance'.[56] The romance, then, works like a 'daydream' to satisfy the reader's 'nameless longings'[57] – it is, in effect, a narrative dream-machine.

From the beginning, romance is a gendered genre. Pervasive in the critical accounts is the assumption that the romance is a more healthily masculine form than the realist novel. Contemporary discourses of degeneration, and jeremiads about the decline of the true British racial stock are relevant to this generic gendering.[58] Victorian *littérateur* Andrew Lang, for example, presented the romances of Haggard and Stevenson as an antidote to the feminizing – and thus morbid – effects of the virus of French realism.[59] The fiction of Zola and the Goncourts 'makes one feel uncomfortable in the reading, makes one feel intrusive and unmanly'.[60] Similarly, recalling the contemporary reaction to the Romantic Revival, William Phelps describes the 'relief' at turning 'from the close, foul mugginess of naturalism to the invigorating air of the ocean'.[61] Linking the 'umanliness' of naturalism and realism with degeneration, Lang conjures up a vision of a degenerate hairless and toothless 'Coming Man' whose diet will consist of 'pap', literary and alimentary. Romance on this model is the raw meat that appeals to the wild man within, variously described by Lang as 'the natural man within me, the survival of some blue-painted Briton or of some gipsy', '[T]he savage within us', 'the old barbarian [concealed] under our clothes'. The reader who is still wild at heart, who is in effect a survival of an earlier age, displays a healthy appetite for the 'few modern romances of adventure', that are ' "savage survivals" ' at the level of literature.[62] Rather paradoxically, the road back to a more genuine, more masculine

Britishness that the romance provided appeared to involve a detour through the savage Other. The romance, then, could at once purify British fiction of foreign contaminants and *remasculinize* it. While eighteenth-century Gothic had invited the invidious attention of contemporary critics as a genre putatively written by and for women, the late Victorian romance was in no such danger.

If the romance offered an alternative to unhealthy foreign realism, it was also welcomed as putting an end to the rule of the home-grown realism of the domestic novel.[63] Again, the romance was presented as restoring the manhood of British fiction, too long tied to the apron strings of the domestic novel. The romance's apparent dethroning of domestic fiction conceals a more complex relation, however. As I shall describe in chapter 3, the romance actually reworks some of the tropes of the domestic novel to do its own cultural work. In the mummy fiction that flourished at the *fin de siècle*, the relations between subjects and objects, consumers and commodities are imagined as undergoing an inversion. But by figuring the fetishized commodities as feminine, and their relations to their owners as erotic, these same stories imagine the restoration of the power of people over goods. These most *unheimlich* stories have to revisit the domestic novel to produce their own narrativized commodity theory.

There is another aspect to the realism/romance debate though, one that it is easy to ignore if we confine ourselves to the version of literary history expounded in the essays of Stevenson, Lang and their peers. Whoever won the critical debates in the columns of *The Contemporary Review*, *Longmans* and other periodicals, the romance *sold* better than the realism or proto-modernism of Conrad and James. Stevenson's *Jekyll and Hyde*, Haggard's *King Solomon's Mines* and *She*, Du Maurier's *Trilby*, to name only a few, were bestsellers. Moreover, they were publishing successes at a time when the publishing industry itself, as I mentioned earlier, was undergoing major change.[64] The romance, then, appeared at the same time as a publishing boom that looked forward to the mass-publishing trends of the twentieth century.[65] But before we can come to any conclusions about the connections between the appearance of the romance and the expansion of the market for fiction, we have to look a little harder at the nature of the literary market in this period.[66] This will also enable us to come to a better understanding of the relations between the romance and the modernist text.

Two phenomena were particularly important in the reformation of the publishing industry: the 'new journalism' of the 1880s and 1890s, reminiscent of the earlier 'new journalism' of the 1860s, and the appearance of first editions in cheap single-volume format.[67] Both of these represent a shift from an older mode of literary production, based on the manufacture of expensive literary goods (the three-decker novel) for sale to a rather restricted elite market, and for borrowing from the circulating libraries, to a mode in which cheaper literary goods are produced for sale for a vastly expanded market. As the number of new novels published per year increased dramatically, circulating libraries such as Mudie's found themselves obliged to give up the three-decker novel, which they had sustained and been sustained by for much of the nineteenth century. While still very much forces to be reckoned with, the libraries were losing their stranglehold on a more heterogeneous literary market. They were also, of course, losing their ability to shape the contents of new novels: when the three-volume novel sank, a certain brand of Victorian literary reticence went down with it. Kipling recalls this vanishing coyness, 'We asked no social questions – we pumped no hidden shame – /We never talked obstetrics when the Little Stranger came', in his somewhat tongue-in-cheek elegy for the three-decker.[68]

As Peter Keating has shown, the increase in the number of new novels, the expansion of the market for periodicals and for cheap newspapers provide an index of the changes. From 1875 to 1885 the average number of new novels for adults published was 429. In 1887, 762 new novels for adult readers appeared. As Keating describes: 'By 1894, the year when the circulating libraries announced the death of the three-decker novel because they could no longer keep up with the amount of fiction being published, 1,315 new adult novels appeared.'[69] At this time the Publisher's Circular ceased to distinguish in their statistics between adult and juvenile titles, but it is still possible to see a steady increase, with the average for the years 1895 to 1914 being 1,618. Much of the new fiction appeared in periodicals rather than in volume form, of course, and the same market expansion is visible in the numbers of new periodicals appearing. The increase in journal titles is part of a longer historical trend going back to mid century, but there was a considerable boom in the late nineteenth century: the *Newspaper Press Directory* recorded 643 weekly, monthly and quarterly periodicals in 1875, 1,298 in 1885, 2,081 in 1895 and 2,531 in 1903.[70] The sharpened appetite for print also reveals itself in the appearance of halfpenny daily newspapers: the *Daily Mail* in 1896, the *Daily Express* in 1900 and the *Daily Mirror* in 1903. Other indices of market expansion are provided by the appearance of the Society of Authors, the rise of the literary agent, and the appearance of numerous 'how to' books for aspiring young authors, and a plethora of other literature on the business of professional writing.[71]

To speak of a mass market is of course misleading: one of the principal features of the expansion of the periodical press, for example, was a new diversity rather than a homogenization, as publishers competed in what was effectively becoming a 'niche market'.[72] Purchasers of the *Graphic* didn't expect the same literary fare as the readers of *The Savoy*, and for the most part their expectations were satisfied. Of course this specialization was still in its nascent period, and some unlikely author–journal matches were made, as when Joseph Conrad's *Nostromo* was serialized for the unsuspecting readers of the popular *T. P.'s Weekly* – or 'TP's horror', as Conrad termed it.[73] Writers had to suit their work to the carefully targeted readership of a particular periodical, and to trim the length of their text to suit that periodical's format. As Norman Feltes gloomily describes, 'The writer's work was produced in a journal within relations of production analogous to those prevailing in a textile mill.'[74] Conan Doyle's Sherlock Holmes stories exemplify the new periodical fiction. In Peter Keating's words, their success was predicated on 'the special conjunction of the *Strand Magazine*, [Conan Doyle's] own mythopoeic imagination, and the mind of a fictional detective that could work out ingenious puzzles within the space of 9,000 words'.[75] In book publishing, champions of the 'romance revival' such as H. Rider Haggard and Robert Louis Stevenson were to the vanguard in the shift to first-time single-volume publication. Cassell's decision to publish a series of 'one-volume adventure stories selling at 5/- each' was amply rewarded by the enormous success of *Treasure Island* and *King Solomon's Mines*.[76]

In their eulogies of the romance, Haggard, Stevenson, Andrew Lang and others ignore the role of the new fiction in modernizing the literary market, stressing instead its long lineage – romance appears as the original core of the novel, and a link to a universal and timeless human fascination with narrative itself.[77] In an essay of 1887 Lang uses contemporary anthropological thought to claim a provenance for romance in primitive human culture. Romance appeals to the traces of primitive consciousness in the modern self, it appeals to the 'old barbarian' in us beneath the superficies of civilization.[78] He accords storytelling – producing strongly plotted narratives – an almost ritual cultural role, and distinguishes it from modern, and for him decadent novel-writing. But far from appealing to Lang's 'barbarian', the romances of Haggard, Stevenson, Stoker, Hope, Doyle, Du Maurier and others were aimed at an expanded middle-class readership, possessed of a certain amount of leisure and money, and increasingly drawn to spend the latter on the former. What is being represented here as a form of primitivism is much closer to being the literary equivalent of the burgeoning consumer culture that W. Hamish Fraser describes in British culture from mid century on.[79] In other words, we appear to be closer to the realm of the 'culture industry' than to storytelling around the campfire.

Yet there are problems with the use of the term 'culture industry', which like Norman Feltes's account of the periodical-as-textile-mill seems to conjure up a stable opposition between commercial literature and formally difficult 'real' literature that is neither critically enabling nor factually accurate for this period. As the party at Brede Place serves to illustrate, 'commercial' and 'serious' writers still saw themselves as part of the same profession at the turn of the century. In fact, it is at this very moment in literary history (in Britain at least) that this opposition begins to develop in critical discourse, and it is not until modernism achieves full institutional recognition that Andreas Huyssen's 'great divide' becomes part of critical common sense.[80] We will have to treat this account with some scepticism in order to see how modernism and the adventure romance, despite their apparent mutual hostility, are rooted in the same historical soil. Once we do so, it becomes clear that the romance has much more in common with modernism than with eighteenth-century Gothic.

The story of modernism told by the first generation of modernist critics has a certain amount in common with Andrew Lang's account of the romance. Where Lang sees the romance as a necessary barrier against a tide of degenerate foreign literature, modernism represents itself as an island of 'real' culture in a sea of homogeneous and international mass culture. In F. R. Leavis's terms, which find echoes in the work of Adorno and Horkheimer, T. S. Eliot and the American New Critics, the opposition is between a bland 'mass civilization' and an embattled 'minority culture'. But just as the definition of the romance as a vigorous 'primitive' form dissimulates the extent to which it is a specifically modern and commercially successful form, this rather melodramatic account of modernism's heroic resistance to commercial culture conceals a more complex market dynamic. In fact, as Thomas Strychacz has argued, the difficult, experimental modernist text *depends* on an expanded market for literary goods.[81] A mass market is not necessarily a homogeneous market, and it may be more accurate to think of modernism as one specialization within a fragmenting and increasingly diverse literary market rather than an escape from a world of homogeneous cultural production. In short, modernism depends on, and contributes to, the same transformation of the literary market as does the romance.

Modernism and the romance share some of the same genre-policing strategies. By linking the 'unmanly' fictions of Zola and the Goncourts to the 'pap'-addicted Coming Man, Lang hints at an equivalence of the feminine and consumption that becomes much more explicit in the discourse of modernism. The 'positioning of woman as avid consumer of pulp [fiction]' is, as Andreas Huyssen has pointed out, one of the central paradigms of modernism from *Madame Bovary* on.[82] Into the cultural imaginary of the late nineteenth century popped the figure of woman as reader of trashy novels, a sister to the woman who loved to shop: consumerism, whether of stories or of more tangible goods, was early gendered feminine. Under either aspect, the consuming woman was posed as the icon of everything that modernism opposed. One aspect of this equation of woman and consumer culture was modernism's antipathy toward – and dependence on – the sentimental. In Suzanne Clark's words, 'The term sentimental makes a shorthand for everything modernism would exclude, the other of its literary/nonliterary dualism.'[83] The romance too partly defined itself in opposition to more 'feminine' genres, but in this it was to be outflanked by modernism, which rejected not only the affect-laden realm of the domestic but also the emotional register of patriotism, and the more 'manly' feelings exploited in the adventure romance. Somewhat ironically, modernism treated the romance as another tinny variation on the same old sentimental theme.

That these two apparent opposites are twins formed in the same historical matrix is further suggested by their common reliance on the language of primitivism. As Marianna Torgovnick has shown, a wide variety of modernist practices, from the statues of Brancusi to the novels of D. H. Lawrence, depend on the discourse of primitivism.[84] While certain schools – the Futurism of Marinetti, Russian Constructivism – embraced technology and modernization, other strains of modernism found in the savage Other an escape from what they represented as the smothering effects of modernization and mass culture. Not only did the 'primitive' spaces of the earth offer to the modernist imagination a perch from which to heap scorn on the sterility of modern life, but 'primitive' object-culture offered the modernist artist an image of a non-commodified aesthetic practice. But the romance, as we have seen, was also theorized as a form of primitivism, appealing to a basic appetite for narrative incident. Even more striking though is the extent to which modernist primitivism depends on a similar global imaginary to that created in the fictions of Haggard, Stevenson, Stoker and their fellow-writers, as I will discuss in chapter 4. The dark continent of the unconscious mind, the earthy working-class culture evoked by Lawrence, or the more exotic primitivism of Gauguin's Polynesia, do these not occupy an analogous position in the cultural imaginary to the unexplored territories of Haggard's *She* and *King Solomon's Mines?* With some important changes of shading, the map of the world unfolded in the late Victorian romance and modernism is remarkably similar.

THE CULTURAL WORK OF THE ROMANCE

Once we recognize the romance and modernism as part of the same moment, we can begin to understand the serious cultural function of the romance; the romance, the 'novel of incident', or 'novel of adventure', far from being the commercial pulp that it is labelled by modernist literary history, actually possesses a theoretical backbone. Not just a reflex of the expanding publishing industry, the romance revival provided the narratives and the figures that enabled late Victorian middle-class culture to successfully accommodate certain historical changes, notably modernizing processes. David Harvey argues that modernism provided 'ways to absorb, reflect upon, and codify' various facets of modernization; the romance, I will argue, did likewise (cf. Jameson's account of modernism as 'retraining' above).[85] The particular modernizing processes that I focus upon here are the rise of professionalism, the search for new global markets in the 'new imperialism', and the rise of consumer culture, all of which are also, of course, important contexts for high modernism.[86] A particular romance narrative accompanies each of these processes: the vampire story links to professionalism, the expedition/treasure hunt to the 'new imperialism', the mummy story to consumer culture.

Before I outline the chapters to follow, a few words more about what I am calling 'narrative theory' may be necessary. Perhaps Louis Althusser's notion of 'descriptive theory' most closely approximates the hybrid of narrative and theory that I recognize in the popular romance. For Althusser a descriptive theory provides a way of explaining almost all of the observable facts in the case to be explained, but it remains essentially metaphorical. For example, the Marxist social topography of base and superstructure is a metaphor, or a model, and not a description of an actual society, but it nevertheless explains a great deal about the way a society works, and is a stage on the route to further theorization. This metaphorical – or for my purposes, narrative – stage is not adequate in itself, but it cannot simply be sidestepped.[87] In the stories I will be discussing, descriptive theories are put forward as to the relation of Britain to its colonies and the behaviour of objects in a global economy, among other things. In other words, through its narratives and figures popular fiction provided its readers with a *working* knowledge of Britain as a modernizing imperial society.

Althusser's 'descriptive theory' can be seen to bear a close family resemblance to the category of myth as it appears in the work of other structuralist thinkers.[88] As Gianni Vattimo has argued, myth has become a central concept in contemporary critical theory although there exists considerable ambiguity around its epistemological status. In Vattimo's terms Althusser's 'descriptive theory' resembles a form of 'tempered irrationalism' or 'limited rationality': as a form of theory it is not seen to be completely antithetical to rational or scientific thought, but rather to differ from the latter through certain formal features – it is essentially narrative or figurative.[89]

Althusser ultimately envisages a distinction between 'descriptive theory' and another more purely self-conscious theoretical practice; he assumes the existence of a form of theoretical thought that is neither narrative nor figurative. Since what I am evidently offering is also in the end a *story* about British popular culture as much as a theory of it, my project cannot offer the epistemological certainties Althusser's terms suggest. No doubt readers will be able to tease out political fantasies as well as cultural theories in my story, just as I have attempted to do in the case of Stoker, Haggard and their peers. But if Althusser's assumptions set up a certain dissonance with my own, the hybrid of theory and narrative involved in his 'descriptive theory' appears to me to have a certain usefulness, and for that reason I retain it.

The first three chapters explore three different subgenres of popular fiction: the vampire story, the imperial treasure hunt and the mummy story, each of which corresponds to a particular facet of modernization. Respectively, they provided readers with an origin story for the new professionalism, a means of relating the metropolitian reader to imperial space, and a theory of imperial commodity fetishism. Chapter 1 takes issue with the characterization of the *fin de siècle* as a period of anxiety and crisis for Britain, and suggests that this was a time of imperial expansion abroad, and of the extension of state power at home, as an interventionist twentieth-century state began to replace the liberal Victorian model. Rather than reading the best-known vampire story, Bram Stoker's *Dracula*, as the mirror of *fin-de-siècle* British anxieties, then, as critics have tended to do, I argue that the novel is an origin-tale for a new professional class. These new professionals resemble the experts that the expanding state increasingly relied upon to renegotiate the borders between public and private, between the state and the domestic sphere. *Dracula*'s relation to this historical shift is that it represents the appearance of these new men as the necessary consequence of an external threat, a threat that then becomes embodied in the story's female characters. By the end of the narrative the vampire has been defeated, but the team of professional men lives on.

I raise some broad theoretical questions about the historical embeddedness of the revival of romance in chapter 2, which deals with another important variety of the romance: the expedition/treasure hunt. Where *Dracula* primarily shows the team of men in action at home, reconceiving the possibilities for professional intervention in the domestic sphere, the expedition/treasure hunt narrative unfolds in Britain's potential or actual overseas territories. Coinciding with the new imperialism, stories like *King Solomon's Mines* and *Treasure Island*, among the most successful novels of the 1880s, use the imperial adventure story to establish a particular relation between the domestic reader and imperial space. The home-made (though this is a misleading term) maps that appear in these narratives of imaginary mobility rearticulate the known space of the metropolitan subject and – from the point of the view of the metropolis – the abstract and invisible space of Britain's colonial possessions. Most notably in *King Solomon's Mines*, the 'private map' encodes a libidinal relation between the masculine imperial subject and the feminized and eroticized body of Africa. However, Bram Stoker's reworking of the treasure-hunt romance, *The Snake's Pass*, shows the limits of this cultural narrative. Set in Ireland, and written at a time when the Land War of the 1880s was still fresh in popular memory, this tale of treasure and inter-ethnic marriage fails to present Ireland as a properly manageable imperial setting. Stoker's version of the imperial treasure hunt becomes entangled with older narratives of

Anglo-Irish relations, as well as with historical accounts of the recent agrarian violence of the Land War, and the resulting romance cannot provide the closure of the more exotic narratives of Stevenson or Haggard. *The Snake's Pass*, then, forces us to think about what it means to historicize the revival of romance, and prevents us from assuming that we can interpret the cultural significance of individual romances in terms of some homogeneous English culture.

If the treasure narrative provides one way of bridging the gap between the disjunct spaces of metropolis and colony, the mummy story, the focus of chapter 3, seems to be *founded* on that same disjunction. The mummy fiction that appears at the end of the nineteenth century recounts what happens to a category of ambiguous foreign objects/ bodies when they enter the British economy. In such tales as H. D. Everett's *Iras, A Mystery*, Conan Doyle's 'The Ring of Thoth', and Bram Stoker's *The Jewel of Seven Stars*, mummies come to life, and, unlike the vengeful mummies that Hollywood has bequeathed to popular culture, in some cases even become romantically involved with their new owners. These mummies behave very much like the animated commodities that Marx describes in 'The Commodity Fetish and its Secret' in volume 1 of *Capital*, whose uncanny semblance of life he attributes to the alienated conditions of production under capitalism. Mummy fiction advances a similar theory of the behaviour of objects in a commodity culture, but it explicitly deals with the inverted relations of objects and people within an *imperial* global economy. Mummy stories offer a fantasy of the restoration of human mastery over the world of things through their gender logic; married to the commodity, the (masculine) consumer once again enjoys the upper hand over the feminized object, though this fantasy, too, is not without its dangers for the consuming subject.

The final chapter takes as its point of departure the way in which modernist literary criticism, through its devaluation of the popular romance as a completely commodified form, has made it difficult for us to perceive any critical dimension to the romance. Through an account of modernist primitivism, I argue that modernism's putative hostility to popular fiction dissimulates the degree to which the two embody the same cultural logic. In particular, this chapter shows that the experience of empire, and the status of objects in a commodity economy are as much concerns in the early modernist drama of the Irish Literary Revival, and in the modernist fiction of Ernest Hemingway, as they are in *King Solomon's Mines* or in a mummy narrative like *Iras, A Mystery*.

DEFINING AN ERA

Insofar as this is an account of late Victorian transformation rather than crisis, it will perhaps already be clear that I am siding with those historians who question the extent to which the history of modern Britain can be summarized as a tale of decline from Victorian strength to twentieth-century weakness. What Gordon Martel describes as a 'neo-Gibbonian' chronicle of 'Victorian grandeur, Edwardian sunset, Georgian decline, and Elizabethan disintegration' has had considerable currency in both academic and popular circles, and comes in conservative, liberal and leftist versions.[90] Martin Wiener's *English Culture and the Decline of the Industrial Spirit, 1850–1980*,[91] in which he argues that Britain fails as an industrial power through the innate anti-modernity of its culture (especially as fostered in its public schools), is one of the best known of these narratives of decline. In recent years, though, such teleologies have been treated more sceptically, for example by W. D. Rubinstein in *Capitalism, Culture, and Decline in Britain, 1750–1990*, and in essays by Gordon Martel, Keith Nelson and others. What these revisionary accounts suggest is that not only does Britain's economy continue to perform well even after the turn of the century, but also that Britain maintained its role as a global power up until World War 2.[92]

In selecting three facets of British modernization and not others, I am not attempting to define the essence of late nineteenth-century modernity, still less the modern itself.[93] While the three facets that I have chosen are, I think, relatively uncontroversial, others could be added: technological change, for example, was another important component of late Victorian modernization, developing its own fictional equivalent in the 'scientific romances' of H. G. Wells among others; immigration produced its own narratives, such as George Du Maurier's highly successful – and highly xenophobic – *Trilby*. Other lacunae could be pointed to. While Bram Stoker looms large, I have devoted but scant space to some of the most successful romancists: R. L. Stevenson and Anthony Hope for example. *The Strange Case of Dr Jekyll and Mr Hyde* and *The Prisoner of Zenda* could sustain a chapter apiece. Nor have I said very much about the connections between the adventure romance and some of the other best-selling strains of the time, such as the historical romance or the religious romance. Such authors as Stanley Weyman and Marie Corelli may not have really been part of the romance revival, but they all benefited from it in terms of readership. In defence of these absences, I can only maintain that the chapters that follow gesture at rather than attempt a panorama of turn-of-the-century literary culture. For better or worse I have forsaken a more inclusive account to devote the bulk of this study to showing how particular historical processes connect to particular narratives, and it is on the success or failure of those essays in connection that I would wish this study to be judged.

To return to the theatrical metaphors with which I began this introduction, then, what I have attempted to do is to offer a series of tableaux, as it were, from this chapter in cultural history, out of which I hope the reader may be able to imagine the full dramatic production. But I find myself already regretting the theatrical metaphor – it smacks too much of the comfortable image of the Victorian past that Hollywood has often offered us, all gaslight and hansom cabs. Given the dates with which we are concerned, it might be more appropriate to think in terms of film-stills rather than theatrical tableaux. The photographic image perhaps better captures the odd mixture of cultural proximity and distance, of *déjà vu* and the melancholy of historical separation, that I think a reading of these popular romances conveys. *The Ghost* itself has, appropriately enough, disappeared, and the specific literary culture that produced it, poised on the brink of a massive market expansion, yet cosy enough for the collaboration of its more popular as well as its more daunting authors, has vanished too. And yet the phenomena that the romance tried to absorb and theorize in narrative form, professionalism, imperialism, a global commodity culture, these have not vanished, no more than the vampire, the team and the mummy, however changed, from our popular cultural imaginary.

I am not telling a ghost story: I am not hinting at the existence of some ghostly essence, some Victorian spirit that survives from the nineteenth century to animate twentieth-century international popular culture. But to the extent that the contradictions that produced these romances have not altogether disappeared, we can still see the latter to some degree as *our* stories. To that same degree the historical view that they open up does not offer an altogether stable perspective; if we have the power to survey their historical context, there is also the danger of a sudden attack of vertigo, of the historical ground rushing up to meet us.[94] That, I think, is why these stories are worth reading and studying.

CHAPTER I

Incorporated bodies: Dracula and professionalism

> The dinner was very long, and the conversation was about the
> aristocracy – and Blood. Mrs Waterbrook repeatedly told us that if
> she had a weakness, it was Blood.   *David Copperfield*

In the romances of the *fin de siècle* we have tended to see a literature of
anxiety symptomatic of some more general cultural crisis. The monstrous anachronisms of such novels as *She, Dracula* and *Dr Jekyll and Mr
Hyde* consequently seem to mirror a whole set of anxieties: the collapse
of empire, the degeneration of the race in the light of evolutionary
theory, and the rise of the New Woman, to name but a few. These are
indeed anxious texts, but I want to argue that they may produce and
manage anxiety as well as express it. In this chapter I will give an
account of the way one of these romances, Bram Stoker's *Dracula*, uses
anxiety to produce as both necessary and natural a modern form of
professional, male, homosocial combination – the team of experts.[1] I
will also be advocating a reconsideration of the *fin de siècle* as a period of
crisis. Despite an increasingly shrill rhetoric of decline, Britain was in
fact far from collapse. On the contrary, the British empire grew dramatically during this period, while at home state power was also undergoing a phase of expansion. This latter phenomenon depended on the
existence of a new class of experts, and the adventure romance played a
part in the formation of this professional class. The immediate context
for *Dracula*, I will argue, is what Harold Perkin has called the 'rise of
professional society',[2] a historical shift that links such apparently disparate phenomena as the dramatic increase in the number of professional
associations at the end of the nineteenth century, the expansion of the
state sector, and the emergence of the specialist literary languages of
high modernism. If as a literary artifact Stoker's novel looks back to the
Gothic romances of Horace Walpole and Ann Radcliffe, ideologically it
belongs to a specifically modernist culture that we associate with the
work of Joyce, Woolf and Eliot. To this extent *Dracula* is part of what Jon

Thompson calls 'a larger culture of modernism that includes popular culture and is not limited to institutionalized high art'.[3]

Attempts to historicize the 'revival of romance' too often take the *fin de siècle* at its own estimate. Patrick Brantlinger's assessment of the 'revival' in *Rule of Darkness* typifies this approach. Arguing for the use of the term 'imperial Gothic' to describe the romances of Stoker, Haggard and others, Brantlinger suggests that after the mid-Victorian era the British found their own myths of progress to be increasingly unconvincing. Instead they began to worry about 'the degeneration of their institutions, their culture, their "racial stock"'.[4] He continues: 'Apocalyptic themes and images are characteristic of imperial Gothic, in which, despite the consciously pro-Empire values of many authors, the feeling emerges that "we are those upon whom the ends of the earth are come".' Images of cultural and physical degeneration certainly did circulate widely in the late nineteenth century, abetted by theories which built on Darwin's speculations on the possibility of species 'reversion' in *The Descent of Man*. Max Nordau, analyst of cultural morbidity, found a wide audience for his *Entartung* (1892), published in English in 1895 as *Degeneration*. Drawing on the criminological work of Caesar Lombroso he sought to show that degeneracy had set its stigma on the literature, music and visual arts of the period. 'Degenerates are not always criminals, prostitutes, anarchists and pronounced lunatics: they are often authors and artists', he proclaimed.[5] Where Lombroso traced the signs of degeneration in the facial asymmetries, hare-lips and strabismus of his subjects, Nordau identified the stylistic correlatives of such traits in the work of the Pre-Raphaelites, the symbolists, Nietzsche, Zola and others. Not one to pull his punches, he warned that 'We stand now in the midst of a severe mental epidemic; of a sort of black death of degeneration and hysteria.' Civilization had become 'an immense hospital ward'.[6] Bram Dijkstra's recent study of the female body in *fin-de-siècle* art is just one account that demonstrates how pervasive such theories were in late Victorian culture.[7] The rhetoric of decline became familiar enough for Oscar Wilde to recast it in an ironic light in the following well-known exchange from *The Picture of Dorian Gray*. Lady Narborough, like many late nineteenth-century commentators, sees changes in sexual mores as the harbingers of decline:

'Nowadays all the married men live like bachelors, and all the bachelors like married men.'
'*Fin de siècle*,' murmured Lord Henry.
'*Fin du globe*,' answered his hostess.

'I wish it were the *fin du globe*,' said Dorian with a sigh. 'Life is a great disappointment.'[8]

Wilde appears to be keenly aware of something that Brantlinger and other present-day critics overlook – that reiterations of crisis and imminent apocalypse may conceal real continuities.

I would go further and suggest that the spectre of decline may be put to work during periods of development. The heyday of Brantlinger's 'imperial Gothic' coincided with a period of actual imperial expansion. Anxious or not, Britain added to its empire some 750,000 square miles in Asia and the South Pacific, and another 4,400,000 square miles in Africa beween 1870 and 1900.[9] In fact Britain would retain most of its empire until after the Second World War. Within Britain's own borders, these same years witnessed an extension of state control into regions previously treated either as part of the private sphere or as part of the free market. The decline of liberalism as an ideology was accompanied by a marked increase in the willingness of the state to concern itself with the family and with the relations of employers and employees. In part this was a transformation within liberalism itself, some of the cries for state action emanating from within the Liberal party, from 'New Liberals' such as L. T. Hobhouse and C. F. G. Masterman.[10] A wave of social legislation was one symptom of this shift; the appearance of an army of experts familiar with new theoretical tools such as psychology and eugenics – that is to say, a group capable of overseeing the new relations of the state and the private sphere – was another.[11] In turn this shift can be understood in the context of Britain's economic fortunes. It is often argued that Britain was losing ground to Germany and the United States by failing to undergo fully the 'second industrial revolution' associated with the use of electricity, the internal combustion engine and chemicals. But as W. D. Rubinstein has shown it is quite misleading to represent Britain's (partial) decline as an industrial power as a general economic crisis. Despite its mid-Victorian reputation as the workshop of the world Britain's prosperity had since the eighteenth century been based on 'a commercial, financial and service-based' economy, and what we see at the end of the nineteenth century is the reassertion of the dominance of this tertiary economy, within which the professional was an increasingly important figure.[12]

Widespread warnings that things fall apart, then, coincided with signs that the centre was not only holding, but actually entering a phase of expansion. This apparent paradox may be resolved by taking a look at one historical example. Seen through the lens of crisis the Boer war appears as a traumatic national event; fears for the degeneration of the race and the security of the nation were apparently borne out when considerable numbers of British recruits were rejected as unfit for service.[13] Nevertheless, the end result of the war was not only management of the trauma but also an expansion and consolidation of certain power structures. Evidently, anxiety provided the occasion for state intervention on a grand scale. While the Committee on Physical Deterioration set up after the war found *no evidence* of actual physical or mental degeneration, it did see environmental factors as affecting the health of the poor. The outcome was new legislation whose influence Harold Perkin describes in these terms:

The Report on Physical Deterioration was one of the most influential social documents of the age, and many of its recommendations, including school meals for poor children, medical inspection, physical education for both sexes, cookery and domestic science for girls in schools, tighter control of the milk supply and food adulteration, social education of mothers by midwives and health visitors, juvenile courts, and a ban on the sale of alcohol and tobacco to children, all passed into law before the [1914] war.[14]

Fears there may well have been for the decline of Englishness within England, as well as for assaults from without, but these fears had the effect of buttressing – not enfeebling – the power of the state. Of equal importance, these fears established a mission for a new group of professionals in human management, whose area of expertise would extend into that which liberal ideology had once designated as the private sphere.[15]

While we cannot ignore the existence of a *fin-de-siècle* discourse of crisis and anxiety, neither can we take it at face value. As I suggested in my Introduction, additional problems attach to the labelling of late nineteenth-century adventure fiction as Gothic, or Victorian Gothic, or imperial Gothic. Accounts of Gothic have tended to view it as a literature of crisis, in which the anxieties of a culture find their most explicit expression. The Marquis de Sade may have been the first to impose this construction on the Gothic fiction of 'Monk' Lewis and others, describing it as 'the fruit of the revolution of which all Europe felt the shock'.[16] More recent criticism endorses the general tenor of the Marquis's comments, while offering different views as to what revolutionary crisis is at stake. Thus David Punter, for example, suggests that Gothic reflects the social trauma of the industrial revolution.[17] Psychoanalytic criticism treats Gothic fiction in the same way, while effectively privatizing the revolution; Gothic becomes the textual arena in which the sexual anxieties of an age are rehearsed. Whether in its Marxist or psychoanalytic/feminist versions, the basic theory of the functioning of fiction remains the same: anxiety exists 'out there' some-where beyond the text, generated by some impending crisis in the culture; the dominant representations of a culture obscure this, but in Gothic this anxiety returns as the 'repressed' of the culture. Criticism's role, then, by an etymological coincidence,[18] is to identify the particu-lar crisis that bubbles below the surface of any given culture, and to show how the anxiety generated by this crisis is expressed in a particu-lar text.

A glance at critical accounts of *Dracula* from the last twenty or so years confirms that this theory of Gothic fiction, which we might call anxiety theory, has dominated the interpretation of Stoker's sensational tale. For a novel that enjoys a rather ambivalent relation to the canon, *Dracula* seems to solicit interpretation, and critics have been generous in obliging. Psychoanalysis, Marxism, feminism, gender studies and other varieties of critical thought have each taken at least one turn at reading the text. In this respect the critical fate of *Dracula* resembles that of *Frankenstein*, a text in which the monster who dominates the action has been seen to embody threats ranging from the emerging working class to language itself.[19] In the pandemonium of interpretive activity around Stoker's novel, Count Dracula has appeared as the embodiment of fears about degeneration, the influx of eastern European Jews into late Victorian England, a subversive female sexuality, reverse colonization, nascent media culture, male homoeroticism and monopoly capital, among other things. However, the apparent diversity of critical con-clusions masks a broad consensus that Stoker's text *reflects* certain anxie-ties, be they late Victorian or universal. The reading practice that accompanies this theory of Gothic fiction is allegorical: the text mirrors extra-textual anxieties; the vampire is the figure in the text for those anxieties; criticism decodes the figure to reveal its real referent. For example, Richard Wasson writing in 1966 argues that 'Count Dracula . . . represents those forces in Eastern Europe which seek to overthrow, through violence and subversion, the more progressive democratic civilization of the West.'[20] It may be easy to smile at this, to say the least, overdetermined reading, which tells us more about cold-war America than about Stoker's novel, but the same basic trope recurs again and again in the criticism. Writing eleven years later, Phyllis Roth sees the novel as reflecting pre-Oedipal anxieties, while Judith Weissman sees it as representing a fear 'that women's sexual appetites are greater than men's'.[21] More recently still, Christopher Craft confidently traces the novel's origins to 'Victorian culture's anxiety about desire's potential indifference to the prescriptions of gender'.[22] The tenor in these readings of the monster becomes more complicated, but the basic tenor/vehicle relation returns in a way that is itself more numbing than uncanny.

The tendency to see *Dracula* in relation to specific late nineteenth-century historical contexts marks the most recent accounts of the text. Stephen Arata describes his essay on the novel as moving from the psychoanalytic to the historical in order to identify the text with a late Victorian 'anxiety of reverse colonization'.[23] *Dracula*, he argues, is one of the stories that culture tells itself in order to 'assuage the anxiety attendant upon cultural decay'.[24] Jennifer Wicke takes the refreshing tack of seeing the novel as looking forward to the twentieth century rather than back to the nineteenth. Yet she too is drawn into allegory, this time rewriting the text as a liminal modernist artefact: 'the social force most analogous to Count Dracula's as depicted in the novel is none other than mass culture, the developing technologies of the media in its many forms, as mass transport, tourism, photography and lithography in image production, and mass-produced narrative'.[25] It may be doing a certain violence to Wicke's careful prose to read her characterization of the novel as 'refract[ing] hysterical images of modernity'[26] as yet another version of the anxiety story, but that is what it seems to be, nonetheless.

In what follows, I will try and leave the anxiety story behind, reading the text as more performative than reflective, as providing a cultural narrative that reshapes society rather than mirroring social anxieties. Questioning the separation of text and history, I will be taking for granted that, as Ann Cvetkovich puts it, 'the work of . . . novels is itself a part of Victorian history'.[27] In the end it may appear that I am simply producing another allegory of the text, one with the 'little band of men' at its centre in place of the monster. The difference between a reading that places the text outside of the historical processes it supposedly reflects and a reading that makes it part of those processes is in practice a difficult one to maintain – *Dracula* as myth of origins may look very much like *Dracula* as historical allegory. But if the text still appears as an allegory in my account, it is an allegory of the future, or rather an allegory that helped to construct the future that its own narrative could then be seen to reflect.[28]

In suggesting that this is the way to read *Dracula*, I am also proposing that we treat late nineteenth-century romances as part of their moment – the moment of modernism. If we pay less attention to the formal links to Gothic fiction and stress instead the way in which such a narrative engages its moment, we can discover what *Dracula* shares with novels included in the canon of modernist fiction. The emergence of modernism was accompanied by a new concentration of metropolitan power, a new imperialism, the spread of consumerism, and the expansion of a culture of experts. While all of these are at some level related, it is on this last aspect of modernist culture that I want to concentrate here.[29] As Thomas Strychacz has shown, the culture of the expert, when translated into the field of literary practice, possesses its most obvious equivalent in the specialized languages of experimental modernism. As Strychacz puts it: 'If a body of formal knowledge underpins a professional's power within a mass society, then the idiom of modernist writing – arcane allusion, juxtaposition, opaque writing, indeterminacy, and so on – performs precisely this function within mass culture.'[30] The rise of a culture of experts, then, coincides with the appearance of texts that seem to demand of the reader an ability to master their private languages. Joyce's *Finnegans Wake* is perhaps the ultimate product of this trend, but the pattern is established much earlier, in the work of James and Conrad for example. In this chapter, however, I will be arguing that *Dracula*, a text more often seen as the polar opposite of the modernist novel, is equally concerned with the culture of the expert. Specifically, *Dracula* provides a myth of origins for such a culture.

THE POWER OF COMBINATION

Where does one begin a reading of *Dracula*? Well, why not at the end? If the text has accomplished something, let us catch it tallying up its gains. The last word lies with Jonathan Harker, in a note appended to Mina's typewritten account of the adventure and the other vestiges of seven years before. Harker begins his note thus:

Seven years ago we all went through the flames; and the happiness of some of us since then is, we think, well worth the pain we endured. It is an added joy to Mina and to me that our boy's birthday is the same day as that on which Quincey Morris died. His mother holds, I know, the secret belief that some of our brave friend's spirit has passed into him. His bundle of names links all our little band of men together; but we call him Quincey . . . We could hardly ask anyone, even did we wish to, to accept these as proofs of so wild a story. Van

Helsing summed it all up as he said, with our boy on his knee:-
'We want no proofs; we ask none to believe us! This boy will some day know what a brave and gallant woman his mother is. Already he knows her sweetness and loving care; later on he will understand how some men so loved her, that they did dare much for her sake.'[31]

The novel ends with Quincey, son of Jonathan and Mina; he is at once a sign of the promise of the future and a souvenir, through his 'bundle of names', of the past.[32] But we know that other blood flows in his veins. The giving and taking of blood throughout the novel means that more than the original Quincey Morris's spirit 'has passed into him'. Mina has drunk Dracula's blood, Dracula has drunk Lucy's, Lucy has had transfusions of blood from all the novel's main characters except Jonathan.[33] In other words Quincey stands as a record of the adventure in more than his 'bundle of names'. But this also means that the vampire's blood flows in little Quincey's veins, which suggests, not to put too fine a point on it, that Quincey is part-vampire. What then has been accomplished? Society has been saved from the vampire; Quincey, emblem of the society of the future, *is* – at least partly – a vampire.

This would scarcely seem to represent a triumph over the nosferatu. But what if we consider that the real accomplishment of the novel is bringing that 'little band of men' together? What if the threat of the vampire has largely been an instrument for the formation of an association between these men? As the ending of the novel shows, the team of men doesn't simply wither away once the vampire has been destroyed. The little band is also brought together by their common love of Mina ('some men so loved her, that they did dare much for her sake'). To avert a threat posed by a monster, to save a 'gallant woman' from that monster: this is the charter for this league of men. I want to argue that the vulnerable woman is, like the vampire, needed by the narrative.[34] At the same time, though, as we shall see, the celebration of the mother of the future generation dissimulates the text's investment in producing an exclusively male (and disembodied) model of social reproduction. The female body becomes in fact the exemplary object for the expertise of the team of men. Not surprisingly, then, the home, the 'feminine sphere' for the Victorian middle classes, becomes the privileged site for their activities.

Let us consider the sorts of men who are united by their loathing of the vampire and their love of Mina, and consider also the way their positions change in the course of the narrative. Jonathan Harker introduces himself to us first as a young solicitor, and becomes in the course of the narrative the successor to his employer, Hawkins. Upon the death of Mr Hawkins, the Harkers become wealthy beyond their modest dreams with a suddenness that shocks Mina:

It seems only yesterday that the last entry was made, and yet how much between them, in Whitby and all the world before me, Jonathan away and no news of him; and now, married to Jonathan, Jonathan a solicitor, a partner, rich, master of his business, Mr Hawkins dead and buried . . . The service [sc. for Hawkins] was very simple and very solemn. There were only ourselves and the servants there, one or two old friends . . . and a gentleman representing Sir John Paxton, the President of the Incorporated Law Society. (206)

One generation passes away, and another succeeds it. But succession is not based on biological ties between father and son: one professional man replaces another, the transition sanctioned by the relevant professional body, in this case the Incorporated Law Society. The biological body yields to the legal body as the agent of reproduction.

This is not the only case of succession in the novel, nor is the older 'biological' model completely defunct, as least in the case of non-middle-class characters. Throughout, there is the sense that one social formation, as represented by one generation, is being replaced by another. Mr Hawkins's death occurs at the same time as two others: that of Lord Godalming and that of Mrs Westenra, Lucy's mother. Arthur in turn becomes Lord Godalming, the new generation of aristocrat. Lord Godalming is the team's equivalent for the 'Sir John Paxton, the President of the Incorporated Law Society' who appears by proxy at Hawkins's funeral: his presence confers a suitable air of dignity and respectability on the business in which he is engaged, in this case the hunting of Dracula.[35] Lucy does not replace Mrs Westenra in this way, of course; as Lucy herself dies at the same time (due to the depredations of Dracula), Arthur, Lord Godalming, comes to inherit that estate too under Mrs Westenra's will. Male succession seems to be a far less problematical matter than female succession, for reasons that I hope will become apparent.

Consider the novel's other 'leading men': Dr Seward, Professor Van Helsing and Quincey Morris. Two of the three, Seward and Van Helsing, are, like Jonathan, professional men, experts in their fields.[36] Seward is the new medical professional: an alienist and physician, at an early age it would seem he has reached the top of his profession, having charge of his own asylum for the insane. He is also, in a sense, the professional offspring of Van Helsing, as he has learnt his craft at the latter's feet. He is Van Helsing's 'disciple' even according to the rules of vampiric influence, as he has on an earlier occasion sucked Van Helsing's blood to save him from infection after a surgical accident. For Seward, the latter is 'my old friend and master, Professor Van Helsing' (137). Van Helsing also thinks fondly of those good old days, while acknowledging Seward's full professional status in the present: 'You were always a careful student, and your case-book was ever more full than the rest. You were only student then; now you are master . . .' (146). Van Helsing is the professional *ne plus ultra*. He is 'the great specialist' (144). In addition to his qualifications as a doctor and scientist, we also learn that he is a qualified lawyer: 'You forget that I am a lawyer as well as a doctor' (197). Thus it is that this super-professional is the natural leader of this new social group composed largely of professional men.[37] It is interesting to note that among the characters originally planned for the book were 'a detective – Cotford', and a 'psychical research agent – Alfred Singleton', two further variations on the expert theme.[38] These roles do not really disappear from the finished text, though; rather they are assumed by the polymath Van Helsing. The proliferation of professional men would seem to suggest that the men are, as David Glover suggests, 'members of a liberal bourgeois order'.[39] Yet as we shall see the novel undercuts the traditional values of liberalism, in part through its deployment of the idea of professionalism itself.

Quincey P. Morris, the Texan adventurer, is the only real outsider in this group and, significantly, he is also the only expendable member of the team. But his inclusion is by no means fortuitous, and it is interesting that he is one of the characters who also appears in the original notes (though he does change from 'An American inventor from Texas' to 'A Texan – Brutus M. Marix' before assuming his final identity). The novel's investment in professionalism is nowhere as clear as in Quincey's removal from the winning team. It would be easy enough to imagine a novel of which Quincey and Lord Godalming would provide the centres of interest, but *Dracula* is not that sort of novel. Indeed, Quincey and Lord Godalming might best be considered less as individual characters than as fragments of an older idea of masculine heroism which the novel replaces with the idea of the heroic professional. The novel preserves some of the prestige of that older heroic model in the character of Godalming, who, as I have suggested, adds a certain traditional gloss to the new professional team, but in killing off Quincey it clearly rejects the heroic amateur values of what Martin Green has called the 'aristo-military caste'. Thus in Stoker's first novel, *The Snake's Pass*, the professional man, Dick Sutherland, plays second fiddle to the landed amateur adventurer, Arthur Severn, but *Dracula* reverses that pattern. Quincey is not dispatched before he proves his usefulness, though. When the team finally tracks Dracula back to Transylvania (a romance territory that might be thought of as a nightmare version of Anthony Hope's Ruritania), it is Quincey who finally 'stakes' Dracula. As Mina tells us: 'on the instant, came the sweep and flash of Jonathan's great knife. I shrieked as I saw it shear through the throat; whilst at the same moment Mr Morris' bowie knife plunged in the heart' (447). This staking is a necessary task for the closure of the narrative, but one that it skirts around gingerly. In Mina's account the weapons themselves seem to be doing the work without the effort of the men who wield them. While Jonathan's decapitating of the monster is part of the protocol, it is clear enough from the earlier 'saving' of Lucy that it is the actual staking that is symbolically central. But whereas elsewhere in the novel this symbolic penetration is performed on females by males, here the act is male–male. This seems to threaten the homosocial arrangement of the text, and it should not be surprising that Quincey, who is 'only too happy to have been of any service' (448), does not survive to take a part in the new order.

I have not yet explained Mina's role in this new professional order. Mina, evidently, is not part of the 'little band of men'; rather she is meant to be the ideal centre around which it revolves. She is, however, related to the society of professionals who ostensibly protect her. In fact if Seward, Van Helsing and Harker resemble the new ruling class, an elite group of 'experts' whose power lies in education and affiliation to various incorporeal bodies, Mina may be seen as a soldier in the army of cheap (here, free) female labour that sustains that group. Mina begins the narrative as a teacher, more accurately as an 'assistant school-mistress' (70), one part of the cheap female labour force, but in the course of the novel she becomes stenographer, typist and nurse to the band of men.[40] Thus she resembles the New Woman in her skills, but she is a New Woman with no desire for equality. Women were themselves becoming independent professionals at the end of the nineteenth century, and forming their own professional associations (including the Society of Women Journalists in 1894), but Mina is happy to leave professionalism to the men. One can, of course, interpret Mina's position in a more optimistic light. David Glover, for example, argues that Mina recalls a number of late Victorian women 'whose contradictory response to the suffrage movement gave them a strategic position in late Victorian society'.[41] Yet in terms of the novel's 'team' ethos, it is difficult

to see that her skills entitle her to the same claims to status as the men.
The narrative needs her to be more vulnerable than the men, for her
defence comprises their raison d'être.

Mina's work for the team is not viewed as in any way exploitative in
the text: Mina's interests are seen to be literally married to Jonathan's.

I have been working very hard lately, because I want to keep up with Jonathan's
studies, and I have been practising shorthand very assiduously. When we are
married I shall be able to be useful to Jonathan, and if I can stenograph well
enough I can take down what he wants to say in this way and write it out for him
on the typewriter, at which I am also practising very hard. (71)

Later, too, she happily embraces her secretarial work for the team; after
all, as Van Helsing himself tells us at the end, the men are daring all
for her sake, like knights of old.[42] While the non-professional Texan is
ultimately killed off, and while Mina's gender disqualifies her from
team-membership, their selflessness is nevertheless entirely in keeping
with the logic of the new order. Part of the novel's ideological programme is the abnegation of simple self-interest. Van Helsing's final
eulogy on the men's 'salvation' of Mina ('some men so loved her, that
they did dare much for her sake' [449]) places their self-sacrificing
mission on a par with the divine ('And God so loved the world . . . ').
Earlier, one of the greatest compliments that Van Helsing finds to
bestow on Mina is that she is not selfish:

She is one of God's women fashioned by his own hand to show us men and
other women that there is a heaven where we can enter, and that its light can be
here on earth. So true, so sweet, so noble, so little an egoist – and that let me tell
you is much in this age, so sceptical and selfish. (227)

This occurs in a conversation between Van Helsing and Mina's husband, Jonathan. Vertiginous heights of homosocial rhetoric are
reached, and once again Mina's role, even – or perhaps especially – in
her absence, is to bond men emotionally. Jonathan is nearly overcome:
'We shook hands, and he was so earnest and so kind that it made me
quite choky' (227).[43] Selfishness is in fact a vice of the generation/social
formation that is displaced by the new professionals. The self-centred-
ness of the dying Mrs Westenra is partly responsible for her negligence
in caring for Lucy after the latter has become the Count's victim.
Seward is inclined to take a benign view of this sort of egoism:

Here, in a case where any shock may prove fatal, matters are so ordered that,
from some cause or other, the things not personal – even the terrible changes in

her daughter to whom she is so vitally attached – do not seem to reach her. It is something like the way Dame Nature gathers round a foreign body an envelope of some insensitive tissue which can protect from evil that which it would otherwise harm by contact. If this be an ordered selfishness, then we should pause before we condemn any one for the vice of egoism. . . . (147)

Subsequent events prove the dangers of this magnanimous view of things: through her ignorance of Lucy's condition Mrs Westenra is on more than one occasion responsible for the vampire's access to Lucy. Not once, but twice does she remove the garlic flowers from Lucy's neck, the first time opening the window as well to inadvertently admit Dracula. The defensive selfishness that Seward sees at work in her behaviour turns out to be fatal to others.

It would appear that Mrs Westenra is 'decadent' in the sense developed by Paul Bourget, whose ideas circulated in England in the 1880s and 1890s in the work of Havelock Ellis. The pseudo-scientific language used to define decadence is that which also comes to be the master discourse of *Dracula*. Here is Ellis's version of Bourget on decadence:

A society should be like an organism. Like an organism, in fact, it may be resolved into a federation of smaller organisms, which may themselves be resolved into a federation of cells. The individual is the social cell. In order that the organism should perform its functions with energy, but with a subordinated energy, and in order that these lesser organisms should themselves perform their functions with energy, it is necessary that the cells comprising them should perform their functions with energy, but with a subordinated energy. If the energy of the cells becomes independent, the lesser organisms will likewise cease to subordinate their energy to the total energy and the anarchy which is established constitutes the *decadence* of the whole. The social organism does not escape this law and enters into *decadence* as soon as the individual life becomes exaggerated beneath the influence of acquired well-being and of heredity.[44]

The sort of thinking that *Dracula* produces, then, is coming to be familiar to an English readership in this period from other discourses. Mrs Westenra's egoism, however excusable it may seem initially to Seward, causes damage to the social organism. Her behaviour links her to the text's ultimate egoist, or ego-maniac in Max Nordau's terms, Dracula himself (Mina, at least, has been reading Nordau, and identifies the Count as 'a criminal and of criminal type . . . Nordau and Lombroso would so classify him').[45] As Van Helsing describes it, the fight against the vampire is the struggle of 'combination' against selfish individualism:

we too are not without strength. We have on our side *power of combination* – a power denied the vampire kind; we have resources of science; we are free to act and think; and the hours of the day and the night are ours equally . . . We have self-devotion in a cause, and an end to achieve that is not a selfish one. These things are much. (my emphasis)

Van Helsing, and the professional middle-class fraction from which he comes, are not above learning a lesson from the working class, it seems. Combination, which as E. P. Thompson shows once evoked middle-class and aristocratic fears of Jacobin conspiracy as well as of unioniz-ation, is here reborn as the cornerstone of professional middle-class power.[46] If the aristocratic prestige of a Lord Godalming can be re-modelled as a useful tool for this enterprise, some of the collectivist practices of the working class can be similarly appropriated. What is involved in this collectivism is not so much a rethinking of the relations of self and society, in which the self must give more ground to society, as what Patrick Joyce describes as the late Victorian recognition of 'the social' conceived as a system with laws of its own. As part of this process, the Victorian ethos of independence and 'self-help' yields to one in which 'rights and obligations [are] seen in terms of collective solidarities and responsibilities, and articulated in a language of "exter-nal", extra-personal, social responsibilities [and in which] individual needs [are] now seen as "social" needs'.[47] The new class of experts would more and more combine to define what those 'social needs' were.

THE RISE OF PROFESSIONALISM

Franco Moretti has argued that Dracula represents the threat of mon-opoly capitalism itself, against which the more 'traditional' forces repre-sented by Van Helsing's team set themselves.[48] Similarly, in a recent essay that lends support to my own view that *Dracula* is a tale of professionalism, Jani Scandura sees the Count as representing some-thing new, 'a socially and economically aspiring Other who scales the slippery facade of free enterprise'.[49] But from what we have seen of the text it seems more likely that the meanings that congeal around Dracula designate him as dated, as last year's model. It is in his archaic or traditional individualism that he is most monstrous. By contrast, the little band of men formed in the text are an emergent formation; they are part of the emergence of monopoly capital, in the specific form that takes in the professional monopolies.

Professionalism is a rather difficult concept to pin down.[50] Histories of professionalism run the risk of assuming a false continuity between its pre-industrial and its nineteenth-century varieties, or between its relatively independent nineteenth-century practitioners and the modern corporate professional. The sociology of the professions has to strive to distinguish between the objective attributes of professionalism and the professions' own self-image. Magali Sarfatti Larson provides a useful definition of professionalism as 'the attempt to translate one order of scarce resource – special knowledge and skills – into another – social and economic rewards'.[51] This translation cannot work without certain conditions, notably state endorsement of the particular monopoly of resources being established. Even for the most 'traditional' of the market-oriented professions (which excludes the military and the clergy), these conditions aren't established until well into the nineteenth century. The Law Society was not established until the Solicitors Act of 1825; in medicine the complicated system of physicians, surgeons, apothecaries and apothecary-surgeons was finally rationalized by the 1858 Medical Act.[52] Of more concern to us here, though, is the remarkable rise of occupations that reinvented themselves as professions in the late Victorian period. There are two different processes at work in the rise of professional ideologies in the late nineteenth century. On the one hand, there is a considerable increase in the number of what we might call dependent professionals. (This is an awkward usage, since it is the way in which these groups begin to define themselves as professionals that is of interest – potential professionals might be a better term.) As Harold Perkin describes, these

were growing with the expansion of service occupations during the Victorian age. By 1911, if we add the lesser professionals and technicians to the higher ones, the professions were 4.1 per cent of the occupied population, not much short of the 4.6 per cent who were 'employers' in the census of industrial status, and if we add 'managers and administrators' the figure rises to 7.5 per cent, larger than the category of 'employers and proprietors' (6.7 per cent).[53]

What is more significant for our purposes, however, is that more and more individuals who depended for their livelihood on the marketing of particular specialized knowledges began to amalgamate along the lines of the existing 'liberal professions', such as medicine and law. At work here is the professional ideology of the self-regulating organization of experts, but also the more general collectivist ethos of the late nineteenth century. The last quarter of the nineteenth century is generally recognized as the moment of combination in industry and business, of the formation of cartels, syndicates and trusts. Even Britain, which was losing ground as the pace of industrial and economic development increased elsewhere, participated in this international trend towards concentration of capital. As Eric Hobsbawm puts it: 'From 1880 on the pattern of distribution was revolutionized. "Grocer" and "butcher" now meant not simply a small shopkeeper but increasingly a nationwide or international firm with hundreds of branches.'[54] There was a similar tendency towards combination among those who possessed educational 'capital'. Professional associations of all sorts proliferated. To name only those involved in the sphere of literary production, the late nineteenth century sees the appearance of the Associated Booksellers of Great Britain and Ireland (1895), the Publishers' Association (1895), and the Society of Authors (1883). Perkin charts the dimensions of this transformation:

To the seven qualifying associations of 1800 – four Inns of Court for barristers, two Royal Colleges and the society of Apothecaries for medical doctors – the first eighty years of the nineteenth century had added only twenty more, for solicitors, architects, builders (not successful as a profession), pharmacists, veterinary surgeons, actuaries, surveyors, chemists, librarians, bankers (another unsuccessful attempt), accountants, and eight types of engineer. From 1880 down to the First World War there appeared no less than thirty-nine, from chartered accountants, auctioneers and estate agents, company secretaries and hospital administrators to marine, mining, water, sanitary, heating and ventilating, and locomotive design engineers, insurance brokers, sales managers, and town planners. To these we should add the non-qualifying associations . . . which often combined professional aspirations with something of the character of trade unions or employers' associations.[55]

A large section of the middle class who were not owners of capital in the traditional sense, and who clearly did not see themselves as clerks, began to define themselves in the terms of expertise that had only relatively recently been fully appropriated by the 'real' professions. As Perkin suggests, the dream of professionalism is of resources (knowledge and skill) which in theory at least are susceptible of almost infinite extension: everyone can be a capitalist where human capital is in question. Medicine (and to a lesser extent law) was the profession that offered the dominant model for the new groups of experts to aspire to: high social status, the ideal of public service, self-regulation, and the idea of expertise based on a developing scientific field were all highly attractive to these groups.[56]

Medicine's role as a master-profession is important for an attempt to understand the particular contribution which *Dracula* makes to the late Victorian imaginary. While, as I have noted, its protagonists are for the most part professionals of the (somewhat) more established sort, this narrative of the deployment of expertise and the power of combination spoke to all those other groups for whom medical expertise provided the ideological image of their own specialized knowledge. The men's collectivity of Stoker's text, then, speaks to a more general movement in middle-class England, providing them with a collective origin myth and with a fantasy of control through expertise. Rather than representing the last gasp of liberal English culture against monopoly capital, as Franco Moretti would have it, the group led by Van Helsing *are* the new men, an increasingly fraternal, or associationist, and in specific ways patriarchal, group. The threat that ostensibly unites them is, so to speak, a back-formation; and the woman in whose defence they claim to be working also provides the secretarial and other support services that sustain them. It is in this sense that we can speak of the text's *using* fear toward a particular end, rather than expressing it.

In his illuminating study *Thrillers: Genesis and Structure of a Popular Genre*, Jerry Palmer traces the origins of the thriller to the mid-nineteenth century, specifically to the rise of ideologies of competitive individualism and a new, class-based, hostility to economic crime.[57] The figure conjured up as the appropriate hero for the new genre is the professional, especially the detective as a crime-expert. The isolated, self-reliant, professional is defined against two other types: the bureaucrat, who unlike the professional is incapable of unplanned activity, and the amateur, who does not understand anything (thus the trio of Sherlock Holmes, Lestrade the police bureaucrat and Watson). The professional hero defends the natural order of society against the unnatural criminal conspiracy, and anything that he does, however 'criminal', is justified in advance by this greater evil that he opposes. Palmer's analysis is convincing as far as it goes, but the slightly awkward combination of structural analysis and the sociology of genres leads him to overlook the appearance at the end of the nineteenth century of a species of professional heroism that does not correspond to ideologies of competitive individualism. *Dracula* and the other 'team' novels of the 1880s and 1890s indicate a shift away from the values of laissez-faire, competitive individualism, and a subsequent equation of professionalism with a more associationist ideal. Like Moretti, Palmer assumes that individualism is a value enshrined in popular fiction, but the message of *Dracula* is that competitive individuals are a menace to be destroyed: the new hero is corporate. H. G. Wells's *The Invisible Man* (also 1897), where the lone megalomaniac scientist, Griffin, is finally surrounded by the crowd and literally kicked and beaten to death is in this respect an even more graphic instance than Stoker's novel.

THE VAMPIRE AS FIGURE

While I am arguing that we can to some extent decode the significance of the 'little band of men', I also want to insist that the figure of the vampire is better understood as just that – a figure. In other words, I want to shift the emphasis from what the vampire and vampirism might represent to the mode of representation, to the particular form that the vampire gives to danger. In the vampire we confront a monster whose primary usefulness depends on his capacity to *embody* threats, not so much in his own body, which remains elusively protean, but in the bodies of his victims, specifically women. Once a threat has been properly embodied, it can be dealt with. We can best understand the vampire's incorporative power by considering Stoker's own earlier 'monster', which appears in *The Snake's Pass* (1890), a text that we will study in more detail in chapter 2. In this, his first novel, he blends adventure romance after the fashion of H. Rider Haggard with an inter-ethnic marriage plot. His English hero, Arthur Severn, becomes embroiled in a land dispute and a search for treasure while visiting the west of Ireland. Severn eventually marries Norah Joyce, the daughter of an Irish peasant.[58] One of the most striking aspects of the text, though, is the amount of space devoted to describing the peculiar shifting bog which dominates the landscape. An old schoolfriend of Severn's, Dick Sutherland, is engaged in research into the bogs of Ireland, and through their conversations we are given a wealth of bog-lore. While the novel has a conventional villain, the money-lender Black Murdock, the only force in the text analogous to the threat of Dracula is in fact the shifting bog. The bog is, in its own way, a monster, as the following dialogue between Severn and his old schoolfriend shows:

'Is it a dangerous bog?' I queried.
'Rather! It is just as bad a bit of soft bog as ever I saw. I wouldn't like to see anyone or anything that I cared for try to cross it . . . [b]ecause at any moment they might sink through it; and then, goodbye – no human strength or skill could ever save them.'
'Is it a quagmire, then? or like a quicksand?'

'. . . Nay! it is more treacherous than either. You may call it, if you are
poetically inclined, a "carpet of death!"' . . . It will bear up a certain weight, for
there is a degree of cohesion in it; but it is not all of equal cohesive power, and if
one were to step in the wrong spot –' He was silent.
'. . . A body suddenly immersed would, when the air of the lungs had escaped
and the rigor mortis had set in, probably sink a considerable distance; then it
would rise after nine days, when decomposition began to generate gases. . . .
Not succeeding in this, it would ultimately waste away, and the bones would
become *incorporated* with the existing vegetation somewhere about the roots, or
would lie among the slime at the bottom.'
'Well,' said I, 'for real cold-blooded horror, commend me to your men of
science.'59

In this passage it is clear that the threat posed by the bog is of the
dissolution of identity through a negative version of 'incorporation'. The
bog, like the vampire, has the capacity to assimilate foreign bodies, to
incorporate matter into its own substance. To be drained by the vampire is to have your blood circulate with his, to have your essence
preserved, yet to be personally destroyed. In the case of the victim of the
shifting bog 'the bones . . . become incorporated with the existing
vegetation somewhere about the roots'. The threat of the bog functions
in specific ways in *The Snake's Pass* that don't concern us here, but the
earlier novel does allow us to see how the figure of the vampire is a more
successful reworking of the earlier figure.

The bog is in many ways a greater threat than the vampire, or more
accurately, the text has yet to evolve strategies for its successful control:
the professional ideal is not as effective there as in the case of *Dracula*. It is
not that the ideal is unavailable, as the following passage indicates. Dick
Sutherland is explaining how to reclaim bogland:

'In fine we cure bog by both a surgical and a medical process. We drain it so
that its mechanical action as a sponge may be stopped, and we put in lime to kill
the vital principle of its growth. Without the other, neither process is sufficient;
but together, scientific and executive man asserts his dominance.'
'Hear! Hear!' said Andy. 'Musha but Docther Wilde himself, Rest his sowl!
couldn't have put it aisier to grip. It's a *purfessionaler* the young gintleman is
intirely.' (56, my emphasis)

The draining operations undertaken, though, are on a less treacherous
bog than the one described above. Eventually lime does become available in abundant quantities to further the work of reclamation, but only
when the shifting bog has slid off into the sea: 'scientific and executive
man' can only do their work when the real 'monster' of the text has been

conveniently removed. The monstrous, shifting bog represents a threat that has not been adequately embodied, one that in fact threatens to erase the boundaries of any corporeal self. While the collectivities of *Dracula* seem to provide a version of professional incorporation that is untroubling for the subjects of the novel, the Count himself, like the incorporating bog, threatens the very possibility of identity. The professional organizations offered the possibility of a job for life under their benign aegis, but becoming part of the Dracula corporation means complete self-sacrifice.[60]

Unlike the more properly abject bog, though, the threat of the vampire can be localized and overcome in the bodies of his female victims. We can discern both a continuity with the professional techniques of the engineer, Sutherland, and an advance over them in the shift from the language of the engineer to that of the doctor: cutting and draining are the equivalent to decapitation and staking in the control of the vampire; adding lime the equivalent of filling the mouth with garlic. One process stops the 'mechanical action', the other the 'vital principle'. Significantly, we only have one example in the text of all of these protocols being followed: the staking of the only English vampire, Lucy, in the tomb. As I have suggested, this localization of the danger in the body of women demonstrates the extent to which the threat of the vampire is custom-built for a certain emergent form of power: the collectivity is formed to deal with the threat of the outsider/ foreign body, but its most important activities are directed at extending its power 'at home'. Van Helsing, the vampire expert, but also professionally interested in Lucy as her physician, is the one who explains the means of her 'reclamation' in the following passage.[61] As in the case of Dick Sutherland's account of the treatment of the bog, the master language is provided by science. Professional knowledge distinguishes Seward and Van Helsing from Quincey and Lord Godalming, especially when the medical instruments used take on a strikingly domestic character:

Van Helsing, in his methodical manner, began taking the various contents from his bag and placing them ready for use. First he took out a soldering iron and some plumbing solder, and then a small oil-lamp . . . then his operating knives . . . and last a round stake some two and a half or three inches thick and about three feet long . . . With this stake came a heavy hammer, such as in households is used in the coal-cellar for breaking the lumps. To me, a doctor's preparations for work of any kind are stimulating and bracing, but the effect of these things on both Arthur and Quincey was to cause them a sort of consternation. (256–7)

The techniques of surgery (the operating knives) meet those of the handy-man (solder, coal-hammer, stake), the latter magically transformed by the alchemy of professionalism. There are further rituals: the actual staking, performed by Arthur under Van Helsing's direction, is accompanied by a 'prayer for the dead' (surely inappropriate if Lucy is not yet really dead) before the two doctors add the final touches: 'the Professor and I sawed the top off the stake, leaving the point of it in the body. Then we cut off the head and filled the mouth with garlic' (260). This is a far more elaborate process than that which is required to treat the other vampires, including the Count himself. The staking of Dracula is by comparison a very rushed affair, and even the destruction of the three vampire women who still inhabit Dracula's castle in Transylvania is handled without a number of the steps followed in Lucy's case. The English woman is the only proper object of these techniques. As we discovered through the fate of Quincey Morris, the staker of Dracula, the use of these same professional procedures against males, even against the monstrous Count, is fraught with danger, and runs counter to the logic of the narrative's project. In a very real sense, *Dracula* turns out to be not about Dracula at all: his staking is the least important in the text.

'Reclaiming' Lucy is different from reclaiming bogs in a fundamental respect, of course: Lucy's immortal soul is in peril rather than her body, and the 'surgery' employed is in effect ritual accompanied by prayers. The 'scientific man' of *The Snake's Pass* is replaced by the hybrid Van Helsing, who appears to be priest as well as doctor and lawyer, and who has recourse to a pre-scientific lexis of souls and salvation. This makes more sense if we assume with Nikolas Rose that the 'human technologies' that appear or develop a new importance toward the end of the nineteenth century – not just psychology, but also, for example, theories and practices of education, time-tabling, and statistics – take as their object something that might well be designated as 'the soul'.[62] *Dracula*'s medico-religious rituals provide a dialectical image of this process. As Rose shows, the new class of experts is not solely responsible for the government of the soul, and nor for that matter is the state, though modernist and, indeed, postmodernist fiction will be haunted by the idea of their collusion, condensed in such figures as the hateful psychiatrist of Woolf's *Mrs Dalloway*, Dr Bradshaw, and the sinister forces that combine to exploit Tyrone Slothrop in Thomas Pynchon's *Gravity's Rainbow*.

Vampirism is a back-formation justifying a certain type of intervention, a new type of discipline, a new place for the qualified professional who straddles the public and private realms. Since vampirism is already within the home, the professional must follow it there. Since women are the vampire's natural prey, they must become the special objects of the professional's watchfulness. Besides Dracula's castle, we are offered only two models of domesticity in the novel. The first is the Westenras' home, where the Count's attacks on Lucy necessitate (and this making necessary is very much the text's project) the turning of the home into a hospital: alternatively watched over by Dr Seward and Professor Van Helsing at first, and later guarded by the full male team excluding Harker, Lucy scarcely lives in a private house any longer. Later in the novel, the novel's principal institution, Seward's asylum for the insane, becomes itself a home: Mina and the band of men all come to live in the institution. The domestic merges with the institutional and the institutional merges with the domestic, which of course is only appropriate in a novel where the only marriage, that of Mina and Jonathan, takes place in a hospital.[63] Both of these carefully administered spaces, the institutional house and the domestic institution, have as their ostensible goal the protection of the vulnerable female body from the vampire, yet in both cases the Count manages to enter relatively effortlessly. But in this failure lies the strength of Van Helsing's group: it is only when the vampire-threat comes to be located within the female body that they can properly treat it. Similarly, it is only when the female body has been infected by vampirism that it can constitute a proper object of expert treatment: where there is no crisis, there can be no intervention. Some years later the 'crisis' within the national body announced by the military set-backs of the Boer War would lead to a reconceptualization of the relationship between on the one hand the state and on the other the private home, the family, and women's bodies, developments catalysed by the new science of eugenics.[64]

At a time when Victorian Britain was being transformed by professionalism, combination and collectivity, the Victorian romance conjures up a whole series of teams of men. H. Rider Haggard's *King Solomon's Mines* and *She*, Sir Arthur Conan Doyle's *The Lost World*, and arguably even the latter's *The Adventures of Sherlock Holmes* all lend themselves to analysis in these terms. The crisis-model developed in *Dracula* makes the process of team-formation particularly clear, but the expedition and the investigation, like the struggle against the monster, also posit some obstacle to overcome which requires the energies of the team of men. The ethos of good old-fashioned adventure hides the extent to which the collective characters at the centre of these narratives correspond to a distinct moment of modernization.

Of course the seamless way in which the male team establishes itself in *Dracula* glosses over the far more conflicted process of the consolidation of professional power. The rise of professional culture lacked the strong narrative drive of Stoker's novel: there were subplots and *longueurs*, not to mention problems of closure. Women were by no means content to act as the objects of professional intervention, and the rise of professionalism in fact created many opportunities for women to function outside of traditional domestic roles. While the professional associations were by and large hostile to the idea of women members, their strategies of exclusion were ultimately unsuccessful.[65] Even in the profession of medicine, which the novel makes its master-profession, women disputed male control almost as soon as it was first secured by the Medical (Registration) Act of 1868.[66] Nevertheless, the associationist ideals and the specific disposition of power/knowledge that *Dracula* presents in nascent form have proved to be extremely resilient. Moreover, while the shape of the crisis keeps changing, crisis narratives continue to provide terms in which professional intervention can be explained.[67] While the Count enjoyed an impressive afterlife in popular culture, then, one might argue that the real survivors of the novel are the 'little band of men': in countless films, books and television shows, the model of the team of men, each member possessing some particular skill, is reproduced.[68] Revamped in war stories, westerns and police procedurals, the narrative of professional combination shows no signs of dying out.

Where much adventure fiction unfolds against an exotic backdrop, in *Dracula*, Stoker uses the figure of the vampire to bring the action closer to home: his team of men are as comfortable – more comfortable, I would argue – policing the houses of London as they are tracking the vampire across Eastern Europe. *Dracula* allows us to see that imperial novels also have a domestic address: the professional man at home can see his own exotic reflection in the resourceful imperial team-member. However, romances like *King Solomon's Mines* or *The Lost World* cannot simply be understood in terms of late Victorian ideologies of professionalism. The new imperialism of the *fin de siècle* also generated and was sustained by specific fantasies of its own, and it is to these that we now turn.

CHAPTER 2

The imperial treasure hunt: The Snake's Pass *and the limits of romance*

... the 'sociology of literature' is blind to the war and the ruses
perpetrated by the author who reads and by the first reader who
dictates, for at stake here is the origin of the work itself.
　　　　　　　　Jacques Derrida, *Freud and the Scene of Writing*

If *Dracula* emplots the mutation in public/private space at the metropole, novels like *Treasure Island, King Solomon's Mines* and *She* offer
fantasies about the relations of metropolitan and imperial space. As the
new imperialism emerged in the late nineteenth and early twentieth
centuries these romances equipped the metropolitan subject with an
imaginary model of the territories that were daily added to the British
empire. They depict the conquest of overseas space by the reader's
delegates within the text, the fictional explorers, hunters, soldiers and
engineers who march relentlessly across trackless desert, jungle and
veldt.[1] The expedition was scarcely a new motif in British adventure
fiction, of course, but from the 1880s on that fiction fosters and appeals
to a stronger sense of spatial mastery through the motifs of the survey
and the map. The treasure hunt in particular, most memorably in
Stevenson's *Treasure Island* (1883) and Haggard's *King Solomon's Mines*
(1885), placed the map at the heart of the imperial imaginary.[2] This
marks a departure from *Dracula*'s fantasy of power: where medical
science underpins the new relation to domestic space, the relation to
imperial space is negotiated through the far more haphazard knowledge
given by amateur cartography – by the hand-drawn treasure-map. And
yet the possibility that the map might not be reliable is itself an important part of the imperial fantasy in this period. As Europe's imperial
powers competed for the remaining pieces of Africa and Asia, as the
adventure of empire came to seem more and more like a well-organized
business, officially uncharted territories assumed a new importance in
the European imagination. The clumsily made treasure map – often
written, rather inappropriately, in European blood – is thus a composite

icon of imperial power, representing the exotic territory as at once mysterious and remote and yet ultimately knowable. The 'blank spaces of the map', then, are precisely what the adventure novel maps.

I want in this chapter to unpack the representational strategies of the imperial adventure novel, but I want to approach this task rather obliquely. What would an adventure romance such as *King Solomon's Mines* be like if it were set in Europe? The considered response to this question, in the light of Said's *Orientalism*, might be that Rider Haggard's novel never really leaves Europe, that it provides a European fantasy that is not in the end about Africa. Let us imagine, however, a more literal-minded answer: what if *King Solomon's Mines*, or another adventure romance of this type were set in, say, Ireland? Bram Stoker's first novel, *The Snake's Pass* (1890), gives us some idea of the answer. This novel constructs an adventure romance of the sort made popular by R. L. Stevenson, H. Rider Haggard and others, but using colonial Ireland rather than a more exotic imperial setting. What difference does it make when, as in Stoker's novel, the 'blank spaces of the map' are replaced as setting by the more domesticated, though still colonial, landscape of the west of Ireland? Perhaps the most interesting aspect of Stoker's novel is that its survey and treasure hunt go somewhat awry – *The Snake's Pass* ultimately fails as a fantasy of imperial control. By this very failure, though, as I will show, this novel gives us a defamiliarized knowledge of the textual strategies of the romance. That these strategies are elsewhere more successful in the packaging of colonial space also indicates that imperial space – even imaginary imperial space – is not uniform. Stoker's novel provides, then, a point at which to broach issues of Ireland's peculiar status as a European colony in the era of New Imperialism.

In *The Snake's Pass* a vision of the colonial territory as a virgin page awaiting inscription is complicated by a conception of Irish land, specifically Irish bogland, as an already densely over-written surface. Not only does the bog physically resist the surveyor's project, it also produces from its depths disturbing reminders of the history of the colonial project. The novel's contradictory visions of landscape reveal the representational problems raised by the intersection of the new imperial ideologies of the 'scramble for Africa' and ways of seeing Ireland as a special colonial case, as an old colony with much closer ties to the metropolis. The difference between these two visions – Ireland as imperial territory and as special case – is articulated at a very obvious level in the narrative by the combination of the imperial romance model with another, older textual model of the relations between Ireland and England: the colonial marriage plot that Stoker inherits from the earlier Anglo-Irish fiction. The two subgenres, treasure hunt and courtship story, don't simply exist side by side, however; the failure to package Ireland as imaginary imperial space infects the marriage plot, as it were. Throughout, we have the sense of an inadequation of narrative models and historical materials. To account for this failure to impose form on Anglo-Irish relations, we need to consider Bram Stoker's own liminal position as an Anglo-Irish writer, one who was a moderate supporter of Home Rule for Ireland, and numbered many nationalist figures among his acquaintance, while affiliating with England and the Empire.[3] The spatial fantasies of the adventure romance compete for narrative attention with fantasies that are more clearly those of a particular colonial class, fantasies that are temporal rather than spatial.

The Snake's Pass also raises important questions about the production and reception of the romance. I will be describing Stoker's novel as a migratory text that appears to change its plumage depending on whether one sees it against a colonial or a metropolitan background. If imperial space is discontinuous – and this discontinuity in fact provides the thematics of much imperial romance – so is imperial cultural space. Spatial metaphors may even fail to capture the nature of the dimensions in which the novel originated and functioned. Stoker actually wrote *The Snake's Pass* while he was based in London, acting as business manager for the enormously successful Victorian actor, Henry Irving; but to the extent that many of the text's conversations, muted or explicit, are with Irish colonial discourse, it is also – if the term means anything – an Irish colonial novel.[4] This dual address inscribes itself in the texture of the writing itself, but we cannot imagine a 'pure' reception situation either. There is never, then, a tidy opposition between colonial literary production and metropolitan consumption. An ineluctable hybridity marks both processes: colonial literary production is overdetermined by its awareness of metropolitan readership and metropolitan literary traditions; consumption at the metropole, in turn, never takes place in complete ignorance of the discursive contexts of the colony. The 'truth' of the hybrid colonial text can neither be given exclusively in terms of its origins nor of its destination; both origins and destination remain, in a very real sense, undecidable. The colonial literary artifact, like its postcolonial descendant, resists totalization. What Homi K. Bhabha describes as 'the migrant's double vision' would be needed to bring into focus its extension into different dimensions.[5]

The theoretical rigour such a cultural situation solicits threatens critical rigor mortis. To avoid this fate, I will imagine here a schematized, two-part version of the text's history that in part reproduces its own generic doubling. I will attempt to discuss Stoker's novel as an adventure romance, and I will discuss it as a text which participates in various colonial discourses that are largely outside the problematic of imperial romance. The first half of this chapter, then, gives an account of the novel in relation to the context of its metropolitan reception, the imperial interpretive frame, or 'reading formation', which mediated it for an English audience.[6] This formation relies on, among other things, the specific deployment of landscape that, I am arguing, characterizes the imperial romance, but also specific forms of gender representation and readerly address. In the second part of this chapter I explore those features of *The Snake's Pass* which seem anomalous as long as the novel is seen as an adventure romance, but that make sense as part of a more 'local' intertext. Specifically, this section treats the novel as a vehicle for Anglo-Irish political fantasies – fantasies relating to the Land War of the 1880s, but also fantasies of origins that derive from the peculiar liminal position of the Anglo-Irish as a class. This may seem to be carrying us a long way from the revival of romance. As I hope to show, however, we can discern certain homologies between the cultural imaginary of the Anglo-Irish in this period (specifically in the cultural nationalism of the Irish Literary Revival associated with Yeats and Lady Gregory *inter alia*) and the British imperial ideology expressed by the adventure romance, particularly in their common concern with the heroic past.

The Snake's Pass first appeared in serial form late in 1889 in *The People* and some of the provincial papers, and appeared as a single volume the next year from Sampson Low. The context of the novel's appearance, in which empire was coming to be an increasingly important phenomenon in politics *and* publishing, is suggested by the fact that two of the most successful of Stoker's fellow authors at Sampson Low were G. A. Henty and H. M. Stanley.[7] Stoker's novel can be related in significant ways to the work of both of these writers, though formally it resembles more the imperial romances of Henty. Henty's romances usually concern the adventures of boy-heroes in the exoticized landscapes of the empire (e.g. *With Roberts to Pretoria, With Clive in India*), or in historical settings (*Beric the Briton, Wulf the Saxon*). He was, in other words, writing the sorts of 'boys stories' that writers like Haggard, Kipling and Stevenson were also producing in this period, though these latter authors appealed to children of empire of all ages. We can identify certain motifs that the

most successful of the imperial adventure romances of this period have in
common, such as the journey or expedition, the treasure-plot and the
'male family'.[8] H. Rider Haggard's *King Solomon's Mines* provides a
well-known example of these and other adventure motifs in action: a
band of men set out to find Sir Henry Curtis's lost brother with a sketchy
treasure-map as their only guide; they make a perilous journey through
parched deserts and across icy mountains to a hidden African kingdom;
they come upon untold wealth, and they successfully recover (almost by
the way) Sir Henry's brother. This is imperial romance at its most basic,
which is also to say at its most effective.

Imperial adventure fiction works to reconcile the officially ordered
space of the map and the personal space of the itinerary. The maps that
we meet in adventure fiction are already a departure from the official
imperial map: they are amateurish, provisional, personalized, even
eroticized – mnemonics of space rather than gridworks of place.[9] A case
in point is the map of Kukuanaland in *King Solomon's Mines,* which thinly
conceals the outline of a recumbent female body.[10] The expedition itself
and its moments of panorama further bridge the gap between the
reader's personal experience of space and the official territories of the
empire. The very titles of Henty's novels, *With Roberts to Pretoria, With
Clive in India,* suggest how they position the reader as a subject within an
imaginary landscape (compare later attempts to evoke such a response,
such as Lowell Thomas's *With Lawrence in Arabia* [1925]).[11] As Robert
MacDonald points out, the story of the young protagonist of the typical
Henty tale 'is a dramatisation of the story of conquest'. But it is
important to bear in mind that the adventure novel was part of a more
general effort to construct a metropolitan model of imperial space in this
period. Graham Dawson argues that as early as the Indian Rebellion of
1857 colonial and national imaginaries are drawn much closer together,
but certainly by the end of the century the depiction of colonial space
has become inextricable from the definition of the nation.[12] Imperial
postcards, the illustrated packaging of colonial goods, waxwork tableaux, exhibitions, theatrical spectacles, board games and, towards the
end of this period, film, also assisted in the production of a new scopic
sense of empire.[13] Even the museum culture that emerged in Britain
after mid century positioned the national subject as a viewer of imperial
objects. Thus, as Tony Bennett has recently described, the expansion of
a regime of surveillance charted by Michel Foucault counterpointed the
expansion of a regime of spectatorship, for which the material culture of
empire provided the ideal object.[14]

While being largely off-stage, England is the space that defines, and is defined by, the heterotopias of the adventure novel: to sketch the primitive is also to illustrate the civilized.[15] The stages of the journey through the 'wilderness' of Africa or South America mark a gradual transition from the world of English values to a more primitive social state that offers heroic possibilities long since denied to the civilized subject. Thus the journey through space comes to also represent a journey in time. In *King Solomon's Mines* the temporal journey is further emphasized by a division within the exotic landscape. The daunting mountain range that the adventurers cross in that novel seals off a lost tribe from the progress of the outside world, rather as the steep cliffs of a remote South American plateau allow the survival of a whole prehistoric eco-system in Conan Doyle's *The Lost World*. In place of the African or South American interior, though, *The Snake's Pass* takes as its primitive environment the west of Ireland, where the English tourist-hero, Arthur Severn, falls in love with a local 'peasant's' daughter, Norah Joyce, and embroils himself in a struggle against the local moneylender for land, treasure and Norah herself. Nevertheless, the lines of demarcation between the quotidian world and the space of romance are as clearly defined as they are in Haggard's African romance. Here, for example, Severn describes his journey to the remote district where the action of the novel takes place:

Between two great mountains of grey and green, as the rock cropped out between the tufts of emerald verdure, the valley, almost as narrow as a gorge, ran due west towards the sea. There was just room for the roadway, half cut in the rock, beside the narrow strip of dark lake of seemingly unfathomable depth that lay far below between perpendicular walls of frowning rock. In the wide terrace-like steps of the shelving mountain there were occasional glimpses of civilization emerging from the almost primal desolation which immediately surrounded us – clumps of trees, cottages, and the irregular outlines of stone-walled fields, with black stacks of turf for winter firing piled here and there. Far below was the sea – the great Atlantic – with a wildly irregular coastline studded with a myriad of clustering rocky islands . . . The view was the most beautiful I had ever seen, and accustomed as I had been only to the quiet pastoral beauty of a grass country, with occasional visits to my Great Aunt's well-wooded estate in the south of England, it was no wonder that it arrested my attention and absorbed my imagination . . . Earth, sea and air all evidenced the triumph of nature, and told of her wild majesty and beauty. [16]

The Irish landscape is 'irregular', 'wild', and manifests the 'triumph of nature'; its waters are 'unfathomable', an important concept for the subsequent thematicization of the countryside. In opposition to the wildness of this colonial space exists the 'quiet pastoral beauty' of England, where 'primal desolation' is replaced by the regularity of the 'well-wooded estate'. One still has 'occasional glimpses of civilization' in the west of Ireland, but the general picture is of the ascendancy of 'nature'. The stage is set for Arthur's involvement in a series of adventures which will allow him a form of heroic subjectivity unavailable to him in England: over against the latter's 'pastoral', the colony seems to open a space for epic.[17] The journey back in time becomes also, then, a journey back through the history of narrative form: romance is theorized by its advocates in the 1880s as a sort of modern epic that represents the most basic, and thus the most forceful, of narrative forms.[18]

While the romance produces imperial landscape as antithetical to England's green swards, these imaginary territories are nevertheless presented as susceptible to the power of the explorer's gaze.[19] Images of an imperial sublime co-exist with a discourse of visual dominance. For example, in the following passage from *King Solomon's Mines*, the tension between these positions is developed through the landscape's simultaneous appearance as both infinite and knowable:

Behind and over us towered Sheba's snowy breasts, and below, some five thousand feet beneath where we stood, lay league on league of the most lovely champaign country. Here were dense patches of lofty forest, there a great river wound its silvery way. To the left stretched a vast expanse of rich, undulating veldt or grass land, on which we could just make out countless herds of game or cattle, at that distance we could not tell which. This expanse appeared to be ringed in by a wall of distant mountains . . . The landscape lay before us like a map, in which rivers flashed like silver snakes, and Alplike peaks crowned with wildly-twisted snow-wreaths rose in solemn grandeur, while over all was the glad sunlight and the wide breath of Nature's happy life.[20]

The commensurable ('some five thousand feet') rubs shoulders with the infinite ('vast', 'countless'); the sublime grandeur of the Alps is undercut by an image that links visibility and knowability ('lay before us like a map'). *The Snake's Pass*, on the other hand, develops a more uneasy thematics of imperial vision. Arthur, as a tourist, spends a great deal of his time in visually consuming Ireland; in his eyes the colonial territory is abstracted into a series of reassuring prospects: 'Somehow the view seemed to tranquillize me in some degree. It may have been that there was some unconscious working on the mind which told me in some imperfect way that *in a region quite within my range of vision, nothing could long remain hidden or unknown*' (93, my emphasis). But the novel also thematicizes visual control through projects of surveying and engineering, and here the sense of visual mastery falters. Arthur meets an old school-friend, Dick Sutherland, who is employed as an engineer in the area. Sutherland is also conducting some private scientific research into the bogs of Ireland and their reclamation, and the novel provides extensive accounts of his investigations of the peculiar local 'shifting bogs', which Sutherland hopes to reclaim through a process that involves both mapping and drainage. His account of Irish bogland places it at the edge of British imperial knowledge. Although bogs '[touch] deeply the happiness and material prosperity of a large section of Irish people, and so [help] mould their political action' (55), little, he claims, is known of them. This lacuna in the imperial archive is so serious, Sutherland complains, that 'even the last edition of the "Encyclopaedia Britannica" does not contain the heading "bog" ' (55).[21] The text spends a great deal of time presenting the bog as a problem to be solved through the agency of 'scientific and executive man' (56), but to the extent that Sutherland himself represents this latter figure, the problem eludes such agency. If the African landscape presented by Haggard is mysterious yet ultimately knowable, the bog appears to represent the limits of the text's ability to map colonial space.

In *King Solomon's Mines* and *Treasure Island* the map is a device to produce the empire as an imaginary space for the investment of desire, as well as a way of representing the control of the blank spaces on the map.[22] There thus exists a close connection in the imperial romance between the discourse of surveying, mapping, constructing a sort of visual dominance over the landscape, and another romance topos, the treasure hunt. The ability to map the exotic territory leads directly to the discovery of its treasures. This same linkage recurs in *The Snake's Pass*, where Black Murdock, the villain of the piece and the local money-lender, or 'Gombeen man' (Ir. *gaimbín*, usury), uses Sutherland's engineering expertise in a search for buried treasure. Murdock is searching the bog on his property for the lost gold of the French forces who came to Ireland in 1798 in support of an Irish rebellion against British rule. Again, though, this treasure hunt marks a difference as well as a topical similarity. The mineral treasures of *King Solomon's Mines*, or of *She*, suggest the untold riches that are to be had from the body of the colonial territory; they are a form of 'natural' wealth. Like the teeming wildlife on which Haggard's protagonists test their marksmanship, these treasures signify the colonial cornucopia.[23] In Stoker's text the treasure has a different relation to the ground in which it is found. It is not only that it isn't 'natural' wealth: the Irish treasure has its origins in the history of colonial struggle. Just as the bog challenges the visual control of the subject, the treasure which Irish soil reluctantly gives up tests the edges of the imperial fantasy. England's historical relation to Ireland is too vividly evoked by these spoils of war.[24]

The treasure hunt also leads us to the connections among empire, imperial romance and profit. The characters who populate empire fiction are those whom we may assume to be required by an aggressively expanding nation; in these novels the exotic territory acts as a testing-ground for the manly European subject. But there are also close ties between the expanding empire and the expanding culture industry in this period. Popular fiction and, increasingly towards the end of this period, film make empire pay at home through addressing new readers, new markets for the literary commodity. These novels are engaged as much in producing armchair adventurers, imperial consumers, as real empire builders. While imperial adventure fiction was often portrayed, like empire itself, as an escape from the commercial fug of the metropole (as well as from the cloying atmosphere of the naturalist novel) into the colonial fresh air, packaging the empire for domestic consumption was a very profitable commercial enterprise. If empire was profitable in terms of its provision of raw materials and a market for British manufactured goods, it also became a marketable dream. The treasure hunt partly thematicizes the multiple contradictions in imperial ideology. The novels undercut their apparent rejection of the world of commerce by the way in which they link exploration to the topos of the treasure hunt, as I suggested above: while material gain is rarely the ostensible aim of these adventures (*Treasure Island* is an exception in this respect), it frequently follows.[25] In *King Solomon's Mines*, *She* and Conan Doyle's *The Lost World* it is diamonds; in *The Snake's Pass* the French gold. The only character in Stoker's novel who is motivated by the desire for riches is Black Murdock, the villain of the piece, and he is ultimately a victim of his greed, engulfed by the bog that he searches for the treasure. However, the other 'team', consisting of Arthur, Dick Sutherland (who early on leaves Murdock's employ), Norah Joyce, the heroine, and Norah's father *does* find the treasure, which is left behind when the treacherous bog slides into the sea after a heavy fall of rain. Thus *The Snake's Pass* replays the serendipitous logic of other romances, denying (in the Freudian sense of *Verneinung*) the desire of the character/reader at the same time that it satisfies it; colonial wealth is not sought, but it is found all the same. Arthur and Dick, though, are more impressed with the second treasure found beneath the bog – a golden crown, seemingly dating from an early Irish civilization, which they find in a limestone cavern decorated with ogham writing. We shall return below to the significance of this second treasure, which has no equivalent in other adventure romances.

The central characters of the imperial adventure are, of course, almost invariably male. If the domestic novel revolves around the family and the heterosexual love plot, the adventure romance constructs an all-male 'family' or team, and replaces the heterosexual romance with strong affective (though also hierarchical) ties between men. Anne McClintock has described the colonies as granting a new lease of life to forms of patriarchal organization that were increasingly marginalized by the development of a centralized state bureaucracy in Britain; adventure fiction offered an analogous extended life to certain modes of heroic masculinity.[26] The manly men of these novels recall the Victorian image of the 'Christian soldier', epitomized by colonial heroes like Sir Henry Havelock. The specifically literary origins of 'men's men' like Haggard's modern 'Viking', Sir Henry Curtis, lie in the earlier phenomenon of muscular Christianity most closely associated with the adventure tales of Kingsley and the public school fiction of Thomas Hughes.[27] Indeed, imperial romance heroes often look as if they may be adult versions of the boys in *Tom Brown's Schooldays* (1857).[28] *The Snake's Pass* links 'playing the game', gender identity, and physical force in the following passage, in which Arthur defends Norah's honour from the vile imputations of Murdock:

Here I could restrain myself no longer; and to my joy on the instant – and since then whenever I have thought of it – Norah withdrew her hand as if to set me free. I stepped forward, and with one blow fair in the lips knocked the foul-mouthed ruffian [sc. Murdock] head over heels. He rose in an instant, his face covered with blood, and rushed at me. This time I stepped out, and with an old football trick, taking him on the breast-bone with my open hand, again tumbled him over. (170)

Arthur's reliance on his early training identifies him with imperial adventure heroes such as Stalky of Kipling's *Stalky & Co.*, who brings his public school skills to the North-West frontier, or Bertie Cecil in Ouida's *Under Two Flags*, who 'with the science of the Eton Playing Fields of his boyhood' escapes imprisonment and goes on to blaze a trail of glory in Algeria with the French cavalry.[29] As Michael Denning shows, this connection between sports and more dangerous games survives in the novel of popular adventure well into the twentieth century through the narratives of Erskine Childers, John Buchan and 'Sapper', which also celebrate the muscular Christian, and it even appears in modified form in Ian Fleming's James Bond novels.[30]

While the male team that we encountered in the previous chapter appears to be the appropriate group-subject in domestic adventures, the empire team is usually less clearly marked as 'expert'. Thus in *King Solomon's Mines*, Allan Quatermain is a professional hunter, someone whose chosen area of expertise is indeed Africa, but Good is a naval officer, and Sir Henry Curtis is a country gentleman; they are gentlemanly amateurs both. The idea of professionalism had, of course, some impact on actual British imperialism in later years, in part through the popularity of the technocratic ideology of national 'efficiency'. Beatrice and Sidney Webb attempted to bring together a cross-party group of leading imperialists, experts in various fields of government under the name the 'Coefficients'. The Coefficients never developed into a political party, but as Harold Perkin notes, 'they were an eloquent expression of the professional ideal in its social imperialist phase'.[31] This ideal of science-based professional efficiency never finds full expression in the imperial romances.[32] In *The Snake's Pass*, where Ireland oscillates uneasily between exotic colonial space and domestic space, the expert does appear in the person of the engineer, Dick Sutherland, but Arthur Severn, the gentleman of property, is the real hero of the piece.

The Snake's Pass never develops the fully-fledged 'male family' or team that we find in *Dracula*; it only has two full members, Arthur and Dick, though later in the novel, Norah's father, Phelim, becomes, as it were, an associate member, as to some extent does Andy, Arthur's guide. Arthur and Dick are quite literally old boys, schoolfriends separated over the years but now brought together by their love for the same woman. The triangular relation between Dick, Norah and Arthur recalls a similar structure in Haggard's *She* (and looks forward to the more obvious homosociality of *Dracula*), but here it is overwritten by another narrative pattern, that of the inter-ethnic symbolic marriage. The romance comes to be 'romantic' in the other sense. Arthur, with Dick's assistance, foils the machinations of Black Murdock, and wins Norah's hand, and he sends her off to continental and English finishing schools, which turn the Irish peasant into a 'lady'.

Such a reshaping of the native woman is impossible in imperial romances set in the more distant parts of the empire. These novels do represent the colonial woman as exerting a peculiar fascination, but the exotic sexuality that the adventurers find in Africa is never allowed to

disturb the integrity of the male family.[33] Where, as in *King Solomon's Mines*, or *She*, there is a possibility of the male family being broken up by the attractions of such a woman, the text quickly shuts down this avenue of narrative development: the threats posed by Ustane, Ayesha herself (though it is not clear to what extent she can be described as a 'native'), and Foulata vanish with their deaths. While Haggard is happy to entertain the idea that the savage Briton survives beneath the clothes of the modern British gentleman, there can be no 'going native'. Some later narratives of English masculinity, like the popular myth of Lawrence of Arabia, allow for the imaginative repossession of heroic qualities lost to modernity through a closer identification with the culture of the native other, but in the romance the line between the team and its surroundings must be maintained: Africa itself offers a primitive landscape in which heroic masculinity can be regenerated, but the explorers must never become part of that landscape.[34]

Stoker's text is never altogether comfortable with its own domestication of the romance of empire. Ireland, with its 'almost tropical' rain (215), at times seems a little bit too foreign for the solutions of domestic fiction. In particular, Norah, the Irish heroine, is described by Arthur as being conspicuously dark-skinned: 'I had heard that along the west coast of Ireland there are traces of Spanish blood and Spanish beauty; and here was a living evidence of the truth of the hearsay' (75). She is 'somewhat sunburnt', but clearly 'northern'. Norah's darkness becomes the source of a slightly nervous comedy in the dialogues between Arthur and the car driver, Andy, himself a familiar stage-Irish type. They discuss Arthur's idea of beauty:

'Is she to be all dark, surr, or only the hair of her?'
'I don't mean a nigger, Andy!' I thought I would be even with him for once in a way. He laughed heartily.
'Oh! my but that's a good wan. Be the hokey, a girrul can be dark enough for any man widout bein' a naygur. Glory be to God, but I niver seen a faymale naygur meself, but I suppose there's such things; God's very good to all his craythurs! But, barrin' naygurs, must she be all dark?' (101)

Stoker's narrative circles around this 'impossible' and thus 'amusing' confusion, and Andy's jokes on the subject recur frequently. The English gentleman and his Irish inferior are brought together by their common distance from the 'naygur'. Whether or not Stoker's discomfort with the application of Victorian racial science to Ireland derives from his relative sympathy with Irish nationalism, as David Glover argues, a certain strained quality to the comedy reveals ideological fissures that have not been completely papered over.[35]

The construction of gendered identity in these novels also reminds us that the imperial romance has to be understood in relation to the contemporary metropolitan discourses to which it is opposed. Imperial romance masculinity and femininity conduct an intertextual dialogue with the versions of gendered identity being offered by the New Woman novel and by the literature of decadence. For example, where we see women in imperial romance, it is as love objects or as idealized figures, rather than as protagonists in their own right. It would be an over-simplification, however, to think that the conservatism of these fictions works through a simple reversal of the gender roles presented in the New Woman novels. Rather, figures like Mina Harker (*Dracula*) and Norah Joyce in Stoker, or like Ustane (*She*) and Foulata (*King Solomon's Mines*) in Haggard assimilate many of the 'strong' qualities of the New Woman, only to put these qualities in the service of the texts' men – alternative constructions of gender are not so much expelled as sublated. In *The Snake's Pass* Norah saves Arthur (who has just saved *her* from the evil designs of Murdock) from the moving bog, and the men of the novel erect a tribute to her heroism. In Norah Joyce we might recognize the late nineteenth century's most controversial Nora, Ibsen's Nora Helmer, rehabilitated within the paradigm of romance.

In sum, then, *The Snake's Pass* would have been readily intelligible to a metropolitan readership as an adventure romance. The will to visual power, the treasure buried in the colonial surface, the 'male family', and the role of the colonial woman – all of these would have been recognizable to a readership nurtured on the imperial fiction of Haggard and his rivals. But there are a number of textual features that must have seemed awkward, or anomalous to those readers. There is the shifting bog that resists the visual dominance of the novel's protagonists, and that looms too large in the text to be considered simply as background. The marriage plot and the racial anxiety that surrounds it, and the heavy historical burden that the treasure is made to bear, also point to a certain textual excess over the romance model. And the more one focuses on these discrepancies, the more significant they appear to be. *The Snake's Pass* would seem to be settling scores that are irrelevant to the concerns of the adventure romance. Even if the worrisome bog is eventually consigned to the sea, and the lost treasure found, these troubling details do not vanish with the ending. Ultimately, the textual holiday in Ireland does not go entirely smoothly for the reader. To account for these anamorphic details we will have to leave the imperial romance behind for a moment, and consider the novel as an Irish colonial narrative.

THE POLITICS OF MARRIAGE

The prominence of the love plot in *The Snake's Pass*, usually a minor feature of the adventure romance, if present at all, makes a great deal more sense when we realize that it derives not from the romance but from a long narrative tradition of representing Anglo-Irish relations in terms of inter-ethnic courtship and marriage. The marriage plot offered a way for the Protestant Ascendancy to imaginatively re-cement their ties to Britain. It is not, in other words, a metropolitan imperial fantasy, but rather a fantasy of affiliation with the metropole, usually combined with some sort of imagined assimilation of the remains of the colonized Gaelic culture. The 'marriage' of Ireland and England becomes especially important as a political trope after the Act of Union of 1800, which terminated the existence of a separate Irish parliament. Ireland always gets to play the bride in this international love match, recalling that figuration of the colonized country as female that in its Irish versions is traceable from Spenser's depiction of Irena (Ireland) in the *Faerie Queene* on. In the nineteenth century this use of gender also connects to the ethnographic stereotype of the 'Celts' as 'an essentially feminine race'. As David Cairns and Shaun Richards suggest, the original relatively positive implications of this formula of Ernest Renan's came to be considerably revalued in Matthew Arnold's work, where the feminine Celt is seen as incapable of self-government.[36] Of course this is not a trope confined exclusively to Anglo-Irish fiction: it is as a device for the imaginary resolution of *class* conflicts that the courtship plot comes to constitute an important strand of British fiction, from Richardson's *Pamela* on. In Anglo-Irish fiction (and drama) the resolution takes the form of a marriage between an Englishman and an Irishwoman, or, in some cases, of an Anglo-Irishman and a woman of Irish Catholic 'stock'. Two of the earliest examples of this tendency are *The Wild Irish Girl* (1806) by Lady Morgan, and Maria Edgeworth's *The Absentee* (1812). Lady Morgan's novel already contains all of the essential ingredients. In it, the idle son of an English landowner with large properties in Ireland is smitten by the Irish beauty, Glorvina, the daughter of a decayed Gaelic chieftain. Edgeworth's novel reworks the same basic plot, while placing a much heavier emphasis on estate improvement and the responsibilities of Irish landlords. Closer in time to Stoker's novel, and also closer to its ethos, is Dion Boucicault's comic melodrama, *The Shaughraun* (1874). Written shortly after the abortive Fenian rising of 1867, the play matches a propertied (though financially beleaguered) Irish heroine, Claire Ffolliott, whose brother has been actively involved in Fenianism, and an English officer, Captain Molineux, stationed in Ireland. As in *The Snake's Pass*, land is an important issue, and there too the grasping Irish moneylender, Corry Kinchela, plays the part of villain. *The Shaughraun*, like *The Snake's Pass*, rewrites the iconology of colonial relations developed in Edgeworth and Lady Morgan in its own terms: the *dramatis personae* are simplified to make the principals (who even in the earlier novels are far from being complex characters) equally flawless, all responsibility for their problems falling on the similarly monochrome villain, who must be expelled from the world of the play. With Boucicault's play the politics of the marriage plot move closer to a version of nationalism: while there is a reconciling marriage between Claire Ffolliott and the English Captain Molineux, Robert Ffolliott's Fenianism is never discredited by the play, and the Police agent, Harvey Duff, is as great a villain as the moneylender.

The love plot then, while it may appear to exist uneasily alongside the imperial adventure narrative, also carries colonial political messages; not those of the New Imperialism, which try to reconcile metropolitan subject and imperial space, but those of an older colonial order, in which the colonials imagine their relation to the 'home' country as well as to the 'native' culture. In this respect the Protestant Ascendancy may sometimes see themselves as the Irish bride to be, about to be securely linked to England; and sometimes picture themselves as the English hero, embracing Gaelic culture. The 'imagined community' of the inter-ethnic marriage novel is one in which other political voices, Bakhtin's heteroglossia, are silenced.[37] Ireland is integrated into the larger community of the empire, and the murky origins and the liminal position of the Anglo-Irish are forgotten as they imaginatively affiliate themselves to Britain. The consent of the Anglo-Irish to the symbolic union is taken to represent the voice of Ireland as a whole; dissonant elements are largely unrepresented, and where they do find representation, they are expelled from the harmonious world of the end of the novel.

The Snake's Pass is more than the sum of its subgeneric parts, however. While real heteroglossia are largely silent in the novel, we can hear occasional muted echoes. In fact, the space that would have been occupied by a contestatory voice is taken instead by the doubleness, and indeed interchangeability, that organizes the novel. This doubleness announces itself from the start in the two names of the mountain that looms over the district – it is known as both Knockcalltore and Knock-calltecrore, hill of the lost gold, and hill of the lost golden crown. This same form of doubleness plays itself out in the land dispute between Black Murdock and Phelim Joyce; they have swapped their adjacent farms, so that Phelim now lives in Murdock's house and Murdock in Joyce's, a situation which becomes significant when Joyce's original dwelling is swept away by the bog. Norah exemplifies this logic of interchangeability at the level of character. For a time, Arthur seems to be fascinated by two women: Norah, whom he has heard but never seen, and the anonymous beauty he meets on Knocknacar; but eventually it becomes evident even to him that these are one and the same person. Norah is also the focus of Andy's double entendres: he jokingly refers to Arthur's interest in Norah as an interest in bogs, and 'bog' becomes a coded term for woman in the novel.

That all of this undermotivated doubleness is actually the textual symptom for a submerged political struggle becomes increasingly evident when we look at the Irish political situation in the decade leading up to the novel's publication. The immediate colonial context for *The Snake's Pass*, I want to argue, is the late nineteenth-century Land War that shattered the power of the Anglo-Irish as a class. The Land War pitted financially vulnerable, predominantly Catholic tenants, attempting to improve their position, against their largely Protestant landlords. In part the war can be related to agrarian unrest elsewhere in Europe in the late nineteenth century, the consequence of a substantial decline in prices for agricultural produce, but the struggle took on a specific form in Ireland's colonial situation.[38] On the tenant side it involved activities ranging from the Parliamentary work of the Irish National Land League led by Charles Stewart Parnell and Michael Davitt, to the unofficial violence associated with the Moonlighters (sc. agrarian activists). Contemporary British accounts suggest that the Land War was perceived as a serious threat to colonial rule in Ireland. As such it received considerable – and melodramatic – coverage in the British press. (One of those who felt inspired to action by such reportage was one of the founding fathers of the romance revival, Robert Louis Stevenson, who planned on moving his whole household to Ireland to come to the rescue of a Protestant widow and her daughters whose family farm was being boycotted.)[39] The British government responded with a mixture of coercion (special courts, emergency police powers) and concession (a series of Land Acts). More revisionist accounts now represent the Land War as a complex affair rather than a straightforward anti-colonial movement: the struggle was complicated by disagreement on the part of the League's leadership as to its goals, Davitt wanting no less than national ownership of the land, the more conservative Parnell balking before such a radical step. The tenants in whose name this campaign was fought can be disaggregated in a similar way: one can argue that they were an uneasy amalgam of small farmers seeking to improve their miserable state, and more affluent graziers and strong farmers who represented the emergent rural bourgeois classes, anxious to strengthen their control over their property.[40] Despite its internal tensions, however, it is hard to deny that the Land League presented a formidable challenge to British rule in Ireland in the 1880s, and meant the end of the Protestant Ascendancy as a political force.

Although the novel nowhere explicitly describes the Land War, *The Snake's Pass* is evidently a response to this crucial moment in Anglo-Irish history. That Stoker himself saw the novel as a contribution to debates over the land question is evident from the fact that he sent copies to Gladstone and to Michael Davitt (hoping to secure a favourable review in Davitt's newspaper, *The Labour World*).[41] The events of the story take place in a fictional area of County Mayo, which because of its history of tenant combination, its Fenian activism and other factors (Davitt himself was from Mayo, as it happens), was what R. F. Foster calls a 'vital seedbed' for the land movement.[42] In Westport, Co. Mayo, in 1879 Parnell gave his first speech encouraging non-payment of rents and the National Land League chapter for Mayo was formed in August of the same year. Mayo became one of the major sites of confrontation during the Land War itself, and saw some of its most violent incidents. The intense conflict even gave a new word to the English language: 'boycott', after Captain Charles Cunningham Boycott, Lord Erne's Mayo land agent, who was subjected to a campaign of ostracism during the war. The county's reputation for rough justice would live on into the twentieth century, inspiring J. M. Synge to use it for the backdrop to *The Playboy of the Western World* (1907). There is nothing casual, then in Stoker's choice of this same area as the background for the marriage of the Englishman, Severn (who, I am suggesting, is really more of a representative of Anglo-Ireland), and the Irish 'peasant', Norah. Significantly, the match is also the occasion for a land merger, in which Severn joins the land he has bought to Norah's few acres (though he has already secretly purchased these too) and founds a model estate.[43] Those tenants who are anxious to go are bought out, and the others are allowed to purchase land from Arthur's agent. In effect, Arthur establishes an estate with no tenants:

The estate from which they [sc. the tenants] held was in bankruptcy; and as a sale was then being effected, Mr. Caicy had purchased the estate, and had then made arrangements for all who wished to purchase to do so on easy terms from me. The nett result was, that when certain formalities should be complied with, and certain monies paid, I should own the whole of Knockcalltecrore and the land immediately adjoining it, together with certain other parcels of land in the neighbourhood. (189)

Tenants, and later agriculture itself, are banished from Arthur's new Irish landscape: with the help of the limestone uncovered by the shifting of the bog, he has his engineering friend, Dick Sutherland, turn the estate into 'exquisite gardens' (246). The 'wild' Irish landscape is turned into something resembling the English countryside of his childhood. The text, in other words, evolves an imaginary solution to a political problem, landlord–tenant conflict, that it renders invisible.

On closer examination we see that the conflict is not so much absent as transformed, at once miniaturized and displaced: the love story of the English gentleman and the Irish peasant does take place against the background of a sort of mini-land war, but one between two Irishmen: Norah's father, Phelim Joyce, and the moneylender, Black Murdock. Thus the fight for control of land appears everywhere in the text, but with its colonial dimension completely, or almost completely, occluded. In fact, in a further distortion, the text transforms the historical struggle between Catholic tenants and their largely Protestant landlords into the persecution of the Protestant (but poor) Joyces at the hands of the presumably Catholic Murdock.[44] The English hero, Severn, only involves himself in this purely local dispute between Murdock and Joyce through his interest in fair play, and through his affection for Norah.

'JOYCE COUNTRY'

We can most clearly see how the text transforms the historical material of the Land War by looking at one of the episodes it draws on, arguably the most infamous atrocity of that war. The agrarian violence that accompanied the more official activities of the Land League provided the readers of the London *Times* and other British newspapers with a rich diet of sensation. On 19 August 1882, the first accounts came in of an especially gruesome incident:

Dublin, August 18. Intelligence reached town this afternoon of the most terrible tragedy of which the West of Ireland has ever been the scene. It has been reported to the authorities (as yet only the bare facts are known) that last night a family of four persons, John Joyce and his wife, mother, and daughter were murdered and two boys wounded in their own home at Maamtrasna, in the Clonbur district, near Cong, county Galway. In this district several deeds of blood, commencing with the murder of Lord Mountmorres, have been perpetrated.[45]

It was the first of many accounts of the 'Maamtrasna murders',[46] which became symbolically central in the 'Irish question': for British conservatives they represented further proof of the natural appetite for violence of the Irish; for Irish nationalists, the handling of the trial of the men charged with the Maamtrasna murders came to emblematize the utter bankruptcy of British justice in Ireland. The *Times*'s own correspondent kept interest in the story alive with detailed accounts of his journey to Maamtrasna, on the border of Galway and Mayo, the testimony of the eyewitnesses, the state of the one surviving boy and the inquest. An editorial described the incident as having 'no parallel for absolute barbarity in the modern history, at any rate, of Irish agrarian dispute or vengeance'. The only comparable atrocity, claimed the same editorial, was the infamous assassination of the Chief Secretary and the Under Secretary for Ireland in Phoenix Park in May of that year by the 'Invincibles', an event that would find its own romance echoes in R. L. Stevenson's *The Strange Case of Dr Jekyll and Mr Hyde* (1886).[47]

The most obvious link between the Maamtrasna events and Stoker's story is of course the name, Joyce. One of the more bizarre aspects of the Maamtrasna murders was that a number of the defendants (there were ten in all) were also called Joyce. This particular region of Connemara was widely known as 'the Joyce country' because of the prevalence of that family name in the locality. Stoker's fictional Joyce family, then, had their real-life predecessors not only in the Joyces of Maamtrasna – shot and bludgeoned to death, it was argued, as potential police informants – but also in those other Joyces, tried and executed for their murder. When one reads the accounts of the murders and the subsequent trials one appreciates the amount of *work* that has gone into shaping this material from only seven years earlier, redolent of the brutalities and counter-brutalities of the colonial situation, into the stuff of melodrama and marriage plots. The work of literary production has not only dramatically reshaped these historical materials, it has also almost effaced the traces of that very production.

In the newspaper account, we are first drawn into the landscape by the narrator's description of the depopulated, rugged, mountain-fringed landscape he passes through on his journey (by horse and car) west to the site of the mass murder:

> Maamtrasna, which has now, and not for the first time, earned a place for itself in the blood-stained records of the west, forms part of a wild and lonely valley on the borders of Mayo. It seems shut out from all other life by mountain chains and ranges high, bleak and strangely impressive. It is a succession of bold, desert-looking serrated mountains; once the car leaves the Clifden main road, solitude marks the district as its own. No sign of life is visible anywhere around save now and again a few sheep scattered over the face of the mountain, some nibbling the thin herbage within reach of the driver's whip, others so far above, that they appear but as white specks to the passer by . . . From Maam the road lies chiefly round the borders of Lough Nafevey, a crescent shaped tract of water fed by mountain streams.[48]

Compare Stoker's opening, which we saw earlier as exemplifying the romance novel's use of the journey to mark the transition from the 'real' and civilized world into the romance space. Here, too, the narrator is travelling west by horse-drawn car:

> Between two great mountains of grey and green, as the rock cropped out between the tufts of emerald verdure, the valley, almost as narrow as a gorge, ran due west towards the sea. There was just room for the roadway, half cut in the rock, beside the narrow strip of dark lake of seemingly unfathomable depth that lay far below between perpendicular walls of frowning rock. In the wide terrace-like steps of the shelving mountain there were occasional glimpses of civilization emerging from the almost primal desolation which immediately surrounded us – clumps of trees, cottages, and the irregular outlines of stone-walled fields, with black stacks of turf for winter firing piled here and there. (9, 10)[49]

In both cases, the journey through the wild and desolate landscape marks a transition into an isolated realm where civilized, English values don't hold sway; the implied readership for these accounts is urban, English and 'modern'.

Here the two descriptions begin to diverge sharply. The landscape which confronts the special correspondent is made to function in his narrative as a sort of topography of recent history:

When standing on the mountain looking down at Maamtrasna, the visitor can be shown on the one hand where the bodies of the wretched bailiffs who were found chained together at the bottom of Lough Mask were picked up, on another where Mr. George Robinson, the agent of Colonel Clements, the owner of a large portion of the Joyce country, was fired at about 12 months ago; and on a third, where the lad Gibbons was murdered. Other points of equally fatal interest, no doubt, are embraced within the orbit of the view.[50]

This murderous topography, offering a prospect of 'fatal interest', is replaced in Stoker's novel by Severn's, the visitor/tourist's, first sight of Shleenanaher (the Snake's Pass) and Knockcalltecrore, and the driver Andy's commentary on them:

We were rapidly descending the valley, and, as we got lower, the promontory seemed to take bolder shape, and was beginning to stand out as a round-topped hill of somewhat noble proportions.
'Tell me, Andy', I said, 'what do they call the hill beyond?'
'The hill beyant there is it? Well, now, they call the place Shleenanaher.'
'Then that is Shleenanaher mountain?'
'Begor it's not. The mountain is called Knockcalltecrore. It's Irish . . . I believe it's a short name for Hill iv the Lost Goolden Crown . . . it's a bit iv a gap in the rocks beyant that they call Shleenanaher... Irish it is an' it means "The Shnake's Pass".'
'Indeed! And can you tell me why it is so called?'
'Begor, there's a power iv raysons guv for callin' it that. Wait till we get Jerry Scanlan or Bat Moynahan, beyant in Carnacliff! Sure they know every laygend and shtory in the bar'ny . . .' (14)

This passage performs a series of substitutions: the landscape that tells of legends of lost treasure and the mythical pre-Christian past replaces that which records the history of agrarian violence; the grimly omniscient account of the journalist-narrator metamorphoses into the dialogue of the comic Irish guide and the amused tourist-narrator; the quaint replaces the menacing. Both narrators define themselves as visitors to the strange world of the west of Ireland in similar ways, and for both the landscape is required to 'speak' the past, but they read very different historical meanings from the topography.

In Stoker's narrative, as we noted at the beginning of this chapter, the sublime landscape features of irregularity, vastness and the uncontrollable natural energies of the storm are all present, and placed in contrast with England's pastoral beauty. The strangeness of the scene is interiorized in *The Snake's Pass* in a way it is not in the other account. Severn feels that the storm and the scenery have awakened him: 'I felt as though I looked for the first time with open eyes on the beauty and the reality of the world' (11). In a sort of chiasmus, Stoker's narrative recasts the newspaper's contrast between the landscape and the scenes of violence to which it has been witness as a harmony of subject and setting. But Arthur's initial response to the landscape is premature: the sublime wildness of the landscape proves to be the index of its dangers; and the uncultivated mountain bog must yield to the 'exquisite gardens' (246) of Arthur's model estate before subject and setting can be properly reconciled.

To complete this narrative trajectory, Stoker must reshape the events of seven years before almost beyond recognition. The drowning of two bailiffs (in an earlier incident related to the Maamtrasna murders) becomes in the novel Phelim Joyce's accident returning from Galway, in which he is thrown from his horse into the lake and breaks his arm (35). He does not drown, though he does spend 'nigh three hours' in the water. This diminution-effect typifies the procedures of the novel. Throughout the remainder of the text, elements of what we might call the pre-texts of the Land War and the Maamtrasna murders recur, but in comic miniature. When Andy surprises Severn on the mountains as he waits for Norah, he leaps up 'with a feeling that was positively murderous'. 'Begor! but yer 'an'r lepped like a deer when ye heerd me shpake. Did ye think I was goin' to shoot ye?' (94).[51] Similarly, the agrarian violence of the Moonlighters finds a place in the novel in a comically diminished form. Severn's nocturnal rambles in pursuit of Norah make him the subject of local attention. At his hotel his host warns him about 'the moonlighters who now and again raided the district, and who, being composed of the scum of the countryside – "corner-boys" and loafers of all kinds – would be only too glad to find an unexpected victim to rob' (115), and also of the danger of himself being suspected of being a Moonlighter. The novel represents the Moonlighters as simply local thugs and robbers – a species of less colourful Irish *banditti*. Severn himself comes under police suspicion, and is interviewed about his interest in moonlighting. Again, the novel treats this comically, and Severn and the policeman talk at cross-purposes about moonlight. Severn is at pains to convince the constable that his interest in moonlight is purely aesthetic: 'I mean the view – the purely aesthetic effect – the chiaroscuro – the pretty pictures!' (116). Severn, like the novel itself, is determined to give political questions romantic answers.

While Stoker partly succeeds in transforming historical trauma into a neatly packaged romance plot, one feature seems to place considerable strain on its procedures – the shifting bog. The rhetorical intensity with which the bog is described, and simply the amount of space devoted to it in the novel, at times threaten to derail the narrative. The bog is the central figure in *The Snake's Pass* for what we might designate as an Anglo-Irish anxiety of origins: the resistant texture of the bog makes much more sense when we recognize it as the figure in the text for the colonial past; the bog signals the difficulty of representing the origins of the Anglo-Irish in Ireland.[52] Arthur himself, of course, also figures this anxiety of origins. While Arthur is English, to the extent that he is also Stoker's most obvious representative in the text he may also be seen as having Irish roots. He is an orphan, his parents 'lost in a fog when crossing the Channel' (11). His father 'had been pretty well cut off by his family on account of his marriage with what they considered his inferior' (11). The doubled sense of isolation – his father's disinheritance and his own orphanhood – as well as the suggestion of inferior blood on the mother's side, make Arthur an appropriate figure for a class whose identity might well seem to have been lost overboard, albeit somewhere in the waters between Ireland and England rather than those between England and France. But the bog suggests that what is really at stake in the murkiness of the Anglo-Irish past is the violence of colonial history. The traces of an ancient Celtic order revealed when the bog disappears thus hold out the promise of a culture before political division; and when the bog slides away it carries with it the history that fuels division.

It is worth quoting at some length from the passages in which Sutherland explains to Arthur the nature of the shifting bog, which I pointed to in chapter 1 as prefiguring the mechanism of the vampire:

'It is just as bad a bit of soft bog as ever I saw. I wouldn't like to see anyone or anything that I cared for try to cross it . . . [b]ecause at any moment they might sink through it; and then, goodbye – no human strength or skill could ever save them.
. . .
A body suddenly immersed would, when the air of the lungs had escaped and the rigor mortis had set in, probably sink a considerable distance; then it would rise after nine days, when decomposition began to generate gases . . . Not succeeding in this, it would ultimately waste away, and the bones would become incorporated with the existing vegetation somewhere about the roots, or would lie among the slime at the bottom.' (59)

Here we begin to see what lies behind the earlier hints at the 'unfathom-able' aspect of the Irish landscape. In fact, the bog in the above passage problematizes the very concept of landscape as an object. A landscape feature that is capable of movement and of devouring human life needs to be seen as something of the order of a character, or more accurately, of a monster. In an earlier passage Dick makes the connection between bogs and history, specifically the history of colonization. After describing bogs in general Dick moves on to discuss:

> . . . Irish bogs, beginning with such records as those of Giraldus Cambrensis – of Dr Boate – of Edmund Spenser – from the time of the first invasion when the state of the land was such that, as is recorded, when a spade was driven into the ground a pool of water gathered forthwith. He told me of the extent and nature of bog-lands – of the means taken to reclaim them, and of his hopes of some heroic measures being taken by Government to reclaim the vast Bog of Allen which remains as a great evidence of official ineptitude . . . 'It will be something,' he said 'to redeem the character for indifference to such matters so long established, as when Mr King wrote two hundred years ago, "We live in an Island infamous for bogs, and yet, I do not remember, that any one has attempted much concerning them."' . . . 'In fine, we cure bog by both a surgical and a medical process. We drain it so that its mechanical action as a sponge may be stopped, and we put lime to kill the vital principle of its growth . . . together, scientific and executive man asserts his dominance.' (55, 56)

These passages are striking in a number of respects: the linking of bogs and the colonial project (here, interestingly, described as an invasion); the connection established between the state of the bogs and government malfeasance; the references to Spenser and to 'scientific and executive man' who will control the bogs are all noteworthy. Everything points to the bog as standing in in some way for those aspects of the country which have been most resistant to the colonial project, the bog as that which, while yielding, fails to keep the imprint made by the work of colonization – the spade sinks in, but it leaves no trace when it is withdrawn.[53]

The bog in Spenser is a dangerous bolting hole for the wild Irish, who will not come within the pale of civilization. As Luke Gibbons points out in a recent essay on *The Snake's Pass*, in William King's 'Of the Bogs and Loughs of Ireland' (1685) bogs 'are a shelter and refuge to tories and thieves', and by them the natives 'were preserved from the conquest of the English'.[54] But what threat does the bog pose in the late nineteenth century? Why does Sutherland see the 'vast Bog of Allen' as a terrible example of 'official ineptitude' that can only be put right by 'heroic measures' (56)? No longer a refuge for Irish rebels, it is difficult to see why the bog should seem so maleficent, so in need of the interventions of 'scientific and executive man'. The range and precision of historical reference that Stoker invokes in describing the bog suggest that it is a recording device, a matrix for the storage of history. That is to say, if the bog as literary topos is connected to the history of colonization, the 'real' bog in the text, topographical rather than topical, preserves colonial history.

In his trawling of the bog Murdock, the Gombeen man, is looking for a relic of military history, the lost bullion-chest of the French expeditionary force of 1798. That force was to have joined with the Irish rebels in an effort to overthrow English power in Ireland, but the rising was, of course, brutally and efficiently quelled after some early military victories. Unlike Spenser's dangerous bolting hole, the bog here retains the traces of the historical *success* of the English colonial project.[55] What is threatening about the bog is that it preserves actual pieces of history – it keeps the past present. The hostility of the bog to the protagonists is thus the return in a fantastically inverted form of English colonial hostility to Ireland. In effect, as Gibbons argues, the bog appears to act like the body of one of Freud's hysterical subjects: the history that has been repressed, that of colonial violence, returns with all the force of the repression.[56]

If the hysterical body demands the attention of the professional physician, and Freud's new science of psychoanalysis, Stoker's oddly active bog, and organic history book, solicits the controlling power of the 'scientific and executive man', Sutherland. In the end, though, Black Murdock is the one who precipitates the destruction of the bog through his probing for the treasure. A particularly heavy fall of rain sends the whole mass into the sea, taking Murdock with it, and leaving the bare rock behind. The bog may retain the repressed history of colonial violence, but beneath it lies a more acceptable history for Severn and the others. The lost treasure of the French expeditionary force is revealed, but so too is a cave inscribed with ancient Celtic writing, which Arthur and the others explore:

The cave widened as we entered, and we stood in a moderate sized cavern, partly natural and partly hollowed out by rough tools. Here and there, were inscriptions in strange character, formed by straight vertical lines something like the old telegraph signs, but placed differently. 'Ogham! – one of the oldest and least known of writings' said Dick . . . (241)

Norah finds an ancient Celtic crown in the same cave. The two finds suggest the existence of a long-vanished aristocratic Celtic culture and, moreover, a literate culture (ogham may be inscrutable to Arthur and Dick, but they recognize it as writing). In a dramatic scene of political fantasy the layers of muddy and bloody history, the history of colonial oppression and native resistance, and by implication the more recent agrarian unrest are swept into the sea, leaving open access to a lost aristocratic culture which would presumably have understood the exigencies of sovereignty and the dangers posed by counter-jumpers like Black Murdock.

Stoker's novel can thus be read as part of a more general tendency in late nineteenth and early twentieth-century Anglo-Irish writing – that of Standish James O' Grady, and later the proto-modernist Literary Revival of W. B. Yeats, Lady Gregory, J. M. Synge and others – which offered a similar vision of a submerged heroic past for the Anglo-Irish to claim as their own.[57] The reclamation of this legendary past, in which 'the warlike spirit of the people was high, the imagination aflame, [and] the national idea had laid hold upon the Irish mind', possessed considerable importance for the cultural nationalist project. But in Stoker's novel we can more clearly see an agenda that is often more carefully buried in the work of the Irish Literary Revival: the attempt to supply the symbolic materials for a national culture was also a way for the embattled Ascendancy to find a new historical mission for itself. It was primarily for an increasingly politically marginalized Anglo-Irish group that it was important that the past be both heroic and noble. Like Stoker, O'Grady, Yeats and others wanted to find a mirror for Ascendancy culture in the distant, precolonial past, in the legends of Cuchulain and in the other early Irish sagas. The historical distance of the 'heroic period' made it available as an imaginary common past for Irish and Anglo-Irish alike, making it symbolically – if not logically – possible to a imagine a common precolonial origin. Of course, this historical affiliation is baseless: it is difficult to see how the Anglo-Irish could see pre-Christian Ireland as part of their past in a way that more recent history was not; but as Ernest Renan once noted, amnesia is a vital part of nationalism.

This Anglo-Irish political fantasy sheds some light on just why Black Murdock is such a figure of abhorrence in, and even for, the text, to the extent that he has to be swept off into the sea and out of the narrative. Luke Gibbons has described the peculiar and dysfunctional form that modernization assumed in Ireland, where underdevelopment and commercial penetration went hand in hand, presided over by a landlord caste that had 'anachronistic pretensions of aristocracy, yet presided over the unrestrained commercialization of the Irish economy'.[58] Gibbons assumes that Black Murdock is the figure for this species of landlordism, combining the rapacity of the Gombeen man with a more feudal dimension. Yet it is in fact Severn who is the text's ultimate feudal modernizer, using modern methods to improve the land, while assuming for himself the role of quasi-feudal landlord to the whole region. Stoker may have had Home Rule sympathies, but as David Glover notes there is also a strongly conservative strain to the novel's ending, 'which brings a tranche of the most resistant and unreclaimable region in Ireland under the sway of a benevolent British squirearchy'.[59] This paternalism necessitates the removal of Black Murdock who seems to represent the prosperous Catholic middle classes who later become the Revivalists' rivals for the intellectual leadership of the nationalist movement. The Gombeen man stands in for that group that J. M. Synge will later refer to as an 'ungodly ruck of fat-faced sweaty-headed swine', in marked contrast to his idealized Irish peasants.[60] As Chris Morash has argued, this imaginary division of the Irish rural population into good 'peasants' and bad 'gombeen men' is already apparent in William Carleton's novel of 1847, *The Black Prophet*.[61] We will see in chapter 4 that the Irish Literary Revival develops its own myths of the alliance of landlord and peasant, and the expulsion of the bad modernity of the Catholic middle classes, producing in the process a species of modernist primitivism.[62] Murdock's removal allows the narrative to end with a happy alliance of landlord and peasant; the monied Catholic middle class, and the troublesome remains of recent colonial history, slither off into the sea.

While the historical threads of *The Snake's Pass* may seem to lead us away from the romance, in important respects they lead us back to it. Late Victorian Irish cultural nationalism mirrored the imperial English culture to which it opposed itself. After all, the rhetoric of heroism and the celebration of the heroic past in O'Grady was something with which a romance readership would have been equally familiar. The attempt to find spiritual values in the savage yet heroic culture of the distant past significantly resembles the ethos of heroism, nobility and self-sacrifice we find in the *fin-de-siècle* romances.[63] If the Irish cultural nationalism of the Revival, then, depended in this period on the translation and literary reworking of ancient epic, in England Haggard, Stevenson and other contributors to the 'revival of romance' were trying to create modern epic. Both 'revivals' are distinctly modern movements, yet both represent themselves as being in flight from what we might broadly refer to as modernization: heroism and the nation/empire represent an ideal that transcends petty commercialism.[64]

Notwithstanding the homologies between Irish and English cultural nationalism, the bog is never properly accommodated within the romance frame. Within the colonial context we can read the emphasis on the bog in Stoker's novel as part of a discourse of history and the nation. But this discursive involvement interferes with the presentation of Ireland as a proper space for imperial romance. The degree of energy which the novel expends in explaining bogs, citing authorities on them and in describing their eventual control by man overwhelms the adventure aspect of the narrative. The metaphorics of depth and history that figures at once the complex historical situation of the Anglo-Irish and an imaginary solution to that situation, sits uneasily alongside the fantasy of imperial visual dominance. A properly consumable imaginary Ireland never emerges from this tropic mixture.

ENGLISHMEN ABROAD

The bog's significance as a recording device for colonial history is not without its consequences for the other Ascendancy fantasy that we touched on earlier – the symbolic marriage that guarantees the links between colony and metropole. Though Norah's part in this symbolic marriage is to represent Ireland in its fair and fruitful aspect, she also comes to be closely associated with the treacherous shifting bogs. The novel early links women (specifically Norah) and bogs through the jokes of Andy, the stage-Irish driver. Arthur justifies his repeated visits to Knocknacar in search of Norah (though at this stage he doesn't realize she *is* Norah Joyce) by claiming an interest in bogs. 'Bog', as I mentioned above, comes to function as a code-word between Arthur and Andy for women:

Shure yer 'an'r can thrust me; it's blind an' deaf an' dumb I am, an' them as knows me knows I'm not the man to go back on a young gintleman goin' to luk at a bog. Sure doesn't all young min do the same? I've been there meself times out iv mind! . . . Lukin' at bogs is the most intherestin' thin' I knows. (50)

Phyllis Roth in her critical introduction to Bram Stoker remarks that this association 'doesn't bear looking into', struck, presumably, by the deep strain of misogyny that appears to underlie the linkage.[65] Nevertheless, it is in equating the dangers of the bog and the native woman that *The Snake's Pass* demonstrates how Anglo-Irish anxieties of origin undercut the seemingly optimistic fantasy of political union. One of Arthur's nightmares shows the way in which the initially jocular association of the bog and Norah becomes more threatening:

> The last of all my dreams was as follows: Norah and I were sitting on the table rock in the cliff fields; all was happy and smiling around us . . . Suddenly there was a terrible sound – half a roar, as of an avalanche, and half a fluttering sound, as of many great wings. We clung together in terror, waiting for the portent which was at hand. And then over the cliff poured the whole mass of the bog, foul-smelling, foetid, terrible, and of endless might. Just as it was about to touch us, and as I clasped Norah to me, so that we might die together, and whilst her despairing cry was in my ear, the whole mighty mass turned into loathsome, writhing snakes, sweeping into the sea! (206)

Here Stoker has reworked the available gendered tropes for the representation of Ireland. The earlier fictions of Morgan and Edgeworth produce the figure of the Irishwoman as a desirable colonial object; the emergent bourgeois language of gender differences is used in the colonial context to place colonized and colonizer in appropriate (in the view of the colonizer) positions with respect to each other. Stoker splits the colonial fantasy object into its desirable (the docile colonial subject, represented here by Norah) and undesirable elements (the dangerous bog, the seemingly rootless malevolence of Murdock, and the supposedly wanton violence of the Moonlighters); but this division is undermined by the connections made between Norah and the bog. In the climactic scene of the novel, this tendency for the 'good' and 'bad' colonial objects to collapse finally ends. Norah rescues Arthur from the bog, after he has rescued *her* from Murdock. Norah thus redeems herself from her connection with the bog, and the bog removes itself from the landscape leaving Norah behind as a safe object of desire. As a tribute to her bravery in saving Arthur from the bog, the men inscribe her name in the exposed rock, linking her to the heroic and aristocratic culture of the past.

> On the spot where she had rescued me we had reared a great stone – a monolith whereon a simple legend told the story of a woman's strength and bravery. Round its base were sculptured the history of the mountain from its legend of the King of the Snakes down to the lost treasure and the rescue of myself. (246)

Stabilizing Norah's identity through this act of material writing is for Arthur also, then, the 'rescue of [him]self'. This resolution is only made possible by something of the order of an act of God, however, a second flood which makes it possible for the world to start over again. The novel's drive to closure is evident in this double ending – the removal of the bog and the conclusion of the marriage between Norah and Arthur. This ending strives to contain the 'nightmare of history' figured both in the bog and in Norah-as-bog, but again the effort to do so makes *The Snake's Pass* less and less palatable as a romance. Authorial desire reveals itself too nakedly. We are a long way here from the melioristic world of Maria Edgeworth's *The Absentee*, but we are equally far from the packaging of Africa that Haggard accomplishes. Haggard provides a formula for adventure that can be reused over and over again, but the upheavals necessary for Stoker's ending to work provide no model for the further symbolic containment of the Irish question.

AN ENDING, IF NOT A CONCLUSION

I have separated out the functioning of *The Snake's Pass* within the late Victorian market for adventure romance from what we might see as its other dimension, the Irish colonial situation and the different contexts or pre-texts that suggests. To some degree this is an artificial separation, insofar as some of the material which I have placed in the category of the colonial would have circulated in the metropolis along with adventure romance, and some of the English readers of *The Snake's Pass* in its serial version in *The People* must have seen the shadow of the Maamtrasna murders over Knockcalltecrore. For most, though, this would have been an invisible connection, and the context for the reception of Stoker's work was supplied by other romances, other tales of love or of adventure in seductively unfamiliar settings. If the bogs of Ireland seemed to provide a less effective romance landscape of escape than Haggard's African plains, it is unlikely that this narrative failure could have been traced by them to its origins. The novel evidently to some extent succeeded in its reworking of historical material – one of the few reviews we have of the novel suggests that *The Snake's Pass* was seen as broadly similar to the other literary 'goods' produced for the 'novel-devouring public'.[66] In restoring the colonial dimension of *The Snake's Pass* we have not moved from metropolitan misreadings to the historical truth of the novel, though we have, perhaps, made possible *another* reading of it. Stoker's novel makes us see how in the age of empire and its aftermath, any attempt at a 'whole' reading must be doomed to failure. Such a will to totalize, to emplot the interconnections between metropole and periphery was a pervasive feature of late Victorian culture, and furnished, as I suggested at the beginning of this chapter, one reason for the popularity of the adventure romances of Haggard and his peers.

In the next chapter we will focus on a rather different type of romance, though one that was equally concerned with narrating the relation of England and its outside. But while the adventure romances we have been looking at deal with the subjugation of unruly colonial territories, mummy stories explore the difficulties presented by refractory colonial objects.

CHAPTER 3

'Mummie is become merchandise':
the mummy story as commodity theory

Mummie is become Merchandise, Mizraim cures wounds, and
Pharaoh is sold for Balsoms.   Sir Thomas Browne, *Urne Burial*

In his *Travels*, the English merchant-traveller John Sanderson describes
a visit to the mummy-pits outside Cairo in 1586:

The Momia, which is some five or six miles beyound, ar thowsands of imbalmed bodies, which weare buried thousands of years past in a sandie cave, at
which ther seemeth to have bine citie in tim[e]s past. We were lett doune by
ropes as into a well, with wax candles burninge in our hands, and so waulked
uppon the bodies of all sorts and sised [read sizes], great and smaule, and some
imbalmed in little earthen potts, which never had forme; thes ar sett at the feet
of the great bodies. They gave no noysome smell at all, but ar like pitch, beinge
broken; for I broke of[f] all parts of the bodies to see howe the flesh was turned
to drugge, and brought home divers heads, hands, arms, and feet for a shewe.
We bought allso 600 lb. for the Turkie company in peces, and brought into
Ingland in the Hercules, together with a whole bodie. They ar lapped in 100
doble of cloth, which rotton [rotting?] and pillinge of[f], you may see the
skinne, flesh, fingers, and nayles firme, onelie altered blacke. One little hand I
brought into Ingland to shewe, and presented it my brother, who gave the same
to a doctor in Oxford.[1]

The six hundred pounds of mummy flesh as well as the 'whole bodie'
were later sold to London apothecaries, who prescribed mummy as a
sovereign remedy for bleeding, internal and external. Some two hundred and fifty years later, mummies assume quite a different role in
British culture. Here is an excerpt from the *British Press* of Jersey of 1837,
describing a species of scientific spectacle that became highly popular in
the 1830s and 1840s – the unrolling of a mummy:

The learned lecturer assumed with an air of modest triumph his station at the
table on which the Mummy was placed . . . When the flowers and fillets were

removed the whole body appeared covered with a sheet that was laced at the back in a manner, said Mr P., which might give a lesson to our modern stay-makers (laughter) . . . The work of unrolling now again proceeded until the joyful announcement was made that something new was discovered which had never before been found on a mummy. Mr P. now exercised his scissors very freely, and soon released the scarabeus which was found to be fixed above a plate of metal . . . found to be fashioned in the shape of a hawk . . . The wings of the hawk were expanded, and he held in his talons the emblem of eternal life; it was handed round for inspection and excited much applause and admiration. A new description of bandage now appeared, and the arms and legs were shown to be separately bandaged . . . At length the left foot was displayed to sight, and though black and shrivelled, it excited much applause . . .[2]

This moment passes too.[3]

By the end of the nineteenth century the vogue for the unrolling of mummies was long over, and the mummy's power as spectacle was confined to the museum. At the same time, the appearance of mummy fiction as part of the romance revival indicates that the mummy retains its importance in the cultural imaginary of late Victorian and Edwardian Britain. For most of the nineteenth century mummies possessed little attraction as literary material. Between 1880 and 1914, however, more than a dozen mummy narratives appear, including Conan Doyle's 'The Ring of Thoth' (1890) and 'Lot No. 249' (1892), H. Rider Haggard's 'Smith and the Pharaohs' (1913), and Bram Stoker's *The Jewel of Seven Stars* (1903), as well as pieces which have almost fallen out of literary history, such as Guy Boothby's *Pharos the Egyptian* (1899), H. D. Everett's *Iras, A Mystery* (1896) and Ambrose Pratt's *The Living Mummy* (1910).[4] If the early modern period is marked by the literal consumption of mummies as medicine, and the early nineteenth century by the visual consumption of the mummy as spectacle, the late nineteenth century is fascinated by the mummy as a sign that may be consumed in popular fiction.

I want to argue that just as the treasure hunt and the team of men relate to the new imperialism and the rise of professionalism, the mummy is a figure through which changes in the material culture of Britain in the late nineteenth and early twentieth centuries were articulated. This period sees a shift in the British economy that caused people – intellectuals and popular readers alike – to conceive it in terms of consumption rather than production. Britain's overseas empire participates in this change. Thomas Richards has shown how in the late nineteenth century British exports took on a significance that far ex-

ceeded their humble object nature, to the extent that at times it appeared that commodities themselves were performing the work of
empire without human agency. Imperialists portrayed, in his words,
'commodities as a magic medium through which English power and
influence could be enforced and enlarged in the colonial world'.[5]

This chapter will explore the other side of the story. At home too the
commodity appeared to possess an imperial force. In the aftermath of
the Great Exhibition of 1851, it seemed, again in Richards's words, 'only
a matter of time until this superabundance of things colonized the
country and made committed consumers out of every man, woman, and
child in England'.[6] But what if the things which came to fill the British
home were not in fact British? Mummy fiction provides a new kind of
narrative dealing with this imperial side-effect. The mummy story
emplots the new relations of subjects and commodities, articulating the
connections between the national economy and its less visible imperial
extensions, and so providing a sort of narrativized commodity theory.

STAGING EGYPT

To understand the cultural operation of the fictional mummy, we must
begin with an earlier phase of Victorian culture, where actual mummies
played a significant part in the representation of the relations between
Britain and its outside. Unrollings were all the rage during the 1830s and
1840s.[7] This contemporary description of an unrolling at the Royal
College of Surgeons in 1834 indicates the degree of popularity of such
occasions: 'at twelve o'clock the doors of the theatre were opened from
Lincoln's Inn Fields, and from Portugal street; and all the seats were
soon occupied, and the greatest good order and regularity prevailed.
The windows were soon obliged to be further opened to admit cool air,
and all were perfectly satisfied, though great numbers were obliged to
stand . . . Visitors in considerable numbers arrived very early and filled
the seats; many were obliged to stand; and many others retired from all
the doors who could not find admission.'[8] This same kind of spectacle
provided the floorshow for various intellectual and social events. While
it does not seem inappropriate for Thomas Pettigrew to have concluded
his series of lectures on Egyptian antiquities at the Exeter Hall in 1837
with an unrolling, modern readers must be surprised to hear that this
was also the principal entertainment at an 'At Home' given by Lord
Londesborough – 'A Mummy from Thebes to be Unrolled at half-past
two'[9] – and that yet another unrolling closed the first congress of the

British Archeological Association held at Canterbury in 1844. The reports of the Canterbury Congress suggest that the proceedings were similar to those of the Jersey museum event. Again, the rather grisly mixture of science and theatre seems to have elicited considerable excitement, which increased in pitch as the unrolling proceeded:

All the boxes were filled (the pit had been boarded over), and the most intense interest prevailed throughout these altogether novel proceedings. The *Pictorial Times* says that 'the stage decorations were got up with great care, Mr Pettigrew and the mummy being in the centre, supported on either side by antiquarians [sic] tastefully arranged so as to give full effect to this imposing scene' . . . As the unrolling proceeded the cloth became more and more difficult to unroll, being impregnated by bituminous matter, and it had to be cut away with knives . . . The greatest interest was revealed by the spectators, 'and from time to time pieces of the bandages were handed to the ladies in the boxes', although the cloth 'had a peculiar and disagreeable smell.' 'The dust pervaded the atmosphere and was inhaled by all persons near.' Dr Pettigrew then sawed off the back part of the skull, to see what was inside, and found that the brains had been replaced by pitch. After an hour and a half 'the mummy, which proved to be that of a young man, was raised to its feet, and presented to the company, and was received with enthusiastic applause.'[10]

Wherever they took place, as part of popular science lectures or as drawing-room entertainment, the unwrappings produced this same excitement.

We have here a very specific form of spectacle, a distinct species of visual – and to some extent tactile and olfactory – consumption. Vision, as Martin Jay has remarked, is the 'master sense of the modern era'. Timothy Mitchell argues that vision achieves a particular centrality in nineteenth-century Europe, where exhibitions, museums and department stores joined to present the Western viewer with the world as a picture, as a spectacle (the role of maps in late Victorian adventure fiction is also part of this moment, as we saw in chapter 2). Commodities and artifacts from around the world rendered other cultures as a set of objects to be gazed at by a viewer posited as distinct from and prior to this world spectacle.[11] But the fact that the commodity which comes to represent Egypt is also a *body* suggests that there is more at stake than simple spectacle. In the unrolling of the mummy, a purely visual theatre meets the surgical theatre; the mummy has depth and substance as well as a spectacular surface.[12] The mystery of the mummy resides in the fact that it is wrapped, and therefore resists a kind of knowledge that depends upon sight. If the inability to see the mummy's body constitutes the mystery of the mummy's identity, its sex and age, then uncovering the body, and subjecting it to the techniques of surgery, reveals synecdochically the 'mysteries of the Orient'. In the spectacle of the unwrapping, then, Egypt is confirmed in the part it had long occupied in the Western imaginary as a sort of shorthand for the inscrutability of the Orient, but at the same time it becomes available for a form of scopic possession.

On stage at Exeter Hall, at the Royal Society and at numerous other locations, Egypt was summoned up, objectified, and demystified in the body of the mummy. To (literally) embody the Orient was to render it, at the level of fantasy at least, susceptible to new methods of knowledge and control (cf. the embodiment of vampirism in women's bodies in *Dracula*). Egypt's own techniques for preserving the body became subordinated to a Western technology of the body. Egypt thus became very much an object, not a subject of knowledge. Embodied, made bituminous flesh, mystery came up against the saw, the scissors, the hammer and the chisel. The audience could not only gaze upon this investigative process, its luckier members could take part in it, could handle the very bandages that, stripped away layer by layer, revealed Egyptian mystery incarnate. This is not to suggest that any single unrolling would ever finally disperse the mystery of the Orient: the pleasure of the spectacle lay in asymptotically approaching this point.[13] No two mummies were ever quite the same: if each held out however tenuously the possibility of finally laying bare the truth of Egypt, their very differences suggested that the synecdochic demystification was always necessarily partial – parts may stand in for wholes, but they also evoke the existence of other parts.

The advertisement for the unrolling of a mummy from Giovanni D'Athanasi's collection of Egyptian antiquities gives us a glimpse of the commercial uses of such uniqueness. It is the 'MOST INTERESTING MUMMY that has yet been discovered in Egypt'.[14] The numerous inscriptions that cover the surrounding bandages themselves hold out the prospect of a final knowledge:

The numerous folds of cloth with which the mummy is surrounded are covered with HIERATIC, ENCHORIAL and HIEROGLYPHICAL INSCRIPTIONS and DESIGNS of all the Funereal Ceremonies. The piece of linen now placed round the Mummy is above eight feet in length; it was taken around the feet, and from the mark or character at the end, it would appear that the pieces placed on the breast and other parts of the body were a continuation of it – thus forming the subjects which are usually found in the MS. rolls of Papyrus. It is believed, that these, with the other inscriptions with which the whole of the bandages are covered, include the ENTIRE RITUAL of the ancient Egyptians.[15]

If the possibility of totality could be endlessly entertained, displaced into the body of the mummy, Egypt itself remained finally intangible. But at the same time this intangibility was the enabling condition for the commercial exploitation of the 'mystery of Egypt' in mummy form. Mummy unrolling both staged the unveiling of the Eastern body and produced the East as finally inscrutable. This logic of always deferred satisfaction bears an uncanny resemblance to the motor force of consumer culture itself, as mediated by advertising. In the logic of consumerism each new purchase offers the prospect of an end to desire, but that end is never reached.[16] Indeed, having served as the embodiment of Egypt in rituals of symbolic colonial control, the mummy could be said to assume the new role of the exemplary commodity in British culture, though as we shall see there is something both alien and mysterious about the commodity too.

When the mummy takes on an expanded figurative role within Victorian culture, its actual presence within that culture becomes if anything more ethereal. Mummy unwrapping still presented a relatively close encounter with the other; in the later portion of the mummy's career, that immediacy disappears. The mummy under glass in the museum comes much closer to Mitchell's model of a spectacular object than does the mummy of scientific theatre; any more intimate relation to the mummy is displaced into fiction. This process of derealization resembles that which Allon White sees at work in the progressive attenuation and marginalization of the culture of carnival in nineteenth-century Europe. He argues that the other of the bourgeois self-image, the 'grotesque body' summoned up in carnival, is not so much forgotten as it is banished into the realms of literary culture and privatized consciousness. In effect, there takes place a 'sublimation of a material, physical practice into purely textual semiosis'.[17] This tendency for the literary to displace material practices is also evident in mummy fiction where the ritual encounter of the unwrapping returns as literary fantasy; the exotic object returns as a pure sign. But this process also sets the mummy free to figure a wider range of self and other confrontations; the body of the Oriental other merges with the body of the commodity, as an expanding consumer culture demands narratives to explain the new relations of subjects and objects.

MERCHANDISE AS MUMMY

It has been argued for some time now that Britain's economy undergoes an important change after mid century. If Britain had pushed its way to the front of world trade by developing its *productive* power, after mid century *consumption* assumed a new importance, as if the workshop of the world was becoming the shop of the world.[18] By the 1880s consumerism had fundamentally transformed Victorian culture, a process that occurred in parallel with the gradual shift towards a service-based economy and the rise of professionalism that we discussed in chapter 1. The 1851 Crystal Palace Exhibition announces a new form of public entertainment that unites commercial spectacle with leisure culture. Like the department store that it anticipates, the exhibition establishes what Walter Benjamin calls a 'universe of commodities'.[19] This new visibility of the commodity is also suggested by contemporary theorizations of Britain's economy. With the appearance of neo-classical economic theory consumerism might be said to have its own school of economics.[20] But even before this, Karl Marx had begun to analyse the uncanny power that certain objects had acquired over consumers in a capitalist economy. Commodities, evidently, were on the move. But so too were mummies: toward the end of this period mummies first begin to stalk the pages of popular fiction. The mummy, and to a lesser extent the collector and the detective, are figures around which another theory of the new relations of subjects and objects finds articulation. Indeed, it could even be argued that mummy fictions tell us as much about Marx's model for explaining the inverted relations of subjects and objects in a nascent consumer culture as Marx can tell us about such fictions. While Marx's 'The Commodity Fetish and its Secret' cleaves to a production-centred economic model, the mummy suggests the existence of objects whose commodity nature is not the effect of production.[21] The mummy is the type of the object which becomes a commodity simply because it becomes desirable for consumers, and is thereby drawn into economic exchange. This chasm between production and consumption is thematicized in Conan Doyle's 'Lot No. 249'.[22] The story's title refers to the lot number assigned to a mummy at the auction where it was bought, and the story itself explains how this exchange has transformed the mummy into a pure object: ' "I don't know his name," said Bellingham [the villain of the piece] passing his hand over the shrivelled head. "You see the outer sarcophagus with the inscriptions is missing. Lot 249 is all the title he has now. You see it printed on his case. That was his number in the auction at which I picked him up' (192). The story includes only enough of the mummy's history to mark the disparity between production and consumption: 'This fellow has been pickled in natron, and looked after in the most approved style. They did not serve hodsmen in that fashion. Salt or bitumen was enough for them. It has been calculated that this sort of thing cost about seven hundred and thirty pounds in our money' (192). What makes mummies valuable, though, is not the cost of their production but the fact that people *want* them. If Marx wants to hold onto the rational kernel at the centre of the magical commodity form, to show that the commodity's seeming autonomy is the effect of alienated labour, the mummy narrative implies that the relations of consumers and commodities are fundamentally irrational – or, in other words that they are driven by idiosyncratic desire.[23] Similarly, in the stories of H. D. Everett, H. Rider Haggard, Arthur Conan Doyle and others, the mummy, as a markedly foreign body within the British economy, articulates precisely the imperial dimension of the nineteenth-century British economy that Marx underplays.

COMMODITY STORIES

Marx, in his theorization of the new prominence of the object world in *Capital*, provides a myth of the fall. In the past, the relations between producers were relatively clear, and objects knew their places; but now, through the increasing dominance of commodity production, relations between people appear as relations between the objects they exchange, and objects seem to take on the characteristics of subjects:

The form of wood . . . is altered if a table is made out of it. Nevertheless, the table continues to be wood, an ordinary, sensuous thing. But as soon as it emerges as a commodity, it changes into a thing which transcends sensuousness. It not only stands with its feet on the ground, but, in relation to all other commodities, it stands on its head, and evolves out of its wooden brain grotesque ideas, far more wonderful than if it were to begin dancing of its own free will. (164)

Marx, of course, wants to demystify this bizarre object world, to reveal the magic that animates it. The secret, he reveals, lies in the form of production. Objects begin to misbehave in this fashion when individuals cease to produce goods simply for their own use, or for the use of a knowable community, and begin to produce for an impersonal market:

Objects of utility become commodities only because they are the products of the labour of private individuals who work independently of each other . . . Since the producers do not come into social contact until they exchange the products of their labour, the specific social character of their private labours appear only within this exchange . . . To the producers, therefore, the social relations between their private labours appear as what they are, i.e. they do not appear as direct social relations between persons in their work, but rather as material [dinglich] relations between persons and social relations between things. (165, 166)

There is nothing fortuitous in this process for Marx. Use value is only displaced by exchange value 'when exchange has already acquired a sufficient extension and importance to allow useful things to be produced *for the purpose of being exchanged*, so that their character as values has already to be *taken into consideration* during production' (166, my emphasis).

Things weren't always like this. In feudal society, Marx argues, there was no system of independent and mutually invisible producers: 'Here, instead of the independent man, we find everyone dependent – serfs and lords, vassals and suzerains, laymen and clerics . . . But precisely because relations of personal dependence form the given social foundation, there is no need for labour and its producers to assume a fantastic form different from their reality' (170). The problem then would appear to be one of knowledge or representation: only reveal that the ostensible powers of goods are bestowed on them by the labour of actual men, and the dominion of objects over men should cease. In a completely transparent society, where exchange stayed within clear sight of production, subject/object relations would be unambiguous. However, Marx argues, the spell that objects cast over men may only be broken by *lived* knowledge, not abstract theoretical knowledge: 'The veil is not removed from the countenance of the social life-process, i.e. the process of material production, until it becomes production by freely associated men, and stands under their conscious and planned control' (173). It is not enough, in other words, to simply reveal the relations of the parts to the whole of the economic system: the relations between, and nature of, the parts must be changed.

The story of the mummy suggests that the circulation of objects is more complex than Marx was willing to imagine. What if the chain of production did not lead one back to the factory or the mill? Marx's commodities often have an interestingly homely cast: the weaver sells his linen and ('being a man of the old school' [199]) buys a bible; the bookseller uses that money to buy brandy. What about objects that are not produced for exchange but nevertheless become objects of exchange? What if the relationship between visibility and knowledge is complicated by an immense spatial and cultural gap – of the kind, say, that separated London and ancient Egypt? If Marx had wandered out of the British Museum reading room and visited, say, the Assyrian or Egyptian rooms, he would have seen one of the world's largest collections of such things, things that, regardless of their original roles, had entered into circulation as commodities, before being removed from economic exchange and placed on display within a very different culture. While he does not produce an explicit account of this very different world of goods, it nevertheless makes an appearance in his text.

IMPERIAL FIGURES

In the dancing table allusion I cited earlier, Marx draws on the Victorian craze for spiritualism; his unruly tables resemble the tilting tables of middle-class seances. Marx dismisses such practices at the same time that he draws on them to describe the behaviour of commodities. In the same way *Capital* develops its anatomy of capitalism and the commodity form by substituting the language of religion for that of political economy:

In order, therefore, to find an analogy [sc. for the way commodities appear to alienated producers] we must take flight into the misty realm of religion. There the products of the human brain appear as autonomous figures endowed with a life of their own, which enter into relations both with each other and with the human race. So it is in the world of commodities with the products of men' s hands. I call this the fetishism which attaches itself to the products of labour as soon as they are produced as commodities, and is therefore inseparable from the production of commodities. (165)

Just as human powers become displaced onto supernatural figures with which men are reunited through religious rituals, so in a capitalist economy do the relations between people become projected onto the world of things. Though Marx draws on the work of Feuerbach to make this analogy, it is perhaps more important that he is describing the fetishistic behaviour of certain objects in British culture at a time when British anthropology is developing an interest in the religions of 'primitive' people.

During the 1860s fetishism became a focal point of intellectual interest in the emerging discipline of anthropology. 1866 saw the appearance
of a *Fortnightly Review* article by Edward Burnett Tylor, a founding figure
of Victorian anthropology, on 'The Religion of Savages'. Four years
later the same periodical published J. F. McLennan's 'The Worship of
Plants and Animals, Part 1: Totems and Totemism'.[24] Tylor's pioneering *Primitive Culture: Researches into the Development of Mythology, Philosophy,
Religion, Art, and Custom* appears in 1871, the second volume of which
contains a discussion of fetish objects, which Tylor distinguishes from
the other objects collected by both primitive and modern societies.[25]
Marx's analysis of the commodity form envisages the possibility of its
demystification through an account of its production. But by using the
language of primitive and occult cultural practices to describe the thing
in need of demystification, he pushes these objects beyond the reach of
his narrative account. Objects from 'exotic' cultures were pouring into
Britain during this period for display in private homes,[26] as well as for
collections like the Pitt-Rivers at Oxford (with which Tylor was connected, as it happens). Weapons, tools, ritual masks and objects that would
probably have been classified as fetishes were imported into Britain in
increasing numbers as the net of empire was cast ever wider. These
objects clearly entered the British economy as commodities, yet it is
unlikely that all or even most of them could be described in Marx's
terms. The term commodity fetish, then, as Marx develops it, both
acknowledges and denies the existence of this category of things.

This fetishistic functioning of the commodity in his own discourse is
activated by his transposition of the imperial theme: 'Value . . . transforms every product of labour into a social hieroglyphic. Later on men
try to decipher the hieroglyphic, to get behind the secret of their own
social product . . .' (167). To describe the commodity as a 'social hieroglyphic' is to put in play centuries of discursive production of Egypt as
enigmatic, as a country that is ineffably mysterious – and to occult the
very process of production he is out to demystify. Like the term 'fetish',
itself, his use of such a metaphor betrays the fact that while he describes
the social life of things in *Capital* in nostalgically domestic terms – the
farmer's wheat is exchanged for the weaver's cloth, the weaver's cloth is
exchanged for the tradesman's bible – his account retains the vestiges of
the commodity flow which he is forced to discount in order to keep his
production-centred theory of the commodity. The foreign objects which
begin to pour into Britain in ever-increasing numbers, who could say
how or why they were made? In this light, Marx's focus on properly

English commodities almost seems like a strategy of containment; the origin fantasies that surround the flow of imperial objects are evoked in the language of primitive religion and of Oriental mystery, but the actual analysis disavows the other-worldly nature of these commodities.

THE NATIONAL COLLECTION

At the same time that imperialism was effecting enormous changes in disparate cultures around the world, then, the 'home culture' was also being reshaped in response to the new global system. It is also as part of a new empire of objects that we can understand the museum's new importance in the British social imaginary. The museum is part of the particular spectacular regime of nineteenth-century Europe. This regime, as Timothy Mitchell observes, must be understood as itself an imperial phenomenon, 'since what was to be rendered as exhibit was reality, the world itself'.[27] The museum often provides the setting for exploring subject–object relations in mummy fiction. If, as Susan Stewart remarks, 'the museum . . . must serve as the central metaphor of the collection' this is because it offers the national equivalent of the private collection.[28] The collection provides a way of 'domesticating' objects, making origins and function subservient to a scheme of classification imposed by the collector.[29] Marx tries to imagine the reacquisition of conceptual control over the realm of objects by means of a narrative of origins; the collection seeks to do the same by giving the object a new origin within the collection. In the private collection, the ultimate origin is the collector him or herself: 'Not simply a consumer of the objects that fill the decor, the self generates a fantasy in which it becomes the producer of those objects, a producer by arrangement and manipulation.'[30] The self extends its own boundaries through the disposition of objects. In Walter Benjamin's words: 'for a collector . . . ownership is the most intimate relationship that one can have to objects. Not that they come alive in him; it is he who lives in them'.[31] In the public collection the same principle holds – namely, that objects must be controlled, must be put in the service of the *system* of objects. The British Museum came to represent the ideal of the collection in this period, a world of exotic objects under a domesticating taxonomic regime. In the museum, the imagined body of the nation could incorporate the other, subjecting the unruly parade of foreign objects to the strict discipline of classification. Thomas Richards persuasively argues that the British Museum operates as one of several fantasy images for a total imperial

knowledge.[32] While this may be true of the museum's library, I want to
suggest that the museum operates somewhat differently – as a fantasy
image for the containment of the material culture, the *things*, rather than
the knowledge, accumulated with empire. In this way the national
collection plays an important part in mediating between the national
body and its imperial extensions.[33]

For much of its history the British Museum authorities were more
concerned with keeping people out than luring them in, but the museum
movement of the second half of the nineteenth century reimagined the
storehouse-museum as an instrument of popular education. We can
discern this new conception of the museum in the 1860 'Report of the
Select Committee on the power of Parliament to provide, or of the
House to recommend, the placing of institutions supported by General
Taxation for recreation and improvement of the people'.[34] The committee recommended the adoption of evening opening hours to allow the
working class to attend the British Museum and other institutions. More
was at stake than providing popular entertainment, as is evident from the
section of the report addressing the possibility of setting up a loan scheme
for museum exhibits. Educational recreation was to draw the public
from less acceptable pursuits; indeed not to do so was to risk the
museum's transformation into a forbiddingly exotic, even Gothic space.
Being brought face to face with the objects of empire would disperse the
mystery surrounding them: 'Thus instead of our vast national collections
being virtually *entombed* as at present, or becoming *so vast as to bewilder*, and
yet so crowded as to be *hidden*, profitable recreation would be provided in
the various crowded districts of the Metropolis, which would successfully
compete with places of demoralizing amusement.'[35] The museum as a
vehicle for self-improvement was to be made more accessible, but also
the 'various crowded districts' were to be improved by a judicious
distribution of the equally crowded national collections.

Nor were antiquities the only possible instruments for the diffusion of
culture. The museum movement, aspiring towards the 'diffusion of
instruction and rational amusement', was especially visible in the development of the local and natural history museums.[36] The attempt by one
General Augustus Pitt-Rivers to diffuse culture among the lower orders
is a case in point. Pitt-Rivers, founder of the eponymous Museum at
Oxford (earlier situated in the working-class Bethnal Green district),
assembled a huge collection of weapons and tools from around the
world. He applied Darwinist theories of evolution to this collection,
arranging the artifacts to show the step-by-step development of material

culture. Through his seamless displays of the evolution of common objects he wanted to persuade the working-class museum visitor that world history observes a continuity of development, that '*Natura non facet saltum*'.37 The intelligent working-class visitor would then apply these universal principles of gradual change to politics and realize the futility of political agitation. Pitt-Rivers's project is congruent with that of the Select Committee. Somewhat paradoxically, bringing goods from 'primitive' cultures into working-class London districts was meant to have a civilizing effect on their inhabitants. In the museum, then, we see the point of intersection of different fantasies: what we might designate an explicit political fantasy of the museum as an instrument of ideology, and the less clearly formulated fantasy of the museum as the mediator between the foreign and the domestic. These fantasies are by no means consistent. The former fantasy endowed objects, albeit arranged objects, with the power to influence people; the latter returned objects to the control of the collector or curator, the object expert.

If the Select Committee and Pitt-Rivers were mostly concerned with the effects of a museum culture on people, others considered the effects of this culture on the objects collected. Two poems from the late nineteenth century develop the theme of the fate of auratic objects in the museum collection. In 'To S.C.' (viz. Sidney Colvin, Keeper of the Department of Prints and Drawings in the British Museum), R. L. Stevenson contrasts his own trajectory from Britain (and, indeed, the British Museum, where he had stayed in Colvin's residence) to the Pacific with that of 'island gods' who have ended up in Bloomsbury. Like them Stevenson has been uprooted, but he is 'estranged in body, not in mind'. He urges Colvin to spare a thought for objects that once enjoyed the status of powerful subjects, but have now become mere curios:

> Lo, now, when to your task in the great house
> At morning through the portico you pass,
> One moment glance, where by the pillared wall,
> Far-voyaging island gods, begrimed with smoke,
> Sit now unworshipped, the rude monument
> Of faiths forgot and races undivined:
> Sit now disconsolate, remembering well
> The priest, the victim, and the songful crowd,
> The blaze of the blue noon, and the huge voice,
> Incessant, of the breakers on the shore.
> As far as these from their ancestral shrine,
> So far, so foreign, your divided friends
> Wander, estranged in body, not in mind.38

Colvin explains in a note that 'the allusion is to the two colossal images from Easter Island which used to stand under the portico to the right hand of the visitor entering the museum'.[39] Stevenson doesn't hold out much hope for these translated figures, but Eugene Lee-Hamilton in 'Fading Glories' (1884) gives a rather more complicated account of the social life of auratic things under modernity. He meditates on the path from the cathedral to the museum:

> In or and azure were they shrined of old,
> Where led dim aisle to glowing stained-glass rose,
> . . .
> Where censer swung, and organ-thunder rolled;
> . . .
> And now they stand with aureoles that time dims
> Near young Greek fauns that pagan berries wreathe,
> In crowded glaring galleries of dead art.
>
> Their hands still fold; their lips still sing faint hymns;
> or are they prayers that beautiful shapes breathe
> For shelter in some cold eclectic heart?[40]

Lee-Hamilton is at once aware that if auratic objects have no defences against the commodifying effects of a secular economy, aestheticism itself is in a sense a reconsecration of the object world, though the sacred has shifted its centre from the divine to the individual's taste. The shelter of 'some cold eclectic heart' nonetheless is better than none at all.

Indeed the context in which Stevenson's British Museum poem was written, if not the text itself, also testifies to the possibility that aura may be bestowed as well as lost by collection. The poem was written during Stevenson's visit to the island of Apemama, where Tembinok, the king, was famous for his collection of European goods. '[C]locks, musical boxes, blue spectacles, umbrellas, knitted waistcoats, bolts of stuff, tools, rifles, fowling-pieces, medicines, sewing machines, stoves [and] European foods', all prosaic enough in themselves, acquired a new significance in the context of the royal collection.[41] The mummy stories too, as we shall see, suggest that the individual's encounters with objects may be more complex than Stevenson imagines, though they also show that cold-heartedness may not always characterize the modern viewer.

HOMES AND HOLMES

Tembinok's cluttered store-houses may serve to remind us that the national collection also had its private equivalent, and that eclecticism may make a shelter of the home as well as the heart for all sorts of things. For back in Britain the bourgeois home was becoming itself museum-like, as, from relatively spartan beginnings, it came to be more and more a repository for objects. Nor was Britain altogether alone in this. By the end of the century Max Nordau would identify a new continental acquisitiveness as yet another index of degeneration: 'The present rage for collecting, the piling up in dwellings, of aimless bric-à-brac' was typical of 'an irresistible desire among the degenerate to accumulate trifles', citing with approval Magnan's term for this 'buying craze' – 'oniomania'.[42] Managing these piled-up objects was the province of the middle-class woman.[43] Books on interior decorating and household management such as Charles Eastlake's popular *Hints on Household Taste in Furniture, Upholstery and Other Details* (1868) and the bestselling Mrs Beeton's *Book of Household Management* (1861) simultaneously created and filled a need: as Mrs Beeton claimed, there were 'difficulties in the way of housekeeping, and many modern demands upon it, with which our grandmothers or even our mothers had not to contend'.[44]

One of these difficulties was the sheer increase in the number of *things* in the Victorian home, and thus the number of things about which the domestic woman was expected to know.[45] The home, as a sort of domestic museum for the exotic and antique, becomes a space for the collector's art. Mrs Orrinsmith's *The Drawing Room* nicely illustrates the character of the domestic collection:

In her drawing room there were to be 'shelves with delicate carving on side and edges, tiles and plates on the lowest, and Venetian bottles, old Delft vases or old Nankin cups arranged on the upper shelf'. 'What shall be added next?' ought, she said, to be 'a constantly recurring thought'. The answer was another 'object of taste'. 'To the appreciative mind, not spoiled by the luxury of wealth, what keen pleasure there is in the possession of one new treasure: a Persian tile, an Algerian flower-pot, an old Flemish cup . . . an Icelandic spoon, a Japanese cabinet, a Chinese fan; a hundred things might be named.'[46]

But if the increasing numbers willing to take Eastlake's household hints seem to suggest that the British home was able to take happily to its new role, there are also indications that the house-as-museum was rather less than *heimlich*.

In mummy fiction the division between the home and the museum characteristically breaks down, but often in a disconcerting way for the inhabitants of these spaces. In Bram Stoker's *The Jewel of Seven Stars*, Margaret Trelawny is not sure which space she inhabits: 'I sometimes don't know whether I am in a private house or the British Museum.'[47] Abercrombie Smith of Conan Doyle's 'Lot No. 249' notes a similar transformation of domestic space: 'It was such a chamber as he had never seen before – a museum rather than a study. Walls and ceiling were thickly covered with a thousand strange relics from Egypt and the East. Tall, angular figures bearing burdens of weapons stalked in an uncouth frieze round the apartments. Above were bull-headed, stork-headed, cat-headed, owl-headed statues, with viper-crowned, almond-eyed monarchs, and strange beetle-like deities cut out of the blue lapis lazuli' (187). In another Conan Doyle story, 'The Ring of Thoth', the substitution takes place in the other direction. A Louvre attendant, in fact an ancient Egyptian who has discovered the secret of immortality, makes one of the museum's smaller rooms his temporary home (he has 'prevailed upon [the director] to move the few effects which [he] has retained' into it) while he searches for his lost love, one of the museum's mummies.[48] A similar convergence of home and museum occurs in H. Rider Haggard's 'Smith and the Pharaohs', when Smith is forced to spend a night in the Cairo museum. In an effort to make his surround-ings less intimidating, he seeks out the most domestic of the museum's rooms: 'He was shut in a museum, and the question was in what part of it he should camp for the night . . . He thought with affection of the lavatory, where, before going to see the Director, only that afternoon he had washed his hands.'[49] Both the museum as house and the house as museum stage the exotic interior of an expanding consumer culture that is also an imperial culture. If imperialism brought the forces of modern-ization to bear on the remotest parts of the globe, imposing the stamp of British culture on often recalcitrant nations, Britain itself seems to have felt the cultural recoil. The domestic space in these fictions is increas-ingly experienced as foreign; the present is increasingly infiltrated by what it has designated as archaic.

When the home is experienced as a museum, it is not surprising that the private collector should find a place in fiction. Dickens's novels are perhaps the first to meditate on these changes, and the collection and its designer are already visible in *Our Mutual Friend, Dombey and Son* and *The Old Curiosity Shop*. Indeed, as Dorothy Van Ghent noted many years ago, the world of Dickens's novels is marked by the same personification of objects and reification of people that Marx describes in *Capital*.[50] It is the less surprising, then, that, writing at the threshold of the Exhibition age, Dickens should also be among the first to deploy the figures that come to mediate the experience of a transformed object world. We also encoun-

ter the collector in the novels of Wilkie Collins quite early, as the awful
Mr Fairlie in *The Woman in White*, and as Noel Vanstone in *No Name*. He
is much more in evidence, though, in the later nineteenth century, in the
fiction of Henry James or Oscar Wilde, for example, but also as Stein in
Conrad's *Lord Jim*.[51]

The collector possesses a more adventurous counterpart in the detective. Detective fiction provides us with a clue to what was most problematic about the object-rich interior: these new objects are difficult to read.
Meaning has been drained from the world of objects represented in
detective stories, much as it has in the household guides. Thus the new
object world requires a new hero – someone who can discriminate with
a high degree of accuracy between one object and another by establish-
ing origins, uses and values. Walter Benjamin observes how the thicken-
ing of the fabric of modern life first registers in the detective story. Such
narratives exploit the possible threat to the domestic posed by the
exoticization of interiors:

> Far more interesting than the Oriental landscapes in detective novels is that
> rank Orient inhabiting their interiors: the Persian carpet and the ottoman, the
> hanging lamp and the genuine Caucasian dagger. Behind the heavy, gathered
> Khilim tapestries the master of the house has orgies with his share certificates,
> feels himself the Eastern merchant, the indolent pasha in the caravanserai of
> otiose enchantment, until that dagger in its silver sling above the divan puts an
> end, one fine afternoon, to his siesta and himself.[52]

When the bourgeois subject allows the exotic to overcome the domestic,
'Eastern' appetite displaces educated European taste. The detective
restores the proper relations of objects and contexts. Like the connois-
seur and the tasteful woman addressed by Mrs Orrinsmith, he can read
this highly textured bourgeois interior – he is an expert in objects.[53] The
detective's professional interest in the world of objects suggests that all
three figures – detective, collector and woman of taste – are in part
dependent on the discourse of professionalism that we encountered in
chapter 1.

The detective is anticipated in the work of Dickens and Collins, just as
the collector is. His imperial significance is already evident in Collins's
The Moonstone, which traces the metropolitan consequences of the theft
of a colonial treasure. As if to acknowledge this lineage, one of Sherlock
Holmes's earliest adventures, *The Sign of Four*, is a whittled-down version
of Collins's novel. Holmes's expertise extends over all objects, though,
domestic and foreign. One of the most striking aspects of the Sherlock
Holmes stories is the extent to which the solution of mystery lies in the

proper reading of household objects. For Benjamin, collectors are the 'physiognomists of the world of objects'. One might say the same of Holmes. Boots, tobacco ash, writing paper all reassuringly tell us of their origins under Holmes's inspection. His accounts render the inscrutable object world completely transparent; he deciphers the histories of both foreign and mass-produced objects at a glance. Like the middle-class housewife, the detective obtains mastery over material culture. It is scarcely surprising that Conan Doyle was a great admirer of Mrs Beeton.[54] Even the people who turn up at Baker Street bear the legible marks of their travels, trade and social standing. Seemingly homogeneous commodities are revealed to be as individual as fingerprints, while apparently inscrutable individuals are exposed as ex-sailors, members of particular clerical grades or former colonial officers. To the discerning eye of Holmes, all are mere surfaces for the inscription of the defining marks of their type; from such traces whole histories can be reconstructed.

The museum and the collector provide the framework for experiencing and thus for managing the new object world; the figure of the detective both entertains and contains the possibility that the world of objects can escape from that rational framework. The mummy, I want to argue, takes the relation of subjects and objects in another direction, depicting what happens when the enabling rational classification of objects breaks down. Exhibits take on a life of their own, and collectors face their own objectification. In fact, the fantasies explored in mummy fiction closely resemble Marx's description of the transactions between people and things in his chapter on commodity fetishism. That 'transposition of attributes' already nascently present in the fiction of Dickens becomes the dramatic principle of the mummy story.

THE COLLECTOR'S PASSION

Some stories deal with hostile mummies who revenge themselves on those who have disturbed their original resting places. Others exploit the erotic possibilities of the mummy. Still others vacillate between these categories. However, all feature mummies who come to life or otherwise attain agency in modern Europe. As in Marx's commodity story, seemingly inert objects take on a will of their own, and subjects find themselves in danger of reification. The mummy, as a complex figure sharing both subjective and objective traits, is the perfect vehicle for this narrativized commodity theory.[55] Where Marx describes objects that begin to behave like subjects through the process of commodification, mummy fiction shows how subjects-turned-objects revert to the status of subjects. The fictional possibilities of dancing tables may be limited, but resurrected mummies show considerable narrative flexibility, entering into a variety of relations with the subjects who revive them.

The limitations of the collector as object-expert are evident in one of the very first stories to explore the fictional possibilities presented by the mummy, Théophile Gautier's 'Le Pied de Momie'.[56] Gautier's story deals with Benjamin's Paris rather than Marx's London, but the changes in material culture which the story elaborates are remarkably similar. Gautier's narrator one day enters the shop of a 'marchand de bric-à-brac' in 'an idle mood'. He appeals to the shared experience of the new middle-class shopping culture:

You have doubtless glanced occasionally through the windows of some of these shops, which have become so numerous now that it is fashionable to buy antiquated furniture, and that every petty stockbroker thinks he must have his *chambre au moyen age.* (52)

The description of the shop's contents (much of which he suggests are inauthentic) becomes the occasion for an exercise in style, the dense, noun-laden paragraphs mimicking the space of the cluttered shop:

All ages and all nations seemed to have made their rendezvous there. An Etruscan lamp of red clay stood upon a Boule cabinet, with ebony panels, brightly striped by lines of inlaid brass; a duchess of the court of Louis xv nonchalantly extended her fawn like feet under a massive table of the time of Louis xiii, with heavy spiral supports of oak . . . Upon the denticulated shelves of several sideboards glittered immense Japanese dishes with red and blue designs relieved by gilded hatching, side by side with enamelled works by Bernard Palissy, representing serpents, frogs, and lizards in relief . . . Chinese grotesques, vases of celadon and crackleware, Saxon and old Sèvres cup encumbered the shelves and nooks of the apartment. (52–3)

The description recalls the passage from Mrs Orrinsmith I quoted earlier. In Gautier's shop, however, the random collection of exotica is one that only the taste of a discriminating collector can bring to order.

The story dwells on the contradictory aspects of commodification, where uniqueness is rewritten as exchangeability and thus as costliness. The dealer himself embodies this split between regimes of value: his close attention to his customer is described as that 'of an antiquarian and a usurer'. Usury is suggested again when the dealer is described as of the 'Oriental or Jewish type' (54). Our narrator seeks a paperweight, but he wants one that will distinguish his desk from others: he wants, in effect, to purchase uniqueness. He seeks 'a small figure, something which will suit me for a paper-weight, for I cannot endure those trumpery bronzes which the stationers sell, and which may be found on everybody else's desk' (55). A mummy's foot, described by the dealer as the 'foot of the Princess Hermonthis', seems to fit the bill. The fate of uniqueness within a money economy is again foregrounded in the haggling that follows, as the logic of exchange value struggles with the concept of originality to establish the object's worth:

'How much will you charge me for this mummy fragment?'
'Ah, the highest price I can get, for it is a superb piece. If I had the match of it you could not have it for less than five hundred francs. The daughter of a Pharaoh! Nothing is more rare.'
'Assuredly that is not a common article, but still how much do you want? In the first place let me warn you that all my wealth consists of just five louis. I can buy anything that costs five louis, but nothing dearer . . .'
'Five louis for the foot of the Princess Hermonthis! That is very little, very little indeed. 'Tis an authentic foot . . . Well, take it and I will give you the bandages into the bargain . . .' (57)

Gautier explores the paradoxical effects of the new purchase on the narrator; the process which is meant to bestow the distinction of the object on its owner actually gives the object a new power over him, to the extent that the object appears to become a subject in its own right. Having deposited his new acquisition on his desk the narrator goes out 'with the gravity and pride becoming one who feels that he has the ineffable advantage over all the passers-by whom he elbows, of possessing a piece of the Princess Hermonthis, daughter of Pharaoh' (58). Uniqueness, it seems, has been transferred from the commodity to its possessor. The foot confers upon him a new perception of his superiority to others: 'I looked upon all who did not possess, like myself, a paper-weight so authentically Egyptian as very ridiculous people, and it seemed to me that the proper occupation of every sensible man should consist in the mere fact of having a mummy's foot upon his desk' (59).

However, the foot refuses to accept its part in the narrative he has in mind for it. In his dreams that night he sees the foot come to life: 'Instead of remaining quiet, as behoved a foot which had been embalmed for four thousand years, it commenced to act in a nervous manner, contracted itself and leaped over the papers like a startled frog' (60). Peeved that his acquisition could not be of a more 'sedentary disposition', he is further startled by the appearance of the Princess herself looking for her foot. Having generously returned the foot to her (as a visitor from a less commercial world, she has no money to buy it back), he is rewarded by being taken by her to a gathering of Pharaohs where he asks her father for the Princess's hand in marriage ('a very proper antithetic recompense for the foot'). Rejected as being too young for the well-preserved Princess, he wakes to find a friend shaking him, having come to accompany him to an exhibition. The story ends, then, by returning the collector-hero to the world where expert knowledge gives him domain over objects.

This fantasy depends on an object-rich culture, in particular one where the old and the exotic are valued for their own uniqueness, which in turn suggests that mass-production has already achieved cultural dominance. The collector, the man of taste, someone who can read the object world with a certain assurance is the only appropriate subject for such a culture. However, in the story, while the collector seeks to place the object world at the service of his personality, to make it an emblem of his own depth, the object takes on a life of its own. Having 'leaped over the papers like a startled frog' the foot seems, like Marx's table, to evolve 'grotesque ideas' out of its head, conjuring up its previous contexts (i.e. the missing body of the Princess, and then Egypt itself). The collector attempts to domesticate the foreign part-object, removing it from the world of exchange, and cutting it off, as it were, from its previous associations. It is supposed to behave metaphorically, and will 'stand in' for his own cultural refinement. Instead, the foot conjures up the various wholes of which it was once a part, and a metonymic series overturns his metaphorical scheme. The consumer dreams, and in his dreams the past life of the commodity comes before him. However, if his ascendancy over the object world is threatened, his reaction is not horror, but rather an immediate wish to possess the mummy itself in another way – by means of romance. As we shall see in the later mummy stories, the fantasy of the collector is abandoned for a fantasy in which the Western consumer woos the object world. In mummy fiction – as in advertising – objects begin to behave as sex objects.

The British mummy stories replace the shopper with the Egyptologist. If the shopper represents one type of object expert, the Egyptologist represents his more professionalized avatar. Again, it is the limitations of these experts that are foregrounded, and they are no more successful than Gautier's narrator at controlling objects. H. Rider Haggard's 'Smith and the Pharaohs', for example, follows a similar logic to Gautier's tale, which drags first Princess Hermonthis and then Egypt itself into the narrator's study by the foot. In Rider Haggard's story, though, the commodity world evoked more closely resembles that sustained by modern advertising, where the images of objects rather than objects themselves compel the subject's fascination. Smith, a well-to-do clerk, becomes obsessed with the cast of a statue of an unidentified woman's head after a desultory visit to the British Museum. Rather like Gautier's narrator he 'drift[s] into the British Museum' (150) but following a familiar topos, the dense texture of urban experience seems to ensure that such contingency always turns into narrative. Smith is inspired by his fascination with the woman's image to become an amateur Egyptologist, and he travels to Egypt, which is described to him as a place where commerce rather than romance is in the ascendant. 'I'm afraid you'll find it expensive', a superior at work warns him. 'They fleece one in Egypt' (15). After a number of trips, Smith finds the tomb of the Egyptian queen Ma-Mee, the woman whose image obsesses him.[57] Her body has been burned by a tomb-robber, but he recovers her hand ('a woman's little hand, most delicately shaped' 163), two rings and a broken statuette. After he shows these finds to the Museum Director in Cairo he is accidentally locked in the museum after hours, where he witnesses a convocation of the dead kings and queens of ancient Egypt, among them his love, Ma-Mee.[58] As in Gautier's narrative, the collectible part object seems to generate the lost body and, by way of further metonymic extension, the environment of that body. The collected object, rather than remaining a properly classified and subsidiary part of a whole collection, reproduces its original context outside itself. Smith himself is revealed as a part of the object's lost context when we discover that he is the reincarnation of a sculptor who once loved Ma-Mee. While watching the convocation of Pharaohs, Smith feels that he has become an object of study for the reanimated mummies: 'he became aware that the eyes of that dreadful magician were fixed upon him, and that a bone had a better chance of escaping the search of a Röntgen ray than he of hiding himself from their baleful glare' (182).[59] Where Gautier's story explored the possibilities of the collected object attaining subject status, Haggard's story brings the expert face to face with the prospect of his own objectification.

The objectification of the self – reversing the positions of collector and object – is treated most extensively in two of Rider Haggard's novels, *She* and *The Yellow God*. *She* is in many respects a displaced Egyptian romance, in which the collected object behaves in the same way it does in the mummy tales. The Amahagger, Ayesha's subjects, are very much like the modern Egyptians as the Victorians saw them: epigones, the inheritors of vast and majestic ruins of which they have no proper knowledge. The vanished inhabitants of the city of Kôr are explicitly compared to the ancient Egyptians as a people who 'thought more of the dead than the living'.[60] They use the mummified bodies of their greater predecessors as fuel, much as Mark Twain and other nineteenth-century commentators accuse the modern Egyptians of do-ing.[61] Haggard invites us to read *She* as a mummy story when Holly, the narrator, is presented with the remains of one such burnt mummy, a perfectly preserved foot: 'it was not shrunk or shriveled, or even black and unsightly, like the flesh of Egyptian mummies, but plump and fair, and, except where it had been slightly burned, perfect as on the day of death – a very triumph of embalming' (85). Billali, the leader of the Amahagger party which brings the Englishmen to Ayesha, had fallen in love with the preserved body of this woman in his youth. His mother had burned it to put an end to his folly. Thus, in this story, the mummy fantasy is shared between Billali and Holly, European and native. We hear no more of the foot after Holly stows it away in his Gladstone bag. However, it is possible to see how *She* replays mummy fiction's fantasy of the regenerated body through a species of displacement: Ayesha herself stands in the place of the whole mummy conjured up, as it were, by the fragment. This connection is borne out by Haggard's description of her: when Holly first sees Ayesha she is 'wrapped up in soft white gauzy material in such a way as at first sight to remind me most forcibly of a corpse in its grave-clothes' (110). Moreover, Holly notes her 'swathed mummy-like form' (111). Like the mummies in 'Le Pied de la Momie' and in 'Smith and the Pharaohs', Ayesha threatens the fantasy of the collector at the same time that she evokes it, since she is a collector in her own right. She has preserved the body of her long-lost lover, Kallikrates, which, when revealed to the Englishmen, appears to be identical to that of Holly's companion Leo:

With a sudden motion she drew the shroud from the cold form, and let the lamp-light play upon it. I looked, and then shrunk back terrified, since, say what she might in explanation, the sight was an uncanny one . . . For there, stretched upon the stone bier before us, robed in white and perfectly preser-ved, was what appeared to be the body of Leo Vincey. I stared from Leo, standing there alive, to Leo lying there dead, and could see no difference, except perhaps, that the body on the bier looked older . . . I can only sum up the resemblance by saying that I never saw twins so exactly similar as that dead and living pair. (177–8)

If the strangely attractive preserved foot has metamorphosed into the living and breathing Ayesha, Leo Vincey comes vis à vis with his own objectification. The exotic object becomes a subject; to complete the chiasmus, Leo would have to take the place of his (reified) ancestor. This is the same unsettling prospect which confronts Smith in 'Smith and the Pharaohs' where another Englishman faces a reversal of the rational relations between subject and object.

That what we have here is a fantasy of mummification in reverse is confirmed by Haggard's later reworking of the scene in *The Yellow God, An Idol of Africa* (1908), a novel that combines shady dealings in the City with a more openly misogynistic retelling of *She*. In *The Yellow God*, the character who takes the place of Ayesha is the priestess, or 'Asika', to a bloodthirsty idol, and she chooses husbands as she desires. They conveniently die when she tires of them, whereupon she has their bodies preserved, rather as Ayesha has done with Kallikrates. Again the collector's fantasy is reversed along lines of race and gender: the exotic woman supplants the European collector. The hero, Alan Vernon, is shown the Asika's ex-husbands: 'At first, until the utter stillness undeceived him, he thought that they must be men. Then he understood that this was what they had been; now they were corpses wrapped in sheets of thin gold and wearing golden masks with eyes of crystal, each mask being beaten out to a hideous representation of the man in life.'[62] Alan's native servant spells out what will happen to the Asika's present husband in due course. 'In two month's time he nothing (sic)', he explains, 'but gold figure, *No. 2403; just like one mummy in museum*' (my emphasis). Alan's fate may be the same, since she has fallen in love with him, and must dispose of her present husband in order to marry him. This is the ultimate reversal of the collector's fantasy. Drawn into the history of the object he seeks to collect, the would-be collector is likely to become a collectible object himself rather than enhancing his status as a subject.

The object/commodity turned subject does not necessarily involve the hero's reification, however. *Iras, A Mystery* begins as a smuggling story and ends as a love story; the Iras of the title is in rapid succession a contraband mummy, a young woman, a bride and (again) a mummy. Lavenham, the hero of the piece, illegally imports a mummy in a crate of sponges, which he plans to use for a chemical investigation of the embalming process. In the coffin he finds a tablet identifying the mummy as a young woman who was put to sleep by the priest, Savak, when she refused to marry him. The priest can only claim her if she fails to wake or if he defeats her future lover, who will be 'not of this land or

generation'.⁶³ She does awaken and immediately falls in love with
Lavenham; as in the other mummy stories the attraction of collector and
collected is immediate. Remembering his Shakespeare, Lavenham
names her Iras, for one of Cleopatra's handmaidens. Iras's docility and
unswerving affection for Lavenham, together with this Robinson
Crusoe-like christening, suggest that she is a sort of anti-New Woman.
Lavenham naturally experiences some difficulty in explaining her presence to his landlady, and in procuring modern dress for her, but these
problems are surmounted and the amorous couple take a train to
Scotland to be married. The transition from contraband to marriage
partner does not go quite so smoothly, because the vengeful Savak
follows them in spirit form, seeking to foreshorten Iras's new life by
removing beads from her magical necklace. Their honeymoon in Scotland is disrupted by Savak's attacks, each of which destroys a few more
beads. As a result, Iras fades away, to the point where at times only
Lavenham can see her. Eventually, she re-enters the object world, and
he is discovered delirious in the snow with a mummy dressed in modern
clothes beside him. Even such traces as her signature in the marriage
register begin to disappear. When Lavenham finds her trunk of clothes
intact, with all of the clothes she once wore lying there as if they had
never been worn, he is prompted to speculate on the spiritual life of
objects: 'Have inanimate things souls – spiritual doubles? and could it
have been these she used and I saw?' (224) Not only do such exotic
commodities as mummies have secret lives, then; so do such sensible
materials as tweed.

OBJECTS OF DESIRE

Mummies, like Marx's animated tables, seem to live out the logic of the
commodity fetish. There are, however, crucial distinctions beween the
theory of the commodity advanced by Marx and that developed in the
figure of the mummy. Exploring these distinctions will allow us to
theorize the cultural significance of the craze for mummy fiction. The
mummy stories' contribution to commodity theory relates to the way
they gender the roles of collector and collected, and on their figuration
of empire. In one variety of the mummy story, gender becomes the
category through which the relations of subjects and objects are re-
established. *Iras, A Mystery* is in fact a less unusual mummy narrative
than one might expect. The majority of the late nineteenth and early
twentieth-century mummy stories deal not with the vengeful mummies

popularized by Hollywood, but with male collectors and Egyptologists who fall in love with revitalized female mummies.[64] This basic plot allows for numerous displacements without altering the fundamental fantasy that first threatens and then re-establishes the subject's domination over the object world. In Conan Doyle's 'The Ring of Thoth', for example, the Egyptologist is a voyeur at the scene of resurrection performed on a beautiful female mummy by an ancient Egyptian. The plot of Stoker's *Jewel of Seven Stars* turns on the revival of another royal mummy. Again there is a degree of mediation involved in the fantasy. The narrator is not in love with Queen Tera, but with the daughter of the Egyptologist, Trelawny, who wants to revive the dead queen. Margaret Trelawny, however, is the double of Tera, born at the moment when her father discovers her tomb. The revival in this case goes disastrously wrong, for Queen Tera's body is destroyed and Margaret is killed.[65] Grant Allen's lighter 'My New Year's Eve Among the Mummies' pokes fun at this pattern. The narrator finds his way into an unopened pyramid, where he finds 'a living Egyptian king, surrounded by his coiffeured court', who wake every thousand years to feast.[66] He wastes no time in falling in love with Hatasou, the king's daughter, and in order to stay with her decides to become a mummy himself. A priest will carry out the mummification with the help of chloroform (one of a whole series of jokes suggesting that the ancient Egyptians were more 'advanced' than the people who now study them). When he wakes from the operation, however, the narrator finds himself in Shepheard's hotel in Cairo. As in 'Le Pied de Momie', 'Smith and the Pharaohs', and 'The Ring of Thoth', the hero emerges unsure as to the ontological status of his experience.[67]

Conan Doyle's 'Lot No. 249' appears at first glance to offer an exception to the rule, insofar as the mummy is a vengeful male. A sinister Oxford undergraduate, Bellingham, revives a mummy in order to initiate a reign of terror. Abercrombie Smith, the hero of the piece, at first suspects Bellingham of having a woman in his rooms in flagrant breach of college regulations: 'He knew that the step which he had heard upon the stairs was not the step of an animal. But if it were not, then what could it be? There was old Styles's statement about the something which used to pace the room when the owner was absent. Could it be a woman? Smith rather inclined to the view' (198). Subsequent events prove otherwise, of course, but the presence of the fantasy of the mummy as a love object suggests that the vengeful mummy is a later form of the mummy fantasy, perhaps even a defence against the fantasy of the mummy as love object. In short, then, while the fantasy of the vengeful mummy governs the mummy's appearance in twentieth-century popular culture, the late Victorian and Edwardian imagination seems to have dwelt more on the mummy's romance potential. In these stories the relations of subjects and objects are problematized so that objects become subjects, and subjects come under the spell of objects that embody their desire.

It is important to recognize that the difference between subjects and objects is not so much erased as sublated through this inversion. In a novel like *Iras*, the illicitly imported object becomes a love object: the potentially refractory commodity is replaced by the docile woman. In effect, late nineteenth-century mummy fiction temporarily problematizes the subject/object division only to reinscribe that division at another level, as a 'natural' gender difference. Where the mummy fragment conjures up a female body who does not obey this logic, that body remains a narrative problem – as in *She* where Ayesha's body has to be destroyed before the narrative conflict can be resolved. The relationships between collectors and collected are temporarily suspended, then, but only in order for a stronger domestic narrative to be put into action. The 'romance revival' of the late nineteenth century represents itself as a departure from the domestic fiction that dominated mid-Victorian letters, but what we see here is a retooling of one of the characteristic tropes of domestic fiction, the intersubjective bond, for a new purpose within the adventure romance. We have grown accustomed to thinking of domestic fiction as a vehicle for the rewriting of political dissymmetries in gendered, personal terms; the Victorian novel relentlessly translates class conflicts into relations between men and women, seemingly the most natural and self-evident form of binary opposition.[68] Such figuration thus provides an obvious and convincing strategy of containment, making political conflicts susceptible to narrative resolution through love and marriage without any real disturbance of class divisions. The mummy narrative makes this same trope available for a different sort of problem, the apparently unstable opposition of commodity and consumer.

This narrative solution is not without its own problems, however. That mummy fiction can translate subject/object relations into gender relations also testifies to a new aspect of the relations between consumers and commodities during this period. By linking value to the desire of the consumer, mummy fiction makes explicit a further power that the commodity possesses. The Egyptologist-heroes have a penchant for falling in love with mummified princesses and queens, but it is hardly the high standards reached in their mummification that make these objects so desirable. To the contrary, the attraction is sudden and inexplicable, quite outside of rational calculation. This is most certainly true of Smith's reaction to the plaster-cast of Ma-Mee's head: 'Smith looked at it once, twice, thrice, and at the third look he fell in love' (150). One is reminded of Benjamin's characterization of fashion as the ritual form of commodity fetishism, 'coupl[ing] the living body to the inorganic world'.[69] This translation of the relations between subjects and objects into a sexual relation is double-edged. While it looks back at one of the principal resolving tropes of Victorian fiction, it also looks forward to one of the most pervasive features of twentieth-century commodity culture: the marriage of sex and the commodity under the aegis of advertising. In mummy fiction, as in advertising, the object or commodity is replaced by its fantastic, eroticized image, or rather an intermediate class of things, part object, part image is created. What drives Smith to Egypt in 'Smith and the Pharaohs' is not an object so much as an image endowed with certain powers. Similarly, in the other mummy stories, it is their desire for the objects-as-human, not the objects per se, that threatens to invert the relationship between subject and object. Rather than giving him power over the domain of objects, the collector's gaze threatens to vitiate that power, as the object turned love object draws the subject into its own narrative. In his account of the way consumer culture remoulds human subjectivity, W. F. Haug has described this 'tendency of all objects of use in commodity-form to assume a sexual form to some extent'.[70] Haug locates the origins of this tendency in the nature of the commodity exchange relation itself. Where goods are produced for exchange, it is the moment of sale, not the moment of consumption, that concerns the seller. This results in a tendency to enhance the commodity's appearance of use-value, to emphasize the surface or 'skin' of the commodity, its packaging. In mummy fiction, as in advertising, the object or commodity is replaced by its fantastic, eroticized image, or perhaps it is more accurate to say an intermediate class of things, part object, part image has been created.

In a further step, commodity and appearance part company altogether: 'under capitalist production, the commodity is created in the image of the consumer's desires. Later on, this image, divorced from its commodity, is the subject of advertising promotion'.[71] Under such conditions, the consumer replaces the product as the real subject of this advertising. What is offered to the consumer in exchange for the purchase of the commodity is a feeling, an impression, an association – as we already see in Gautier's 'Le Pied de Momie'. Advertising effects the replacement of the object by a fantasy or dream image in what Haug calls the 'general sexualization of commodities'.[72] While Haug is largely speaking of twentieth-century consumer culture, one can observe the very features he identifies in nascent form in late Victorian culture. The crusades of the conservative National Vigilance Association against certain advertisers suggest that the commercial value of sexuality in commodity-promotion was already seen as a source of moral corruption.[73] Given that mummy fiction seemed to manage the relations of consumers to commodities by rewriting them in terms of gender, then we can understand how such a rhetorical move might have opened the way for another assault on the sovereignty of the British subject. Even if these stories promise control of the refractory object by gendering it female, this same translation into sexual terms grants to that object the power of a seductive woman, which is to suggest that in these stories the moment of modern advertising has already arrived: exotic goods turn into desirable women; the act of purchasing or acquisition is filled with sexual promise.

DREAMS OF EMPIRE

How does the question of object love impinge on the question of empire? Mummy fiction, like Marx's table story, is a species of descriptive theory where the relations of consumption and production, consumers and objects, are worked out as narrative. On the one hand, mummy fiction witnesses that very transformation of the nature of value and desire that neoclassical economics describes. Mummies are valuable objects because someone wants them; the source of value is therefore personal and subjective. On the other, these stories also link the desired foreign body/object to the dissolution of the consuming subject, and thus to England's identity as a productive economy. The revived mummies of *The Jewel of Seven Stars* and 'Lot No. 249' are dangerous. In *She* and *The Yellow God* the subject's own objectification seems to be a possible consequence of the affective relation to the foreign body/commodity; the consumer makes himself vulnerable. In *Iras* the revival of the beloved object brings with it not only a docile woman, but also a threat and a rival in the person of the vengeful priest, Savak.

Does mummy fiction gloomily anticipate the fall of an imperial nation given over to consumption, while production becomes the prerogative of others? I think not. This would scarcely explain the popularity of mummy fiction in these years. Rather, the temporary destabilization of subject/object relations that we find in mummy fiction reconfigures imperial power relations, and offers metropolitan subjects a way of positioning themselves in the new imperial economy, rather as imperial treasure hunt tales like *King Solomon's Mines* allow the metropolitan subject a virtual mastery of overseas space. This is neither to suggest that mummy fiction homogeneously purveys false consciousness, nor that readers of popular and middlebrow fiction read passively and uncritically. As I hope I have made clear throughout this study, I read this fiction as a form of popular theory, not as the degenerate form of some properly critical high culture, nor as the innocent object of our own more knowing reading practice. To the extent that mummy fiction offers a descriptive commodity theory, it is indeed critical or theoretical. If that theory should then turn out to enable rather than militate against certain historical processes, it is no less theoretical for that.

To say that these stories are facilitative is not to deny that they play on the dangers of the consumer's position. While the language of gender offers a partial solution to the problem of the commodity, as we have seen, it also brings its own problems: the collector's gaze becomes the means through which his mastery over the foreign object is undermined rather than confirmed. Fantastic images of objects, foreign commodities turned into Oriental bodies, solicit the expert-collector's desire. The appealing image, divorced from any object body, as in 'Smith and the Pharaohs' leads the subject further into the phantasmagoric world of the commodity. Thus the attempt to re-establish the priority of the subject over the object world in terms of gender is at least in part compromised by the power it confers on the commodity; the commodity aesthetics of advertising threaten to supersede the reassuring gender logic of the Victorian novel. Faced with this dilemma, mummy fiction steps back, as it were, from the commodity fantasy. It makes the subject's encounter doubtful – much as Marx does – by displacing it onto another realm – as afterlife. In *Iras*, where the fantasy marriage of the consumer and the commodity is most fully developed, Iras in the end returns to her object status. Lavenham looks forward to their meeting again after his own death, when they will both exist only as spiritual entities. Smith, of 'Smith and the Pharaohs' is left unsure of the objective nature of his museum experience. Gautier's 'Le Pied de Momie' explicitly treats the narrator's encounter with the animated mummy as a dream. In other words, mummy fiction provides a space in which fantasies of an intermediate category of phenomena, part object and part image, are allowed to enjoy momentary ascendancy over the subject, only to be expelled from the narrative. Because the mummy is so obviously fantastic, it allows for a convincing restoration of normalcy – namely, a distinction between subjects and objects that allows one to dominate the other. At a moment when Britain's expanding commodity culture, increasingly dependent on imports, threatened the British subject's sense of national identity, mummy fiction provides a carefully delimited space for the entertainment of fantasies of the commodity's power.

Advertising, the new department stores, and the other resources of Victorian consumer culture, were combining to annihilate the distinctions not only between subjects and objects, but also between England and its outside. At the same time, mummy fiction, itself part of the expanding culture industry, was attempting to stabilize those oppositions. While mummy fiction is deeply implicated in the disappearance of the earlier structures of Victorian culture, then, it also nostalgically evokes it. Announcing itself as fantasy, representing the dissolution of older hierarchies as the very stuff of make-believe, the mummy story paradoxically makes a plea for the values of realism. In these stories the revived mummy, the animated object, is ultimately represented as a projection of an over-imaginative subject on the object world, and the crumbling of Britain's borders before a protean army of foreign objects is firmly labelled as fantasy. But to speak of projection, of a simple failure of objectivity, is to assume a prior distinction between subjects and objects – which is also to adopt the premises of realism.

In the end, then, the mummy story, like realism, insists on the very opposition between subject and object that was increasingly problematic in an expanding consumer culture. Placing its characters' troubling encounters in quotes, as it were, the mummy story affects to return the reader to a more stable world. Like the late twentieth-century theme park, the mummy story seems to insist that outside its boundaries the real world exists in all its reliable, and even oppressive, density.[74] In her 1925 essay, 'Modern Fiction', Virginia Woolf laments the 'materialism' of her immediate predecessors, the deadening solidity of their characters and settings. Perhaps mummy fiction allows us to see that the fictional universe of 'softly padded first-class railway carriage[s]' that Woolf found so oppressive masked a deeper awareness that such a world had vanished. Yet I suspect that it is in the fantasy stories of H. D. Everett, Rider Haggard, Stoker and their like, and not in the staid novels of Bennett or Galsworthy, that we see the greatest longing for the lost world of solid objects. But as we shall see in the next chapter, if such fantasies may seem like a final flowering of Victorian realism, they also bear a family resemblance to twentieth-century modernism.

CHAPTER 4

Across the great divide: modernism, popular fiction and the primitive

I have been arguing that the popular fiction of the *fin de siècle*, with its mummies, vampires and treasure hunts, challenged the realist novel for the part of principal literary vehicle of middle-class culture, offering its readers a species of popular theory of social change in narrative form.[1] Until recently, however, criticism perceived this as a marginal and even juvenile literature, rather than as something culturally central. More-over – and this is a disposition that hasn't entirely disappeared, despite the new prestige of cultural studies – we tend to view our own activities as critics of this literature as not altogether serious. There lingers what might be termed a fear of going native, of drifting across the border between academic work and the pursuits of the Sherlock Holmes Society. Whence this critical guilt? It may in part be attributable to that more general suspicion of the novel as a lightweight genre that persisted throughout the nineteenth century, and that lives on in the twentieth at the level of curricular hierarchy in many university English depart-ments. A more likely explanation, though, is that literary criticism inherits many of its assumptions from the 'great divide' discussed in the Introduction, taking for granted the existence of a profound gulf be-tween modernism and popular fiction, between 'real literature' and fiction for the masses.

Of course, historically speaking, a divide did open up between high modernism and mass culture, between 'serious' books and mass-mar-keted genre fiction. T. S. Eliot, writing after the great divide, looked nostalgically back to the nineteenth century as a time before such terms as ' "high-brow fiction", "thrillers" and "detective fiction" were in-vented' ': 'the distinction of genre between such-and-such a profound "psychological" novel of to-day and such-and-such a masterly "detec-tive" novel of today is greater than the distinction of genre between *Wuthering Heights*, or even *The Mill on the Floss*, and [sc. Mrs Wood's popular pot-boiler the 1860s] *East Lynne*'.[2] The romance itself flourished before the institutionalization of that division, and was not mass fiction in the later sense; by and large it was written by and for the middle class. At the *fin de siècle*, writers that we now often identify as proto-modernists, James or Conrad, for example, were not perceived to belong to a separate coterie literary culture. But when we look backwards we tend to imagine a continuity between twentieth-century genre fiction (e.g. detective fiction, romances, science fiction) and that earlier popular fiction; and by the same token we tend to imagine an equivalent continuum from late Victorian aestheticism, and such writers as Conrad and James, to high modernism.

Such links do indeed exist, but the existence of a broader culture of modernity of the kind that I have been arguing for in this study would suggest that they exist as much between the late Victorian romance and modernism as between, say, *fin-de-siècle* aestheticism and modernism, or between the romance and later popular forms. In this chapter I will examine one such link between the romance and modernism. Modernism, I will be arguing, depends on the same imperial imaginary as the adventure romance. The map of the world sketched by Haggard, Kipling and Stevenson among others is not so much discarded as transvalued in the modernism of Hemingway, Lawrence and their modernist primitivist peers. In the romance, the 'dark places of the earth' represent the dangerous margins of modernity, though these are also places where real heroism is still possible. While there is a lingering nostalgia for the premodern, romance narratives work to make imperial expansion, and thus the destruction of the premodern, an adventure. In modernist primitivism the margins of modernity are reconceived as places from which to express dissatisfaction with modern metropolitan culture. Writers position themselves outside the modern, on the side of the 'primitive'; for them the 'primitive' embodies a green world of wholeness and authenticity elsewhere lost to modernization. Further, by reversing the magic of the commodity form, these imaginary places enable modernist writers to theorize their own writing practice as something outside the wasteland of commercial culture. If the mummy fiction that sprang up in the 1880s and 1890s imagines a subject in thrall to animated foreign goods, then modernist primitivism evokes a world where subjects once again lord it over commodities. The spell of the commodity is broken by the more powerful magic of primitivism, creating a realm where there is no commodity fetishism. This fantasy of flight from the commodity fetish is also, though, a fantasy of escape from commodified literature, from what are imagined to be the linguistic calcifications of the culture industry, including the romance and its successors. A theory of objects turns into an aesthetic, the primitive object described in the modernist text offering an *en abyme* image of the modernist text itself.

I

In her recent revisionary account of twentieth-century literary history, Suzanne Clark argues that modernism established its own sense of integrity through a rejection of sentimental discourse. Outside its own hard critical carapace, this modernist story of origins maintained, lay the sentimental, associated with popular success, women's culture and an outmoded Victorianism. In Clark's words: 'The term sentimental makes a shorthand for everything modernism would exclude, the other of its literary/nonliterary dualism.'[3] Modernism – a term that for Clark includes the institution of modernist criticism – came to be defined in terms of radical formal experimentalism and disengagement from the quotidian world.[4] Through a violent disavowal, the near literary past, with its baggy, sentimental Victorian monsters, could be rejected out of hand. The sentimental is equated with a debilitating past, and leaving this literary past behind becomes 'homologous with the struggle to grow up'[5] for the modernist writer.

Andreas Huyssen describes the emergence of modernism in similar terms: 'Modernism constituted itself through a conscious strategy of exclusion, an anxiety of contamination by its other: an increasingly consuming and engulfing mass culture.' Again, the basic constitutive moment appears to be one of defence: 'Warding something off, protecting against something out there seems indeed to be a basic gesture of the modernist aesthetic, from Flaubert to Roland Barthes and other poststructuralists.'[6] As his citation of the author of *Madame Bovary* suggests, Huyssen too argues that modernism consistently genders mass culture, locating the latter in a feminine dream-world, and comes to define itself in terms of the reality principle. In contrast to the phantasmagorias of mass culture, offering the reader the possibility of losing him or herself in the story, modernism sees itself as 'self-referential, self-conscious, frequently ironic, ambiguous and rigorously experimental'.[7] Clark's and Huyssen's argument suggests one reason for the declining critical prestige of the romance, for it was not only sentimental feminine culture that was consigned to the ash-heap of literary history. As the modernist aesthetic gained ascendancy over Victorian literary taste, popular, masculine imperial culture and its narrative pleasures went the same way to dusty critical death. The rapid decline in the literary stature of a figure like Kipling, for example, from Nobel Prize winner to children's author, may indicate that the modernist distaste for the sentimental extended to the patriotic zeal and the emotionally charged relations between men that we find in the adventure novel. The very narrative drive of such stories was a mark against them: to lose oneself in a story was no better than to yield to the pleasures of the herd. The success of modernism may have come to mean that popular fiction in general, and not just the 'woman's novel', appeared as immature, an embarrassing stage of arrested literary development.

In ascribing the declining fortunes of the romance to the self-definition of modernism, there is a danger of anthropomorphizing modernism, of assigning the work of many writers a single intention, and erasing the variety of modernist literary practices. As Huyssen admits, the will to modernist autonomy and the antipathy towards the popular were always in competition with other, less separatist, tendencies. Modernism itself was never a monolithic movement, and if some writers viewed popular culture with something akin to horror, others were more attracted than repelled by that culture. As is widely known, James Joyce was interested enough in popular culture to attempt to set up a cinema in Dublin, though it is perhaps less widely known that the young Joyce also tried his hand at writing for the hugely popular *Titbits*, as indeed did Joseph Conrad and Virginia Woolf.[8] As we shall see below, Ernest Hemingway also tried his hand at writing detective stories for the magazines, and even that high modernist mandarin, T. S. Eliot, was drawn to popular Victorian literature, and to popular forms like music hall.[9] Thus while he viewed the 'encroachment of the cheap and rapid-breeding cinema' with some disdain, he saw the death of the music-hall star, Marie Lloyd, as 'a significant moment in English history', and expressed admiration for contemporary music-hall figures like Little Tich and Nellie Wallace.[10]

Nonetheless, we can point to an influential strand of modernism that defined itself against the popular and, perhaps more importantly, to a variety of modernist literary criticism that came to represent high modernism as the last bastion of defence against the depredations of the culture industry. As Huyssen describes, Theodor Adorno is one of the figures who assists in the institutionalization of high modernism, though his actual account of the relations of modernism and mass culture is more complex than is often assumed. Adorno was, after all, prepared to admit that mass culture and modernism were forged in the same historical furnace: 'Both bear the scars of capitalism, both contain elements of change. Both are torn halves of freedom to which, however, they do not add up.'[11] But there is little question which torn half Adorno wished to defend; mass culture sometimes appears in his work as the evil twin threatening to devour alive its more virtuous sibling. For Adorno, the stylistic difficulties of the high modernist canon he helped to create were its best protection from mass culture, representing a reaction to the cannibalizing forces of the culture industry, and the stultified reading habits of the subject of mass culture. In modernist music, for example, he considered the atonal compositions of Schönberg as resisting what he describes in a delightful phrase as the 'sluggish habits of culinary listening'.[12]

Now that modernism itself has become canonical, and has proved itself to be no more immune to commercial use than any other literary movement, such pronouncements appear rather less convincing. Yet present-day criticism often reproduces the terms of modernism's avowed relation to popular fiction, and critics continue to view modernism as the maturely ironic reaction to an overcharged and naïve popular literature. Where Adorno is addressing the relationship between high modernism and a fully developed entertainment industry, the same logic is projected backwards to the moment of the romance itself. Joseph Conrad has become a pivotal character in this story of the rise of modernism. Edward Said, for example, argues that what separates the imperial tales of Conrad from those of his peers is the 'extreme, unsettling anxiety' that emanates from the former.[13] Conrad replaces the 'optimism, affirmation, and serene confidence' of popular imperial culture with the 'ironic awareness of the post-realist modernist sensibility'.[14] Said's laudable intention here is to reveal the radical decentredness of European culture by arguing that the modernist irony attributed to Conrad, and indeed to Joyce, Yeats and Eliot, derives at least in part from the experience of empire. In the context of imperialism, of course, there is little doubt as to which disposition – modernist irony or popular romance commitment – Said finds preferable, and even less doubt as to which we too are meant to find preferable. Conrad, Said seems to suggest, is what adventure fiction becomes when it grows up, and as grown-up critics, we can hardly favour the fictions of Haggard and his fellow fabulists. Said can make room on the modernist life-boat for Conrad, then, but only by pushing overboard the literary culture to which he in part belonged. To this extent Said's account of Conrad represents a more politicized version of the work of the first generation of modernist critics, who rescued James and Conrad for high modernism by abstracting them from their original context.[15]

Many modernists would themselves have endorsed Said's privileging of mature irony over callow commitment. This dovetailing of subject and object of study ought not to surprise us, though, since literary criticism, most obviously in its formalist, but also in its more historical and ideologically sensitive modes, remains very much a modernist venture. Tony Pinkney's discussion of postwar critical thought traces the critical preference for the ironic or demystifying text, the text which 'lays bare', to the influence of what is essentially 'the Brechtian opposition of empathy and active detachment' in criticism and theory.[16] The celebration of detachment over engagement is buttressed by a whole series of theoretical oppositions which echo the modernist binary: Lacan's Imaginary and Symbolic, Barthes's *lisible* and *scriptible*, Althusser's ideology and science, as well as the oppositions implicit in Marx's theory of commodity fetishism, and the Freudian account of sexual fetishism. At some level the critical lexes which these diverse theories have bequeathed to criticism all privilege such modernist aesthetic values as awareness, reflexivity, distance; thin partitions divide the detached Joycean artist, coolly paring his nails, and the theoretically primed poststructuralist critic. Given the extent to which the academy is beholden to modernist critical values, then, it is not to be wondered at that what has been presented as a literary history of modernism has more often been a modernist literary history. Such a history was unlikely to see any kinship between modernism and popular fiction, between, let us say, Haggard and Hemingway, or *Dracula* and *Death in Venice*.

The critical border separating modernism and popular fiction was respected as long as criticism remained essentially modernist. From a different historical standpoint, we have begun to formulate new ways of understanding the relationship between modernism and popular fiction, and recognize that the supposed hostility between the two dissimulates a more complex interaction. The more sceptically we treat tales of an original modernist asceticism, the more plausible becomes a conception of the high modernist text and the popular adventure tale as twin facets of a single moment of cultural production. An expanding and fragmenting literary market meant that literary specialization, whether 'highbrow' or 'lowbrow', could be economically viable, but modernism, abetted by modernist criticism, came to be imagined as more than just another specialized type of literary produce, as more than just a commodity in the literary marketplace. This involved a concomitant assumption that other types of fiction, in effect other specializations within a fragmenting market, could not transcend their nature as cheap goods in that marketplace. Modernist 'difficulty', seen by defenders of modernism as its apotropaic charm against the culture industry's commodifying power, became the principal means of distinguishing it from other literary goods. But once we begin to look past the fetishization of form we can see that the same historical changes that I have been tracking through the pages of popular fiction – the new imperialism, the culture of experts, the relations of subjects and objects under a nascent consumer culture – underlie high modernism. Recent work on modernism and popular culture has made this clearer. Jon Thompson, for example, has argued that detection is an important trope for a common, modern British imperial culture that links Sherlock Holmes, say, with the investigative procedures of *Heart of Darkness*, or with the 'micrological perspective' of *Ulysses*.[17] Likewise working against the grain of literary history, Thomas Strychacz has accounted for the difficulty and the hermeticism of the modernist text as a translation of the same spirit of professionalism that characterizes middle-class culture in general in this period, and that I have described in my account of *Dracula*.[18]

Thompson encourages us to imagine a common imperial culture enveloping both the modernist text and the adventure story, and Strychacz's work suggests that this is also a professional culture. However, the homology suggested between, on the one hand, a modern imperial culture marked by rationalization and professionalism, and on the other, a literary tendency towards technical mastery, is a little too neat. The apotheosis of a dense, professional literary language in the work of Joyce or Woolf parallels the development of a different modernist strain affiliated to the primitive rather than the modern and professional. Primitivist discourse is a body of representations of other, less 'advanced' cultures through which the West has come to imagine itself. Formally in ethnography, but also in travel writing, psychoanalysis, art and literature, primitivism has developed from the nineteenth century on as, in Marianna Torgovnick's words, 'a discourse fundamental to the Western sense of self and Other'.[19] The primitivist impulse within modernism assumes aspects as different as the South Sea paintings of Gauguin and the anthropological borrowings of Eliot in *The Waste Land*.[20] In fiction, D. H. Lawrence represents the type of the modernist primitivist, particularly in the longing for an alternative to modern Western culture one sees in *The Plumed Serpent*.[21] Modernist primitivism evokes the same imperial imaginary that I have discussed in relation to the fiction of Stoker, Conan Doyle and Haggard. Popular fiction presents the 'blank spaces of the map', as potentially threatening regions outside civilized modernity where heroism is still possible; modernism imagines these same places as a sanctuary from a modernity that threatens to suffocate the artist. In the modernist imaginary, this alternative world comes to resemble what Michel Foucault calls a heterotopia.[22] Like a utopia, the heterotopia may hold a mirror up to society, but unlike a utopia it corresponds to a real place – it is 'a kind of effectively enacted utopia in which the real sites, all the other real sites that can be found within the culture, are simultaneously represented, contested, and inverted'.[23] Lawrence's New Mexico, Hemingway's Africa and Spain, are just such spaces, imaginary, and yet found in any atlas. In the looking-glass world that these territories embody, the commodifying logic of the modern world appears inverted. But this also means that modernist primitivism presents a mirror-image of the imperial novel: by continuing to project a map of the world that is, despite its inversion, recognizably Victorian and imperial, modernism reveals its implication in a culture that we often assume it has rejected.

The rest of this chapter will explore the longevity and pervasiveness of imperial culture by tracing the connections between the primitivist imaginary, the status of the commodity and the role of the artist at two different moments of modernism: the Irish Literary Revival, an engaged, anti-imperial, emergent modernist formation, and the heyday of international modernism in the interwar years. At these moments primitivism offered two very different writers, John Millington Synge and Ernest Hemingway, a fantasy of escape from modernization and an idealized image of artistic production. While both of them seem to reject modern commercial culture, and at least one of them is also hostile to imperialism, their primitivist fantasies stay squarely within the parameters of the imperial imaginary first adumbrated in popular fiction. This is as true of their view of the relations of people and things as it is of their conception of space: seeking to escape from the magic of the universe of commodities, these texts end by producing a counter-magic.

II

THE REDUNDANT DETECTIVE AND THE STOCKING:
THE CASE OF SYNGE

In May 1907 the Irish International Exhibition opened at Ballsbridge in Dublin with considerable colonial pageantry and to enormous popular interest. King Edward and Queen Alexandra came to visit in July, and when the Exhibition eventually closed in November of that year, some 2,751,113 visitors had passed through the turnstiles.[24] Among the earliest visitors was Bram Stoker, who wrote a report on it, 'The Great White Fair in Dublin', for *The World's Work*. Part of the Edwardian cult of Efficiency, this publication described itself as 'An Illustrated Magazine of National Efficiency and Social Progress', and devoted its May issue to the Exhibition and the more general subject of the rejuvenation of Ireland through industry and commerce. Like the other contributors, Stoker was anxious to impress on the reader that Ireland was undergoing a process of modernization:

The days of the old Donnybrook Fair and all it meant, the days of the stage Irishman, and the stagey Irish play, of Fenianism and landlordism are rapidly passing away, if they have not even now come to an end. Perhaps there has been some joy of living and much humour lost with the passing of the country fair and its merry-making; but there has come in its place a strenuous, industrious spirit, spreading its revivifying influence so rapidly over the old country as to be worth more than even historical bitterness and sentimental joys.[25]

Stoker's vision of an Ireland where science and industry sweep away the political problems of the land recalls the scientific pastoral that closed his one Irish romance, *The Snake's Pass*, almost twenty years earlier. He evokes the latter in a reference to the natural resources of Ireland, which include 'vast areas of fuel-bog, sufficient alone for national wealth'.[26] Another contributor to this special Irish Number of *The World's Work* seems to have actually lived out the fantasy of *The Snake's Pass*, leaving London to buy a Mayo farm, which he makes profitable in part by reclaiming bog land with lime.[27]

But if Stoker and *The World's Work* wished to read the Exhibition as part of a pageant of Irish modernization, others found in it the vestiges of a very different Ireland. Alongside such 'serious' exhibits as the Canadian Pavilion and the French Pavilion, the Palace of Industries and the Palace of Fine Arts were a variety of side shows, or 'entertainments', which were in many ways typical of international exhibition fare at the turn of the century. These included the water chute, the switchback railway, the 'Helter Skelter Lighthouse', the 'Indian Theatre' featuring 'Ebrahims Sahib's Indian Fakirs', the Cinematograph, and the 'Shooting Jungle'. Among the more exotic features was a replica Somali village, complete with Somalis ('imported from British Somaliland') in native dress, some with shields and spears. The village was a popular attraction, soliciting the attention of both the public and journalists. According to the *Irish Times* reporter, the Somalis were 'good-humored, dark, but not uncomely, and in the opinion of those who have called upon them, by no means relish the climate of the country, though taking singularly little precautions to defend themselves against it'.[28] One of the visitors attracted by the village was John Millington Synge, who described his experience in a letter to his fiancée, the actress Molly Allgood.

Today I went to see Mrs Payne [sc. an actress, married to Abbey theatre director, Ben Iden Payne] after dinner but found the house locked up, so I went on to the exhibition for a while. I didn't enjoy it very much as I was lonesome again, but there are good things in it. *The Somali village especially is curious. A bit of the war-song the niggers were singing was exactly like some of the keens on Aran.* (emphasis added)[29]

The 'keens [Ir. *caoineadh*, a lament] on Aran' were a species of traditional Irish funeral poetry, usually performed by professional 'keeners', that Synge had heard during his visits to the bleak Aran islands off the west coast of Ireland.[30] Synge described the culture of the island people in *The Aran Islands* (1907), and drew on it extensively for his peasant plays, such as *Riders to the Sea* (1904) and *The Playboy of the Western World* (1907). But wandering through the Somali village in Ballsbridge on a May evening in 1907, what struck him was that the culture of the islands was linked to that of east Africa by a common primitive spirit. If Stoker was keen to describe the retreat of traditional Ireland, 'the old country', before the standard of progress, Synge was more interested in imagining the survival of a rich seam of premodernity, a piece of darkest Africa in Ireland.

In the Irish Literary Revival, dating roughly from the 1890s, the Victorian interest in folklore and vanishing regional customs shades into a more exoticist modernist primitivism. While the Revivalists, with the exception of W. B. Yeats, are often excluded from studies of modernism, this primitivism – together with such factors as their group identity and their establishment of alternative circuits of textual circulation and dramatic production – suggests that the Revival was as much a part of the history of modernism as that of Irish cultural nationalism.[31] For W. B. Yeats, J. M. Synge, Lady Gregory and others, rural Ireland and the remnants of Gaelic culture provided the basis for a literary movement apparently hostile to the advances of a modernity portrayed as at its worst in popular British fiction and journalism.[32] These writers scoured the legends and ballads of the 'folk' for characters, plots and a language out of which to construct an alternative, anti-modern and anti-imperial literature. The recourse to the past, then, was oriented towards the future, part of an attempt to forge a national literature in advance of the arrival of the nation itself. At the same time this cultural project offered a form of cultural leadership to an Anglo-Irish formation whose political ascendancy could be seen to be on the wane. Of course for this cultural leadership to succeed, any claims to cultural legitimacy on the part of the Catholic middle class had to be denied. Thus if English consumer culture represented one spectre of bad modernity for the Revivalists, the economic rationalism of the Catholic Irish middle class came to represent another. When the *Manchester Guardian* paid Synge and Jack B. Yeats to write a series of illustrated articles based on a tour of the impoverished parts of the west of Ireland, Synge found that picturesque poverty co-existed with something less attractive to him, as he described to his friend Stephen MacKenna in a letter of 13 July 1905:

There are sides to all that western life, the groggy-patriot-publican-general shop-man who is married to the priest's half-sister and is second cousin once-removed of the dispensary doctor, that are horrible and awful. This is the type that is running the present United Irish League anti-grazier campaign while they're swindling the people themselves in a dozen ways and then buying out their holdings and packing off whole families to America. The subject is too big to go into here, but at best it's beastly . . . In a way it is all heart-rending, in one place the people are starving but wonderfully attractive and charming and in another place where things are going well one has a rampant double-chinned vulgarity I haven't seen the like of.[33]

When nationalist crowds in Dublin jeered *The Playboy of the Western World* (1907) as a slight on the national character, Synge's attitude to this same 'vulgar' middle class hardened further. In another letter to MacKenna he wrote: 'As you know I have the wildest admiration for the Irish Peasants, and for Irish men of known and unknown genius . . . but between the two there's an ungodly ruck of fat-faced sweaty-headed swine.'[34] Fumbling in their greasy tills and greedily adding the halfpence to the pence, this latter group could have no place in the political fantasies of an imagined fusion of Big House ascendancy culture and the noble simplicity of peasant culture.[35]

Synge's antipathy to the Catholic middle class was neither idiosyncratic nor indeed novel. As we saw in *The Snake's Pass*, Bram Stoker, like Synge a scion of the Protestant professional classes, envisioned political harmony for Ireland based on the defeat of the middle-man, or gombeen man, Black Murdock, and the marriage of the landed Arthur Severn to the 'peasant' Norah Joyce. It was W. B. Yeats, though, who turned Synge and Stoker's horrified vision of Catholic, middle-class materialism and vulgarity into the very stuff of myth. In *The Countess Kathleen* (1892), written only two years after *The Snake's Pass*, the Countess sells her soul to two traffickers in souls, who are trying to buy the souls of her impoverished tenants. As David Cairns and Shaun Richards suggest, 'feudalism is vindicated through the actions of the Countess, whose commitment to the peasants is seen as preferable to the deceits of the "devils"; the Merchants from the East whose geographical location embraces both England and "fallen" metropolitan Ireland'.[36] But it is not so much metropolitan Ireland as materialist, middle-class Ireland that is perceived as fallen, I would argue. However different *The Snake's Pass* and *The Countess Kathleen* may appear as literary texts, in both of them the Catholic middle class effectively disappears, bearing away with it all the sins of modernity. Only thus could the peasant be celebrated as an emblem of all that was good in native Irish culture.[37]

Where Lawrence and Hemingway were later to find, or at least imagine, in New Mexico, Africa, or Spain a cultural alternative to the modern West, the Revivalists were thus to build their heterotopia using more local 'folk' materials. But remoteness was also important in the primitivist vision of the Revival. Thus for Synge the bleak Aran Islands off the west coast of Ireland, the most westerly region of Europe, were the privileged site of the survival of a primitive European culture, a sort of miniature anti-Britain, whose modernizing example lay off the east coast.

Synge himself came from a once-affluent Anglo-Irish family who had owned substantial property in County Wicklow. However, by the time that Synge was born the effects of the famine and a whole series of land reforms had attenuated the power and wealth of the landlord class, and the fortunes of the Synge family did not escape unscathed. His father, a barrister, died within a year of Synge's birth, but his mother still enjoyed £400 a year from property in Galway, and largely through this was able to raise her children 'in a style conservative but befitting their class'.[38] After education at Trinity College, Dublin, where Synge learned Irish (taught at the Divinity School because of its potential usefulness in proselytizing among Catholics in the Irish-speaking west of Ireland), he made a series of trips to continental Europe to study music and foreign languages. December of 1896 found him in Paris on one such trip, and while staying at the Hotel Corneille in Paris he was introduced to a fellow-resident who happened to be another Irish expatriate, W. B. Yeats. Yeats's account of the meeting gives it something of the significance of Stanley meeting Livingstone:

[Synge] had learned Irish years ago, but had begun to forget it, for the only language that interested him was that conventional language of modern poetry, which has begun to make us all weary . . . I said, 'Give up Paris, you will never create anything by reading Racine, and Arthur Symons will always be a better critic of French literature. Go to the Arran [sic] Islands. Live there as if you were one of the people themselves; express a life that has never found expression.' I had just come from Arran and my imagination was full of those gray islands, where men must reap with knives because of the stones.[39]

As David Kiely notes, if this is what actually happened, Yeats's words would appear to have had no immediate effect, and almost a year and a half would pass before Synge actually visited the islands.[40] In the meantime, though, he became more interested in the folklore of the Celtic fringe, attending the Sorbonne lectures given by Anatole Le Braz on Brittany and its vestigial Celtic survivals, and reading Pierre Loti and Ernest Renan.[41]

Paris, like London, was a breeding ground for all sorts of societies, literary and political, and Synge was drawn to *L'Association Irlandaise* started by Maud Gonne, dedicated to the cause of Irish independence, of which Yeats was also a member. Synge's reading in the socialism of William Morris and others perhaps made him more receptive to nationalism, which was, on the face of it, a rather unlikely choice for a young Anglo-Irishman whose stay in Paris was partly made possible by the rent paid by his mother's tenants.[42] In *fin-de-siècle* Paris, politics, literature and psychic research appear to have formed a heady cocktail in the cultural life on the fringe of the *Association*. In 1897 Synge was reading some of Yeats's work, including *The Countess Kathleen* and *The Secret Rose*, but also the *Jail Journal* of the Irish nationalist, John Mitchel, and the work of George Russell (AE). According to his laconic diary entry for 19 February of that year political and psychic phenomena sometimes interpenetrated: 'Meeting Irish League. Saw manifestations.'[43]

Synge eventually visited the Aran Islands in May 1898, and returned for four more visits in the following summers. He made a number of friends among the people of the islands, who told him local stories, explained local customs, and exchanged letters in English and Irish with him when he left the islands. Synge's island visits were quite literally the basis of his subsequent success as a dramatist: a story told to him by a local man, Pat Dirane, on Inishmaan later formed the basis of *In the Shadow of the Glen*; there too he heard the true story that he used for *The Playboy of the Western World*; and an episode in the kitchen of the McDonough family provided the core of *Riders to the Sea*. The people of the islands even provided practical help in the staging of the plays: one of Synge's correspondents, Martin McDonough, sent Synge various island 'props' that he had requested for the staging of *Riders to the Sea* in 1904.

But if Synge was at times happy to think of the people of the islands as his friends and his peers, it was what he saw as the 'primitive' flavour of island life that really attracted him.[44] Synge's account of his first four visits to the Islands, published in 1907 simply as *The Aran Islands*, repeatedly deploys primitivist tropes – timelessness, superstition and orality, for example. In a familiar *et in Arcadia* gesture he notes that even these remote Islands have been disappointingly modernized. This should not have come altogether as a surprise to Synge, since his own family had played some small part in this disappointing modernization: his uncle, the Reverend Alexander Synge, had come to the islands as a missionary, and supplemented his income by buying a motorboat and hiring a crew to compete with the local fishermen. Nonetheless many years later, the younger Synge was consoled by the existence of an outside to the outside of modernity: on one of the smaller islands, Inishmaan, he was satisfied that 'the life is perhaps the most primitive that is left in Europe'.[45] His journey there is doubly an escape from the modern, as even the means of his flight is primitive: 'It gave me a moment of exquisite satisfaction to find myself moving away from civilization in this rude canvas canoe of a model that has served primitive races since men first went of the sea' (57). He is convinced that the stories he hears and records on the island connect the culture of the people to the 'pre-ethnic period of the Aryans' (65 n.1). This island culture is quite literally timeless for Synge: they have neither clocks nor sundials, he claims. In fact by his own account he brings them the gift of time, making a present of an alarm clock, the first on the island, to one of his new friends.[46]

In Synge's description of the islands, anthropology vies for space with aesthetic theory. At the heart of his enchantment with the islands is the Schillerian critique of modernity as an alienating force that can be overcome in art, continued and modified in the nineteenth century in the work of Wordsworth, Carlyle, Ruskin, Dickens and others, and which persists in the twentieth century in such forms as T. S. Eliot's account of the 'dissociation of sensibility', and the nostalgia for organic community in the criticism of F. R. Leavis and the *Scrutiny* group. Thus Synge sees the islanders through the lens of a whole theoretical tradition that equates modernization with the loss of human potential. They interest him because they seem to come close to embodying the aesthetic idea of a wholeness of life lost in modernization. This makes of them natural artists:

It is likely that much of the intelligence and charm of these people is due to the absence of any division of labour, and to the correspondingly wide development of each individual, whose varied knowledge and skill necessitates a considerable activity of mind. Each man can speak two languages . . . His work changes with the seasons in a way that keeps him free of the dulness that comes to people who have always the same occupation. The danger of his life on the sea gives him the alertness of a primitive hunter, and the long nights he spends fishing in his curagh bring him some of the emotions that are thought peculiar to men who have lived with the arts. (132–3)[47]

The description of the islanders here is inseparable from an attempt to theorize an art that would not be an art of alienation. Elsewhere he speaks of the way their environment has created 'an affinity between the moods of these people and the moods of varying rapture and dismay that are frequent in artists, and in certain forms of alienation' (74), but what fascinates him is the very absence of any conception of a separate artistic vocation among the people of Aran. The islanders are made to embody Synge's fantasy of an artist who would not be a specialist, not just one expert in a culture of experts. Because, in Synge's eyes, the primitive economy of the island makes every islander a sort of rustic Renaissance man, it suggests to him the possibility of a modern art that would escape the effects of modernization.[48]

Synge's plays, especially *Riders to the Sea*, continue the theorization of the relations between the worker in the primitive economy and the artist.[49] *Riders* is based on a real and rather macabre incident in which the body of a drowned islander found off the coast of Donegal was identified by sending a parcel of his clothes to Inishmaan. Synge expands the anecdote into a fully-fledged tragedy of the battle between the islanders and the impersonal forces of nature, focusing on an old woman, Maurya, who has already lost five sons and a husband to the sea, and in the course of the play loses her one remaining son, Bartley. Synge uses his knowledge of the material culture and everyday activities of the islanders to good account, but the naturalistic presentation of island life is juxtaposed with plot elements from a heightened theatrical register, such as Maurya's description of her ghostly vision of her drowned son, Michael, 'with fine clothes on him, and new shoes on his feet',[50] riding on a gray pony behind the doomed Bartley. The fabric of island life is there, but it is used as a canvas on which Synge paints in the dark hues of Greek tragedy.[51]

Tragedy, however, is only one of the generic components of the play – there is also a detective story, or rather an anti-detective story. In fact, *Riders to the Sea*, as a play that deals with the decipherment of human identity through a reading of the individual's possessions, has a good deal in common with *The Adventures of Sherlock Holmes* (we are reminded that one of Synge's original titles for *The Playboy of the Western World* was *Murder Will Out).*[52] Like Conan Doyles's tales it produces a commodity theory, but the commodity theory it offers is also an aesthetic theory. The curtain rises on a cottage kitchen, in which the way of life of the islands is suggested by various details. Maurya's daughter Cathleen is finishing her baking and beginning work at the spinning wheel – evidently this is not the home as bourgeois private sphere, but as a place of production. Synecdochic details like the nets and the oilskins hanging in the kitchen further sketch in the island mode of production. The play is making sure we realize that this is not a modern consumer economy: people bake their own bread, make their own clothes, catch their own fish; for Synge's audiences in Dublin and London this is a primitive culture.

Cathleen and her sister Nora have a parcel of clothes taken from a drowned man washed up on the shore in Donegal, and are trying to establish if they belong to their lost brother, Michael. But if the clothes have come to substitute for the man, this is not an account of the fetishism that troubles Carlyle in *Sartor Resartus*, or Marx in his account of commodity fetishism in *Capital*. This is a commodity-poor culture, where objects are clearly individuated: a rope is 'the bit of new rope . . . [that] was bought in Connemara' (85). A stick is described as 'the stick Michael brought from Connemara' (89). These objects may have personal histories, but they are not about to evolve into persons in their own right; the relations between objects and people are transparent. While Synge describes the people of the islands as being superstitious (another primitivist topos), then, and all too ready to see the object world as invested with certain powers, they are immune from one form of fetishism, the fetishism of the commodity. The play rehearses the proceedings of detective fiction in Nora and Cathleen's attempt to establish the identity of the deceased through his clothing, but we are quickly apprised of the fact that this is a culture that has no need of the detective's expertise in objects. Nora is able to establish at a glance that the parcel contains a stocking she knitted for Michael:

CATHLEEN (taking the stocking): It's a plain stocking.
NORA: It's the second one of the third pair I knitted, and I put up three score stitches, and I dropped four of them. (90)

There is no need for the special object-expertise of the detective, Synge suggests, because goods are made for use here, rather than exchange. Sherlock Holmes establishes the provenance of cigar ash, or rare types of mud, through his encyclopedic yet specialized knowledge of the object world, but Nora can immediately trace the history of the stocking because she can recognize the marks of *her own labour* in it. Labour is visible and concrete here, not invisible and abstract. Tables cannot evolve out of their wooden brains grotesque ideas, as in Marx's story of the commodity,[53] nor can objects assume human form and become romantically involved with their owners, as we saw in mummy fiction. People still control objects on the islands; everyone is an expert in material culture, and can put objects in their place.

Synge spared no efforts in putting the hand-made material culture of the islands on stage in Dublin and London, making rather a fetish of authenticity itself. Lady Gregory was able to secure a real spinning wheel for the kitchen, and Synge wrote to his island friend, Martin McDonough to obtain real pampooties, the home-made leather moccasins used on the islands, and specimens of the locally used flannel cloth. Indeed, things were becoming a little too real for Lady Gregory. When it appeared that the fake pampooties might have to be substituted due to delays in getting the real thing, she expressed her relief in a letter to Yeats: 'the pampooties will have to be made in Dublin, a very good thing too, there is no object in bringing local smells into the theatre'.[54] Lady Gregory's olfactory worries suggest the difficulty of recapturing now the intensity that *Riders* must have possessed for audiences weaned on very different theatrical fare. A stunned review of the London production in the *Leader* gives us some idea. The play's combination of kitchen-sink realism and pervasive mortality proved too much for the reviewer who thought *Riders* 'hideous in its realism . . . the most ghastly production I have ever seen on a stage. It had all the horrors of a nightmare and reminded me of a visit to a dissecting room.'[55] The primitive could be *too* real.

Ironically, though, Synge's interest in the real textures of material life on the islands is at least in part derived from the metaphor it offers him:

the primitive, hand-made commodity (or non-commodity) culture of the islands provides him with an image of *artistic* production. He observes in *The Aran Islands* that: 'Every article on these islands has an almost personal character, which gives this simple life, where all art is unknown, something of the artistic beauty of medieval life' (58–9). Synge uses Nora's production of humble but unique objects, to dramatize this idea, not because he wants to recall the middle ages – Synge is not, in the end, an Anglo-Irish William Morris – but in order to image his own activities as a modernist writer.[56] Her primitive production – the manufacture of highly individuated objects in a seemingly premodern economy – is his model of modern artistic work. As a unique object not designed for exchange, the modernist artifact will be doubly removed from commodification; it will have nothing in common with the tide of mass culture which the Irish Literary Revivalists saw as flowing from the British presses.

However, this rejection of the market cannot be taken at face value. David Harvey has suggested how this central ideology of modernist creativity dissimulates the marketability of the modernist art object: 'Modernist art has always been . . . what Benjamin calls "auratic art"', in the sense that the artist had to assume an aura of creativity, of dedication to art for art's sake, in order to produce a cultural object that would be original, unique, and hence eminently marketable at a monopoly price.'[57] Synge takes the 'art for art's sake' disposition in an unusual direction through the discourse of primitivism. The essential move that Synge makes is the location of the essence of the primitive in a certain type of production. Once reconceived as a mode of production rather than a special place, or form of society, the primitive can be reproduced by the individual. In the modernist text it is primarily the uniqueness of the primitive object, as exemplified by the personal style – the visible labour – of the modernist auteur, that is sought. The modernist text, like the primitive object, is thus imagined as an anti-commodity. More tentatively, through the identification with Nora, the image of the artist as primitive producer, Synge can posit the existence of an artist who would be a community artist, neither alienated modernist auteur nor slave to the masses.[58] For a moment, at least, in *Riders*, the primitive provides a space adequate to Synge's dreams of an ideal aesthetic practice. The subsequent drama never recaptures this optimism: *The Playboy of the Western World*, for example, deals with an artist-figure, Christy, who ultimately finds that the primitive community can stifle as well as encourage the creative individual.[59] Language itself appears to

offer Christy an alternative home, but cut off from any linguistic community it is difficult to see how that language will survive.[60] The ending
of the *Playboy* thus troubles the aesthetic dreams of *Riders* by posing a
question the earlier play shrugs off: *for whom* is the artist as primitive
producer writing?

III
CANNED GOODS, THE CULTURE INDUSTRY
AND PRIMITIVIST MAGIC

Two decades later we see a similar concern with the primitive, the
commodity, and artistic production in the work of an American expatriate writer, Ernest Hemingway. To move from the 1900s to the mid
1920s is to pass from the period of modernism's hesitant entrance into
the high cultural arena to the period of its hegemony. By that time such
landmark texts as Joyce's *Ulysses*, Woolf's *Jacob's Room*, Lawrence's
Women in Love, and T. S. Eliot's *The Waste Land* had all appeared.
Alternative publication circuits had been established: this was the era of
the 'little magazines' – Harriet Monroe's *Poetry*, *The Dial*, Harriet
Weaver's *The Egoist*, *The Little Review*, Ford Madox Ford's *transatlantic
review*, Harold Loeb and Alfred Kreymborg's *Broom*; and many others.
Principally aided by Ezra Pound, Hemingway took full advantage of this
alternative track: six of his early poems first appeared in *Poetry* in 1923;
six of the prose vignettes that would later form part of *in our time* (1924)
were published in *The Little Review*, also in 1923; Hemingway himself
acted as editor for Ford's *transatlantic review*; and a series of his other early
poems appeared in a German magazine, *Der Querschnitt*. Hemingway's
first books also benefited from the existence of such niche publishing:
Three Stories and Ten Poems appeared in 1923 under the imprint of Robert
McAlmon's Contact Editions; and *in our time* was privately published in
1924 by William Bird's Three Mountain Press as part of a six-volume
'inquest' into the state of American prose edited by Ezra Pound. Only in
1925, with the publication of Boni and Liveright's edition of the expanded version of *In Our Time*, could Hemingway be said to have
entered the commercial publishing market.

But perhaps to a greater extent than any of his more experimental
sponsors, Hemingway managed to make modernism pay. The critical
and commercial success of *The Sun also Rises* (1926) secured Hemingway's
reputation, and seemed to indicate that there was a readership ready for
modernism – at least for a certain variety of modernism – vastly in

excess of the readership of the little magazines. While I have used the term 'popular modernism' to describe the adventure romance, Hemingway is a popular modernist in quite a different sense, bridging the world of Gertrude Stein and Hollywood. He appears to have adopted this role quite self-consciously. In a letter to Horace Liveright he reassured the publisher of his commitment to commercial success: '[*In Our Time*] will be praised by highbrows and can be read by lowbrows. There is no writing in it that anybody with a high-school education cannot read.' Hemingway had considerable admiration for e.e. cummings's *The Enormous Room*, but he mentions it to Liveright as an example of a 'fine book' that 'was written in a style that no one who had not read a good deal of "modern" writing could read . . . [which] was hard luck for selling purposes.'[61] Hemingway would develop a style that would do very well 'for selling purposes'.

Yet in *In Our Time* Hemingway is also attempting to produce a form of fiction that will escape the clichés of genre fiction. If on the one hand he wants, like Synge, to escape from the airless world of art for art's sake, on the other, like the more experimental modernists, he also wishes to escape the *idées reçues* of popular literature. He was certainly familiar enough with the formula fiction that the American popular magazines published, and even tried his hand at writing for that market. One of Hemingway's pre-Paris stories, 'The Ash Heel's Tendon', is a crime story recounting how a big Irish cop, Jack Farrell, brings down Hand Evans, a professional killer: 'Back in the days before cocktails were drunk out of teacups Hand Evans was a gun . . . A gun has not a single one of the gunman's predominant characteristics. Instead he is a quiet, unattractive, rather colorless, professional death producer.'[62] The compulsory twist in the tale occurs when the icy Hand Evans, whose real name turns out to be Guardalabene, hears a recording of 'Vesti la Giubba' from *Pagliacci*, and this unmans him enough to enable Farrell to handcuff him. The story is an odd combination of idiosyncratically vivid prose, and the formulas of the pulp detective magazines. There is some continuity with his later work – the story deals with the world of men, guns and violent death – but it is made of very different stuff to *In Our Time*.

Much critical ink has been spilt over the question of the origins of Hemingway's own unique and highly influential style, whether it evolved out of his journalism, or more directly out of the high modernist influence of Gertrude Stein and Ezra Pound, or a number of other contemporary figures.[63] Certainly his use of repetition seems to follow the example of Stein, and his eschewal of adjectives may derive from Pound's precepts. The pared-down sentences may even owe something to the 'Cablese', the 'maximum of information compressed into a minimum of space', that Hemingway learned as a foreign correspondent.[64] At any rate the sojourn in Paris as the correspondent for the *Toronto Daily Star* (for whom he wrote, *inter alia*, scathing accounts of Parisian bohemianism) seems to have affected his work as dramatically as Synge's trips to the Aran islands did his; to create their rather different modernisms the one writer appears to have needed Paris as much as the other needed to escape it. It is, of course, possible to overstate the role played by Paris and its expatriate literary culture. After all, even before he fell under the influence of Stein and Pound, Hemingway had already written a draft of 'Up in Michigan', which shows him working in a different direction to the genre fiction of the magazines. But his exposure to the experimental literary culture of expatriate Paris would encourage him to move further in this direction, and to develop a style as idiosyncratic as that of any of the experimental modernists, if less obviously 'difficult'. Hemingway would develop a modernist style, not by embracing the professional hermeticism of Joyce, but by adapting modernist primitivism.

Hemingway's Paris was the Paris of Joyce, Gertrude Stein, Ford Maddox Ford and Ezra Pound. If Joyce, Stein and Pound seem to point the way forward, Ford and Pound in different ways bridge the gap between the modernism of the 1920s and an earlier phase of British modernism, Pound through his involvement with imagism, Ford, then Ford Maddox Hueffer, through his friendship and collaboration with Joseph Conrad (*Romance* [1903]). Ford, a sort of literary Melmoth the Wanderer, who survived numerous literary movements and changes of avant-garde personnel, also acts as a direct link to the romance revival – it is one of those significant coincidences of literary history that he was one of the mourners at Bram Stoker's funeral at Golders Green in April 1912. Later he would find a rather unfortunate immortality as the comical Henry Braddocks of Hemingway's *The Sun also Rises*.

But this was also the Paris of Constantin Brancusi, Josephine Baker and Nancy Cunard. This trio belonged to, or were perceived to belong to, a multifaceted movement that drew its energy not from modern metropolitan life, but from 'primitive' cultures – from African or Pacific art, from black American culture, or other 'premodern' sources.[65] Primitivism was scarcely something new in the visual arts in the 1920s: Gauguin's Polynesian paintings date from the 1890s; and Picasso had drawn on the iconography of African masks and ancient Iberian art for his *Les Demoiselles d'Avignon* as early as 1907. Brancusi's work also adopted the visual conventions of African sculpture for representational pieces like *Mlle Pogany* (1912), or the totem-like *Adam and Eve* (1921). Parisian primitivism also took more popular forms: on 25 October 1925 Josephine Baker and Joe Alex performed their 'Danse Sauvage' at the Revue Nègre, creating a sensation as great as the 1913 performance of Stravinsky and Diaghilev's *Rite of Spring*. One critic attempted to explain the Parisian fascination with Baker's performance, which united the dance routines of modern, urban black American culture with exoticist fantasy:

Our romanticism is desperate for renewal and escape. But unknown lands are rare. *Alas, we can no longer roam over maps of the world with unexplored corners . . .* We lean on our unconscious and our dreams . . . These blacks feed our double taste for exoticism and mystery. (my emphasis)[66]

Nancy Cunard's mammoth anthology of black literature and culture was still almost ten years away in 1925, but by then she had already begun to acquire African and Oceanic artifacts, including her trade-mark ivory bracelets, scouring the docks and bars frequented by sailors to add to her collection.[67] Like Picasso and Baker, Cunard's history suggests a growing awareness of and interest in ethnic culture as a facet of modernity.[68] The modernist primitivist vogue that these three very different figures represent was not confined to Paris. Richard Huelsenback's recitation of his 'umbah-umbah' poems, or 'Negergedichte', at the Cabaret Voltaire in Zurich were part of the moment of dada.[69] Elsewhere, a sense of the depletion of white civilization and the need for an infusion of energy from other sources was expressed by writers as different as Sherwood Anderson and D. H. Lawrence. Wyndham Lewis would write a scathing account of this modernist primitivism in his *Paleface* (1929), taking Anderson and Lawrence as its literary exemplars.[70]

When Hemingway's *In Our Time* appeared in October 1925, Paul Rosenfeld described it in a *New Republic* review as part of the new primitivism. Hemingway's spare prose belonged 'with cubist painting, *Le Sacre du Printemps*, and other recent work bringing a feeling of positive forces through primitive modern idiom'. *In Our Time* heralded the emergence of 'a new tough, severe and satisfying beauty related equally to the world of machinery and the austerity of the red man'.[71] It seems unlikely, though, that Hemingway wished to be seen as part of any such movement. His satirical novel of 1926, *The Torrents of Spring*, was partly written to extricate himself from his contract with his publishers, Boni and Liveright, since he knew that they would not publish it, thus freeing him to contract with Scribners for future books. But Hemingway also wrote it with a view to putting some distance between himself and his putative mentors. In particular he pokes fun at the primitivism of Sherwood Anderson's novel, *Dark Laughter*. Since Anderson celebrates the 'earthiness' of black American culture, Hemingway goes one better, and throws in a few 'Indians' as well:

Behind the bar, Bruce, the Negro bartender, had been leaning forward and watching the wampums pass from hand to hand. His dark face shone. Sharply, without explanation, he broke into high-pitched uncontrolled laughter. The dark laughter of the Negro . . . Red Dog looked at him sharply. 'I say, Bruce', he spoke sharply; 'your mirth is ill-timed.'[72]

There is not much trace of 'the austerity of the red man' in that passage, and elsewhere in *The Torrents of Spring* 'the world of machinery' comes in for some hard knocks too.

Hemingway scorned his fellow expatriate's modernist primitivism with equal brio: 'What *Broom* and the Skyscraper primitives will die of is what Dada is dead of: impotence', he wrote.[73] Presumably he had in mind poems like Lew Sarett's 'Maple-Sugar Song', published in *Broom* in November 1921:

> Hó-yo-hó-yo! Hó-yo-hó-yo! yo-ho!
> Wáy-nah-bo-zhóo, big spirit of our brother,
> Come thou and bless us, for all the maple flowers,
> And the Moon-of-Sugar-Making is upon us.[74]

In a note on the poem Sarett explains that this piece is not a translation, but rather 'an interpretation . . . of the spirit and the emotional content of the chants' sung at a native American sugar-making ceremony at harvest time. Elsewhere he describes his 'whole literary life [as being] dedicated to the task of capturing [the] wild . . . spiritual power' of 'the Indian'.[75] This is a world away from Hemingway's decidedly anti-romantic deployment of native Americans in such stories as 'Ten Indians', and 'Fathers and Sons'.

But Hemingway's attitude to primitivism was by no means as straightforward as *The Torrents of Spring* and his comments on 'skyscraper primitives' suggest. If he was sceptical of the sentimental celebration of 'the black man' and 'the red man' by others, he himself was not immune to the spell of the primitive. As sketched by Hemingway, Africa, Spain and the American outdoors offer possibilities for encounters with a nature that lies outside of modernity. He represents the escape from the modern as a recovery of the instrumentality of objects, and of the appetites of his subjects, reaching back beyond Synge's vision of a precapitalist, domestic mode of production to a mythical world of hunting (if not gathering). The primitive scene in Hemingway is decidedly non-domestic: women are a part of the modern that must be left behind, whether men go to face the lion, the bull, or the trout, Hemingway's primary metaphors for direct encounters with the natural. Where Synge imagines a rebirth of the object, and thus of the art object, through a certain form of primitive production, Hemingway hopes to break the spell that commodification has cast over the object world by relocating modern objects in primitive places. Synecdochically rendered as the gun, or the knife, or the fishing rod, the world of commodities is reborn through use, and manufactured goods take on the naturalness of their surroundings. In the final story of *In Our Time*, 'Big Two-Hearted River', even those goods which Andy Warhol will later use as icons of mass production – tinned foods – can be transformed by the right surroundings. Tinned food had already become modernist shorthand for the ersatz life of the modern city in *The Waste Land* ('The typist home at teatime, clears her breakfast, lights/ Her Stove, and lays out food in tins'), adding point to Hemingway's use of them in his own muted parable of modernist salvation. Hemingway's Nick Adams, tucking into tinned spaghetti and pork and beans at his solitary campsite in a remote part of Michigan, somewhat defensively assures himself, that he has 'got a right to eat this kind of stuff if [he's] willing to carry it'.[76] The dislocation of modern convenience food from the world of commodities purifies 'this kind of stuff', even to the extent that it can be awarded the supreme Hemingway adjective: 'The beans and spaghetti warmed. Nick stirred them and mixed them together. They began to bubble, making little bubbles that rose with difficulty to the surface. There was a *good* smell' (215, my emphasis). Like Eliot's typist at teatime Nick may lay out food in tins, then, but he is emphatically *not* at home, and far from the wasteland-city.[77]

A later story like 'The Short Happy Life of Francis Macomber' (1936) works a similar magic with the commodity, though this time Africa provides the primitive backdrop. Hemingway's Africa is not the Africa of H. Rider Haggard; the blank spaces on the map have been filled in and the continent has been opened up to rich tourists like the Macombers. And yet, it still has the power to surprise and to test its jaded urban visitors. In this much-interpreted story, Macomber sheds his fear of death – and of his faithless and manipulative wife – before being killed by her in a shooting accident. Whether it actually was an accident has been the subject of much of the critical commentary, Hemingway's own pronouncements on the story suggesting that Macomber's wife has to kill him because she loses her hold over him when he conquers his fears. The most important agent in the story is Africa itself, though, and its capacity to transform whatever comes under its influence, both people and things. Africa makes Macomber 'come of age' (32), in effect makes a man of him by administering a healthy dose of the primitive. He is liberated from his effete civilized ways and restored to a 'proper' masculinity. (In later life Hemingway himself seems to have experienced Africa as equally liberatory, even to the point of 'going native' himself on his 1954 safari, shaving his head, hunting with a spear, and taking a Masai lover.[78]) He is not the only one who is altered by this encounter, though – the things he brings with him undergo a transformation too. This time, rather than Nick Adams's tinned beans, it is primarily brand name goods by Springfield, Gibbs and Mannlicher – guns – that achieve a certain dignity when they are wrested from the universe of commodities and relocated in the 'primitive' environment of Africa. There they can pursue their true vocation, the killing of big game, including in the end Macomber himself, of course. But even more mundane Western goods undergo a metamorphosis when they are taken on safari. After a successful hunt from a car, the laconic professional white hunter, Wilson, a sort of latter-day Allan Quatermain, muses on how Macomber's first proper kill has made a man of him, taking account of the importance of the familiar in this rite of passage: 'Beggar had probably been afraid all his life. Don't know what started it. But over now. Hadn't had time to be afraid with the buff[alo]. That and being angry too. Motor car too. Motor cars made it familiar. Be a damn fire eater now' (33). If the familiarity of the automobile makes the strangeness of Africa less frightening for Macomber, the car emerges similarly transformed, taking on, like the guns, some of the mystique of the primitive. Thomas Richards has shown how in the late Victorian travelogues of H. M. Stanley the world of Western manufactured goods seems to perform the work of colonization outside of any human agency, becoming 'the spearhead of English material culture in the campaign against the anarchy of the dark continent'.[79] The commodity, in other words, projects its own commercial aura into the African interior. In Hemingway this magic is reversed – Africa and other 'primitive' environments render once fungible commodities unique; they 'resingularize' commodities, to use Igor Kopytoff's term.[80]

The corollary of the rehabilitation of the commodity is the recovery of the subject's natural appetite. One of the most striking aspects of 'Big Two-Hearted River', and of the fishing chapters of *The Sun also Rises/ Fiesta* is the delineation of eating and drinking. Paris may be a moveable feast, but it is to the remote corners of the earth that men go to sharpen their appetite. This ideological project provides the structuring contrast of the novel, where the mysteriously wounded Jake Barnes, not a 'whole' man since the war, is tantalized by his longing for the vampish Lady Ashley (whose appetite for men makes her seem like a descendant of Bram Stoker's Lucy Westenra as well as kin to Mrs Macomber). Hemingway emphasizes the sterility of this unconsummated (and presumably unconsummatable) heterosexual relationship to the point of self-parody in order to heighten the contrast with the men-only fishing trip to the remote Basque region of Spain. Only here can Jake escape the unwholesomeness associated with modern life and recover something of the simplicity and integrity that Synge imagines the Aran islanders to possess. The account of the trip lingers over the pleasures of the local wine and food, and the pleasant tiredness after the 'work' of fishing. Summing up the expedition, Jake stresses the simple oppositions of their vacation world:

We stayed five days at Burguete and had good fishing. The nights were cold and the days were hot, and there was always a breeze even in the heat of the day. It was hot enough so that it felt good to wade in a cold stream, and the sun dried you when you came out and sat on the bank.[81]

The novel contrasts the simple tactile and appetitive pleasures of the primitivist vacation with the postwar mare's nest of relations among Brett and the men who surround her: Jake, Robert Cohn and Mike Campbell.

The recovery of appetite follows a gendered logic: it is only when women disappear from the scene, or when their presence is rendered purely incidental, that Hemingway's principals can really experience the primitive. Hemingway's women are denied this experience because they function in his stories as part of the bad side of modernity itself.[82] Lady Brett's vampish behaviour is a symptom and sign of a more general false appetite in the modern West. Similarly, Mrs Macomber in 'The Short Happy Life of Francis Macomber' is too much an emblem of the modern to be transformed by the experience of primitive Africa. In her case the linkage between female desire and consumer culture is made more explicit. She is an advertising icon, 'an extremely handsome and well-kept woman of the beauty and social position which had, five years before, commanded five thousand dollars as the price of endorsing, with photographs, a beauty product which she had never used' (4).[83] Implicitly, the story links her strong sexual appetite to this consumer-culture role, her ability to stimulate appetite in others.[84] Not the least interesting thing about this story is that Hemingway himself would later lend his name, face and prose to Ballantine Ale, a useful reminder that his relationship to bad modernity was always a complex one.[85]

The stories themselves, though, present a more schematic version of the relationship between gender, modernity and modernist primitivism. Somewhat paradoxically, the gender-coding of the opposition between the modern and the primitive is spelled out most clearly in 'Big Two-Hearted River', a story without women, which describes a fishing-trip to rural Michigan in the aftermath of World War 1. In this story the escape from the modern into the remote countryside is explicitly described as an escape from certain (including sexual) desires, and the recapture of a more basic level of needs: '[Nick] felt he had left everything behind, the need for thinking, the need to write, *other needs*. It was all back of him' (210, my emphasis). The mind once quelled, the body, the subject's personal nature reserve, takes over: 'Nick was hungry. He did not believe he had ever been hungrier' (215). Just as the can of pork and beans is transformed by its relocation in the wilds, Nick's desires have been purified, as it were, in the primitive landscape.

The effect of the recovery of natural appetite is to make possible a new rapprochement between the subject and the world of commodities. We saw in chapter 3 how the romantic encounters between male protagonist and feminized mummy could partially restore the subject's domain over the object world. Hemingway similarly puts heterosexual romance to work by transforming unsatisfactory sexual relationships (associated with the modern) into fulfilling gustatory experiences (associated with the primitive), as in the following sensualized encounter between Nick and a tin of apricots:

While he waited for the coffee to boil, he opened a small can of apricots. He liked to open cans. He emptied the can of apricots into a tin cup. While he watched the coffee on the fire, he drank the juice syrup of the apricots, carefully at first to keep from spilling, then meditatively, sucking the apricots down. They were better than fresh apricots. (217)

On the primitivist picnic, the tinned apricots, synecdochic representatives of a whole modern universe of commodities, are not only redeemed, the fulfilment they offer carries an erotic charge. The modern world that Nick has left behind thus returns in the primitive landscape, but it returns in a new form. An unsatisfying relation to both women and modern culture – both of which threaten to unman Hemingway's modern hero – reappears as a completely satisfying relation to the commodity. Where Marx imagined commodity fetishism coming to an end only with the demise of capitalism itself, Hemingway sees a new relation to objects arising through a qualitative change in the subject, through a mutation in appetite. T. S. Eliot's typically ineffectual modern subject, J. Alfred Prufrock, has to wonder if he dares to eat a peach; his primitive picnic delivers Nick Adams from such anxieties. As the primitive setting transforms consumer goods, in other words, it also transforms the consumer.

Most often in Hemingway it is the instruments that men use in their encounters with nature – guns, rods, even cars as in the Macomber safari – that are shorn of their commodityhood, and as we shall see, language is one of those instruments. In 'Big Two-Hearted River: Part Two', the fishing rod Nick uses becomes in his struggle with a trout 'the now living rod' (224). When a big fish takes the bait, 'the rod [comes] alive and dangerous' (226). To see these as examples of transferred epithet is to at once grasp and miss the point. What is striking is that epithets denoting life can here be transferred to a fishing pole, disrupting Hemingway's ordinarily direct syntax. But as in the case of Synge, Hemingway's account of the salvation of the object world undergirds a theory of his own literary practice. Just as the fishing rod comes alive when it becomes the mediator between Nick Adams and nature, so too is language revived when it is used to describe such an encounter.

The original second half of 'Big Two-Hearted River', 'On Writing', makes the theoretical underpinnings of the piece much clearer. In it Nick Adams begins to meditate on the craft of writing, to assess his contemporaries, and to consider how his own views on writing differ from theirs.

It was easy to write if you used the tricks. Everybody used them. Joyce has invented hundreds of new ones . . . He wanted to write like Cezanne painted. Cezanne started with all the tricks. Then he broke the whole thing down and built the real thing . . . People were easy to do. All this smart stuff was easy. Against this age, skyscraper primitives . . .[86]

Nick rejects the professional modernist language of Joyce, but also the too-easy rejection of modernity, the false 'skyscraper primitivism' that Hemingway himself criticized for its 'impotence'. Yet 'Big Two-Hearted River' itself, like the other stories in *In Our Time*, seems to be an exercise in Hemingway's own brand of primitivism. The story ends with Nick wanting to get back to camp to 'get to work' on 'something in his head'. But Hemingway rejected this material from the final version of 'Big Two-Hearted River', perhaps realizing that it was more of a manifesto than a short story. As James Fenton notes, 'Nobody could infer from the story as published that it ever had anything to do with an ambition to rival Pound and Joyce.'[87] The revised version still contains a literary manifesto, but that manifesto is now implicit, folded into the story itself.

Hemingway, or at least Nick, is impatient with 'all this smart stuff' in contemporary writing. But there is another enemy too, and it is kept in sight in Hemingway's other fiction: the commercialized language of popular fiction and bad journalism. It is there in a later piece, 'Banal Story', for example, which parodies a certain kind of *Reader's Digest* journalism: 'There is Romance everywhere. *Forum* writers talk to the point, are possessed of humor and wit. But they do not try to be smart and are never long-winded. Live the full life of the mind, exhilarated by new ideas, intoxicated by the Romance of the unusual' (361). 'Romance' has become the badge of *réchauffé* mass culture here. *The Sun also Rises* also invokes the spirit of debased romance. On his fishing trip, Jake reads 'something by A. E. W. Mason', whom we met earlier as one of the prime movers in the writing of Stephen Crane's patchwork play, *The Ghost*. Hemingway ironically juxtaposes the sentimental world of Mason's story with Jake's very different experience of modern love: 'I was reading a wonderful story about a man who had been frozen in the Alps and then fallen into a glacier and disappeared, and his bride was going to wait twenty-four years exactly for his body to come out on the moraine, while her true love waited too, and they were still waiting when Bill [sc. Jake's fishing companion] came up' (100). Mason, of course, is hardly a fortuitous choice: his best-known novel, *The Four Feathers*, is in some ways the quintessential imperial romance, and it also, as it happens, depends on a love triangle similar to the one Jake describes. Jake attributes Robert Cohn's foolish pursuit of the indifferent Lady Ashley to his taking seriously the 'splendid imaginary amorous adventures of a perfect English gentleman in an intensely romantic land' (11) in W. H. Hudson's *The Purple Land*. He says of Hudson's book: 'For a man to take it at thirty-four as a guide-book to what life holds is about as safe as it would be for a man of the same age to enter Wall Street direct from a French convent, equipped with a complete set of the more practical Alger books' (11). The language of romance, Hemingway suggests, has ceased to have anything to do with lived reality – it has become completely calcified.

Hemingway seeks to avoid these romantic horrors. For him, language escapes the necrosis of popular fiction and journalism when it goes primitive. Just as Africa, the home of fetishism in the Victorian imaginary, cures commodity fetishism, so too will it provide a remedy for the dead language of mass culture, a different sort of fetish.[88] Of course the equation of a sort of pure state of language with the primitive is scarcely a new manoeuvre, recollecting as it does the Preface to the *Lyrical Ballads* of 1800. There Wordsworth states that he hopes to purge poetic diction of its calcified elements by adapting the more 'philosophical' language of agricultural labourers, whose station in life brings them closer to a life of unmediated experience:

The language, too, of these men is adopted . . . because such men hourly communicate with the best objects from which the best part of language is originally derived; and because, from their rank in society and the sameness and narrow circle of their intercourse . . . they convey their feelings and notions in simple and unelaborated expressions. Accordingly, such a language, arising out of repeated experience and regular feelings, is a more permanent and a far more philosophical language, than that which is frequently substituted for it by poets . . .[89]

Nor is Wordsworth the first to sound this note. As Hugh Kenner has shown, Wordsworth's Preface echoes the language of Thomas Sprat's *History of the Royal Society* (1667), where the latter waxes nostalgic for a time 'when Men deliver'd so many *Things*, almost in an equal number of *Words*', and his advocacy of 'the Language of Artizans, Countrymen, and Merchants, before that of Wits, or Scholars'.[90] It is worth distinguishing among these complaints, though, which from one perspective may all seem to be simply reiterations of Western phonocentrism. Sprat's principal target, as Kenner points out, is the Ciceronian rhetorical tradition. Wordsworth, on the other hand, is already writing within a recognizably modern culture with an expanding print culture, and directs his hostility to a popular culture that threatened to corrupt taste with its 'sickly and stupid German tragedies' and sensational reportage. This myth of an Edenic tongue finds a new currency in the twentieth century, when mass print culture means that language invades the universal problematic in a very particular way. Thus the Wordsworthian lament finds a new currency in the Heideggerian cult of the German vernacular, for example, but it also makes its way in the world of leftist thought, showing up in one of the most widely read critiques of linguistic fetishism, Roland Barthes's *Mythologies*, where Wordsworth's opposition of vivid philosophical and frozen poetic language appears as the opposition of history and myth. For Barthes, when language breaks with history to pursue an independent course, myth is produced. There is one type of language, on this model, which escapes the depoliticizing operations of myth, which 'remains political' (145): 'If I am a woodcutter and I am led to name the tree which I am felling, whatever the form of my sentence, I "speak the tree", I do not speak about it. This means that my language is operational, transitively linked to its object; between the tree and myself, there is nothing but labour, that is to say, an action.'[91] According to Barthes, then, 'the language of man as a producer'[92] is not mythical.

Ernest Hemingway would have agreed, while extending the definition of producer to include hunters, anglers and bullfighters. But Hemingway, unlike Barthes, also sees that second order of language, in which the 'producer' is *described*, as escaping linguistic fetishism. Fredric Jameson captured this aspect of Hemingway's literary project some years ago when he pointed out that its real subject is not hunting, fishing, or pitiless lovers' quarrels between dispsomaniac expatriates, but rather 'the writing of a certain type of sentence, the practice of a determinate style'.[93] In eschewing the representation of urban modernity, and turning to the description of action in a primitive setting, this type of sentence, this style, becomes possible. According to Hemingway's ideology of literature, that is, writing itself becomes an activity that offers a direct contact with nature, the kind of contact that Wordsworth imagines through the figure of the agricultural labourer, Barthes through the figure of the woodcutter. In Jameson's words: 'now conceived as a skill, [writing] is then assimilated to the other skills of hunting and bullfighting, of fishing and warfare, which project a total image of man's active and all-absorbing technical participation in the outside world'.[94] Language on this model becomes a simple tool in the writer's skilled hands. As in Synge's primitivist aesthetic, while literature as a commodity renders the producer's labour invisible, the modernist text allows this labour to appear as inalienable, personal style. Whether one derives the ingredients of the Hemingway sentence from his experience as a reporter, the influence of Gertrude Stein, or even from that of the popular magazine story, it is in this primitivist project that these ingredients find their full significance.

ROMANTIC MODERNISM

Within the imperial imaginary the primitive heterotopia allowed Synge to envisage a form of literature that would be neither engulfed by mass culture nor the walled preserve of an elite – a modern literature that would somehow escape modernity. For Hemingway, the primitive setting held out the possibility of a literary language that could avoid the linguistic calcifications of commercial literature and engage directly with the object of description. Both of them develop these literary fantasies through the representation of the role of the commodity within the primitive space, and the imagination of that other space is essential to their conception of their particular brands of modernism. The invocation of that other country shows their kinship with the popular fiction that elsewhere appears as the very essence of bad modernity. Despite their apparent distance from the world of popular fiction, then, these modernist fantasies remain very much within its problematic. Mummy fiction, like detective fiction, imagines the foreign commodity as potentially fatal to the integrity of England's boundaries, and conjures up strategies to deal with the foreign object within a domestic economy. Synge's work, on the other hand, identifies the foreign object, now perceived as a non-commodity, as an emblem of its own composition. Hemingway, for his part, inverts the tropes of the imperial adventure novel, which sees the deployment of modern techniques and tools within the exotic spaces of empire as a way of civilizing/Anglicizing those spaces. He tries to show that the modern Western commodity – including the modernist text – can be purged of its bad modernity when it is reinscribed in the space of the primitive. This is simply to reverse the magical role of the commodity that we see developed in the fiction of Rider Haggard, and in the travel writing of H. M. Stanley. While the modernist primitives identify with the foreign and the exotic rather than with the domestic, the contours of the imperial imaginary, the delimitations of inside/outside, modern/primitive, remain essentially the same. Ultimately, modernism can no more think its way out of the categories of imperial culture than can popular fiction.

Afterword: the long goodbye

When we prise the narratives of the 'revival of romance' loose from the Gothic tradition and consider them as part of a popular modernist culture, they appear to us under a new aspect. Narratives and figures that remain inscrutable when we try to read them through the conventions of the eighteenth-century Gothic of Walpole, Radcliffe and Lewis, yield up their meaning when read as components of the imaginary of a modern imperial society, a society increasingly characterized, as I have described, by the ideology of professional expertise and by consumerism. The mummy, the team of men, the treasure map – these are historically determinate figures, untranslatable in terms of a Gothic or Romantic lexicon of sublimity, picturesqueness and alienation. But if the modern romance is estranged from its Gothic predecessors, at times it may be more familiar to *us*, as in the case of *Dracula*, where the original text continues to be read alongside numerous adaptations, textual and filmic. Our relation to Stoker's novel is now inevitably mediated by our knowledge of these adaptations, and yet the novel continues to exert a semi-autonomous appeal. Our historical moment is not that of the romance revival, but to the extent that it retains the vestiges of a late nineteenth-century imaginary – in which, as I've argued, the professional team looms larger than the aristocratic vampire – the readerly pleasures that Stoker's tale evokes still work for us in a way that those of, say, *The Castle of Otranto* do not. Presumably these cultural echoes will some day cease to sound, and *Dracula* will confront us as the eighteenth-century Gothic novel does now, as an elaborate clockwork toy with the key missing. But for a time the mechanism of the romance continues to run for us, enabling us to see both its points of departure from our own cultural narratives, and certain regularities.

The distance of that *fin de siècle* from our own is much more evident in the case of a figure like the mummy, which seems to flourish only in the historical microclimate of the late nineteenth century. Unlike the vampire the mummy has no Romantic ancestors, and it plays almost no role in British fiction before the 1880s, when it becomes an overnight success, so to speak. A new figure employed to do new kinds of cultural work, the mummy only appears when it becomes necessary for popular fiction to represent the relations of subjects and objects in a burgeoning imperial consumer culture. Its cultural meanings are thus quite different to those of earlier monsters of reanimated flesh, like Victor Frankenstein's monstrous son. Whatever cultural fears the Frankenstein monster puts in play, they are domestic, whereas the mummy's significance turns on its capacity to figure a distinctly foreign revenant. Moreover, the gender syntax of the two narratives is quite different. Where the Frankenstein story seems to echo the murderous between-men logic of *Caleb Williams*, or *Confessions of a Justified Sinner*, for the most part the mummy story's heterosexual dimension allows for a reconciliation of man and monster under the aegis of romantic love. The cultural problematic that the original mummy stories sprang from seems far less intelligible to us now than that of the vampire. While the mummy still operates as a popular icon, the original mummy tales are now largely unread, and the logic of the few film versions seems to derive more from the 1940s 'mummy's curse' films (owing their origin to the Carter–Carnarvon excavations of 1922–9 and the resulting wave of Egyptomania) than from the cultural concerns of the *fin de siècle*.[1]

In general, though, the figures of romance have proved to be more like the vampire than the mummy in their resilience. In the last chapter I argued that modernism, which seems in many ways the opposite of the romance, is cut from the same cultural cloth as the latter. However, this is not to say that the romance imaginary lives on only in the transmuted form of high modernism. While modernist literary criticism may have speeded the departure of the romance from the precincts of 'serious' literature, the romance did not *disappear* as a form. If the readerly pleasures of the romance seem oddly familiar, this is in part because even after the prestige of authors like Haggard, Stoker and Stevenson had declined, their work continued to feed the stream of twentieth-century popular culture. To take Haggard, for example, his reputation suffered after its peak in the 1880s and early 1890s, but the sales figures for cheap reprint editions of *She* and *King Solomon's Mines* (producing but slim profits for Haggard himself) indicate that even thirty years later there was still an eager audience for his myths of empire, long after Edgar Wallace, in many respects Haggard's successor, had invented a new version of African adventure with his *Sanders of the River* series.[2]

Moreover *King Solomon's Mines* and *She* have not been out of print since, though it is only comparatively recently that they have come in for academic attention, and the consecration implied by an Oxford World's Classics reprint. This is not to say, of course, that these texts continued to signify as they did at the moment of their initial publication. One does not need recourse to any very elaborate theory of reinscription to understand that whatever popular fantasies were put in play by these novels in the 1880s must be somewhat different from those activated in the 1990s. And yet we might also assume that those fantasies are not completely different, that some romance tropes still work for us, even while others have become quite alien; if we cannot assume complete continuity with their initial reception, we cannot assume a complete break either. There is considerable warrant for Stuart Hall's thesis that the 1880s witness something of the order of a cultural shift in Britain that links this period more closely to the present than to the early or even mid-Victorian years.

A NEW MEDIUM FOR ROMANCE

The survival of the romance in cheap reprints does not tell anything like the whole story. It is difficult to discuss the longevity of the romance without mentioning the role played by a new narrative medium: film. To take Haggard again as our example, film gave a new lease of life to his version of Africa, and a nice income to the man himself late in his career (which latter function film also provided for figures like Kipling and Conrad[3]). The film industry seems almost from its inception to have been a bulwark of imperial culture.[4] By 1916 the English film maker, H. L. Lucoque, had bought the seven-year film-rights to six of Haggard's novels, including *King Solomon's Mines*, *She* and *Allan Quatermain*, and Haggard received some £9,000 in royalties from 1915 to 1916.[5] Hollywood also played its part in the preservation of both Haggard's brand of romance and his fortunes. As D. S. Higgins describes, Fox Film Company filmed Haggard's novel, *Cleopatra* (1889), in 1920 with Theda Bara in the title role, paying Haggard £5,000 for what he felt was 'the shameless plagiarism' of his work.[6] Leslie Halliwell records that there were seven silent film versions of *She* alone, as well as sound versions in 1934 and 1965.[7] Nor is Haggard's easy transition to the screen unique. R. L. Stevenson died several years before the Lumières' first film shows in 1895, but his *The Strange Case of Dr Jekyll and Mr Hyde* proved irresistible to film makers: it appeared on the screen in 1921 with John Barrymore in the title role, 1931 with Fredric March, and 1941 with Spencer Tracy, not to mention the more free-wheeling adaptations, like *Abbott and Costello meet Dr Jekyll and Mr Hyde* (1954), *Dr Jekyll and Sister Hyde* (1971), or the recent *Mary Reilly*. *Treasure Island* has been almost as popular (1934, 1950, 1971), and there have also been versions of *Kidnapped* (1938, 1959, 1971), *The Master of Ballantrae* (1953), *The Wrong Box* (1966), *The Ebb Tide* (1937), and 'The Suicide Club' from *New Arabian Nights*.

Dracula provides the most vivid example of the celluloid survival of the romance in twentieth-century popular culture. Bram Stoker died in 1912, too early to see his prose monster become a screen icon. However, Stoker's widow, Florence Stoker, née Balcombe, lived long enough to bring an action against Prana-Film of Germany for producing F. W. Murnau's unauthorized screen version of *Dracula*, *Nosferatu: eine Symphonie des Grauens* (1921), and eventually to profit handsomely from the stage and film rights of the novel, receiving something in the region of $20,000 when Universal finally bought the rights in 1930. The vampire count's tortuous path from novel to film has recently been charted in great detail by David J. Skal, who shows how Stoker's novel became 'one of the great money-spinning literary properties of the twentieth century'.[8] Count Dracula has been represented more times in film than any other literary character, except for, perhaps, another *fin-de-siècle* icon, Sherlock Holmes. A plethora of film versions of Stoker's novel exist, including the first 'legitimate' version by Universal, Tod Browning's *Dracula* (1931), and the recent Francis Ford Coppola's *Bram Stoker's Dracula* (1994). But there are also numerous films that simply adopt the figure (or name) of the Count for narratives that have otherwise very little to do with Stoker's text: *Dracula Meets the Outer Space Chicks* (1968), *Men of Action Meet Women of Dracula* (1969), *Dracula vs. Frankenstein* (1970), *Blacula* (1972), *The Satanic Rites of Dracula* aka *Dracula is alive and Well and Living in London* (1973) and *Dracula's Dog*, aka *Zoltan, Hound of Dracula* (1977), to name just a few. The Count was periodically revived to add a frisson to various moral panics, as in the Hammer production, *Dracula AD 1972* (1972) where the milieu is London teenage occultism (Halliwell records the publicity tag-line: 'The Count is back with an eye for London's hot pants, and a taste for everything').

Equally striking is the myriad of spin-off products, which testify to *Dracula*'s place in popular culture. Skal lists some of the products that exploited Bela Lugosi's famous screen rendition of the Count: 'children's phonograph records, plastic toy pencil sharpeners, greeting cards and talking greeting cards, plastic model figures, tee-shirts, sweatshirts and patches, rings and pins, monster old-maid card games, soap and detergent products, Halloween costumes and masks, enlargograph sets and kits, target games, picture puzzles, mechanical walking toys, ink-on transfers, trading cards . . .'9 In effect, Dracula has become what Tony Bennett and Janet Woollacott term a popular hero, joining a select group of figures who 'break free from the originating textual conditions of their existence, functioning as an established point of cultural reference that is capable of working – or producing meanings – even for those who are not familiar with the original texts in which they made their appearance'.10 This has had knock-on effects for other Stoker texts, so that the less well-known *The Jewel of Seven Stars*, for example, has also been filmed (by Hammer as *Blood from the Mummy's Tomb* [1971]), and has remained available in paperback reprints.

The survival of the narratives of Stoker, Haggard and Stevenson on the screen is part of a more extensive continuity between cinema and the texts of the *fin de siècle*. Stuart Hall's argument for a 'break' in the 1880s receives considerable support from the way in which a wide array of the popular fiction of this time – not all of it romance – provided, and continues to provide, a quarry for the film industry, the major narrative medium of the twentieth century. Even if we assume that these stories changed radically in their incorporation into a new medium, and through new conditions of reception, we still have to explain why these particular tales should have appealed more to film makers than their mid-Victorian predecessors.11 This is not to say that earlier Victorian fiction was viewed as being without cinematic potential. If some mid-Victorian favourites like Trollope and Eliot proved less tempting to film makers, there are certainly many film adaptations (and numerous television adaptations) of the novels of Dickens, for example. Nonetheless, popular fiction written after 1880 appears on the screen in far greater numbers. Cinema has been strongly drawn to such mythic figures as Stevenson's Jekyll/Hyde, Conan Doyle's Sherlock Holmes and of course Stoker's Dracula, as I have outlined, but there is a much longer list of novels from the period 1880–1914 that came to provide grist for the mills of the film industry. In some cases all that survives in the film versions is the narrative germ, in other cases there is more direct indebtedness, but there is strong evidence the narrative elements that attracted readers of fiction up to World War I pulled in cinema audiences well into the second half of the twentieth century. The island Eden of Horace de Vere Stacpoole's *The Blue Lagoon* (1908), the gender transformations of Frank Richards's *2835 Mayfair* (1907), the parent–child swap of F. Anstey's *Vice Versa* (1882), the sensational mesmerism of George Du Maurier's *Trilby* (1892), the gentleman thief of E. W. Hornung's *Raffles* (1899), global invasion in Wells's *The War of the Worlds* (1898), the desert adventure of A. E. W. Mason's *The Four Feathers* (1901), or the paranoid domestic adventure of John Buchan's *The Thirty-Nine Steps* (1915), these all lent themselves to (sometimes multiple) screen adaptations. Horace de Vere Stacpoole's *The Blue Lagoon*, for example, was filmed in 1923, 1949 (with Donald Houston and Jean Simmons) and, of course, in a more fleshly version in 1980 (with Brooke Shields and Christopher Atkins).[12] The gender and age switches of *2835 Mayfair* and *Vice Versa* have appeared most recently in *Switch* and *Big*. *Trilby* has appeared in several versions, as *Trilby* (1914, 1923), *Trilby and Svengali* (1911), and *Svengali* (1931 and 1955).[13] E. W. Hornung's gentleman thief, Raffles, has appeared on screen at least four times, in 1917 (with John Barrymore in the title role), 1925 (House Peters), 1930 (Ronald Colman) and 1939 (David Niven). While Wells's *The War of the Worlds* has only appeared once on the screen in anything like a faithful adaptation (1953), it has inspired a whole generation of Hollywood B-movies about alien invasion, as well as more recent blockbusters like Roland Emmerich's special-effects spectacular, *Independence Day* (1996), which brings Wells's novel up to date by employing a computer virus rather than the common cold to stop the aliens in their tentacled tracks.[14]

The screen success of *The Four Feathers* is worth pausing over. While perhaps not as popular as one of its descendants, P. C. Wren's Foreign Legion adventure, *Beau Geste* (1924), Mason's novel has nevertheless also spawned a series of desert spectaculars (1921, 1929, 1939 and 1955 as *Storm over the Nile*).[15] The success of such desert adventures owes more than a little to what at first may seem like an extra-fictional factor, that is the cult of Lawrence of Arabia. But the popular conception of Lawrence has to be grasped as itself largely a romance, one created by the journalist Lowell Thomas, who turned the far more contradictory materials of T. E. Lawrence's career into an adventure narrative. In an era of modern mass publicity, Thomas's use of familiar romance paradigms helped to make Lawrence into a star, and in turn this process fuelled the market for romances like *The Four Feathers*.[16] As a result of this fictional/publicity cross-fertilization the themes of disguise (even to the point of 'going native') and of guerilla warfare are more prominent in subsequent adventure romances. As Graham Dawson notes: 'The guerilla, the commando, the Special Operations forces, the secret agents, spies and saboteurs who operate "behind enemy lines" . . . these become the characteristic soldier heroes of twentieth-century adventure.'[17] An interesting domestic variant on this theme is provided by John Buchan's *The Thirty-Nine Steps*, which has proved almost as attractive to film makers as Mason's, being filmed in 1935 (with Hitchcock directing), 1959 and 1978.[18]

One can of course adduce a number of possible reasons for the subsequent popularity of these *fin-de-siècle* narrative gems. Most obviously, perhaps, to speak only of dates, both film and the romance stand at the threshold of the new era of mass entertainment; film, after all, appears first only ten years after the beginning of the 'revival of romance'. Given this fact, we might speculate that the first couple of generations of film makers were in part simply attracted to the tales that were most popular when they were growing up. Logistics may also have entered the picture: in terms of length alone the romance lends itself more readily to screen adaptation than the three-decker novel of mid century. In some cases very contingent factors indeed may at least have influenced which adaptations were filmed, if not those that succeeded. Quite apart from the role played by Lawrence of Arabia in popularizing desert adventures, the convenient proximity of Death Valley and the Coachella Dunes of Arizona encouraged Hollywood to make a whole series of desert romances featuring the Foreign Legion, as John Sutherland has suggested.[19]

I want to argue, however, that the fact that film, a new entertainment technology, a 'cultural technology' as Raymond Williams puts it,[20] happens to take over the narrative materials of an older form, the adventure romance, is not purely the result of external factors. Indeed, I would argue that the appearance of both film and romance as components of a new mass entertainment culture is far from a coincidence, and that the imaginary pleasures that film offers follow directly from those developed by Haggard, Stevenson and Stoker. If, as the cultural historian Siegfried Giedion has argued, 'Tools and objects are outgrowths of fundamental attitudes to the world', then it should not surprise us that the technology of cinema that appeared in the 1890s should connect at a fundamental level to the cultural imaginary of that period as it reveals itself in popular fiction.[21] The 'fundamental attitudes to the world' that film expresses as a technology are also, in other words, those that mark the romance. I have described the romance and the modernist text as twins, born from the same cultural matrix, but it would have been more accurate, then, to describe them as triplets, the third sibling being cinema. While the connections between modernism and the cinema have often enough attracted comment, the romance has largely been left out of the picture. Ian Christie has recently touched on one aspect of this series of family resemblances in his account of early cinema history, *The Last Machine*, arguing that the illusion of personal mobility through space and time that the cinema develops was anticipated in nineteenth-century adventure tales: '[Jules] Verne's heroes get ahead of themselves, or travel beyond the end of the map, just as Rider Haggard's explorers in *She* escape from civilisation into the seductive fantasy of eternal youth. What these and many other popular artists created was a cinematic vision before the invention of moving pictures, a space and time machine of the imagination.'[22] Christie, that is, links romance and film in terms of the patterns of pleasure that they develop, and by isolating a particular kind of imaginary mobility as a principal component of this pleasure.

An intriguing historical episode may be taken to emblematize this cultural convergence. H. G. Wells, who it will be remembered was one of the guests at Stephen Crane's century's end party in 1899, had four years before produced *The Time Machine*, a 'scientific romance'. Like such novels as *King Solomon's Mines*, *She*, and *Treasure Island*, *The Time Machine* presents a fantasy of armchair adventure for a society trying to assimilate rapid imperial expansion, modernization and uneven development. *King Solomon's Mines*, or for that matter, *Heart of Darkness*, makes the advance through space also a journey back in time to a more primitive world, but Wells takes this idea a stage further by producing a fantasy of time-travel that allows the traveller to stay (more or less) in the same place while racing backwards and forwards in time. Besides its echoes of imperial romance, though, it is not difficult to see how this fantasy of personal mobility also resembles the experience of the modern cinema-goer, who can live through the American Civil War, or the 1960s, or the year 1999 and still have time to get the last bus home. Certainly the convergence between Wells's novel and the spectacular possibilities offered by emergent technologies of image reproduction was not lost on one contemporary reader. Robert Paul, one of the pioneers of the British film industry, read Wells's novel when it appeared in 1895, and subsequently filed a Patent application for

A novel form of exhibition whereby the spectators have presented to their view scenes which are supposed to occur in the future or past, while they are given the sensation of voyaging upon a machine through time . . . the mechanism consists of platforms for the spectators, with an opening which is directed towards a screen upon which the views are presented.[23]

Through the use of '[S]lides or films, representing . . . successive instan-
taneous photographs, after the manner of the Kinetoscope', the spectator could duplicate the experience of Wells's nameless scientific traveller.[24] As Christie records, this cinematic time machine was never
actually built, 'but moving pictures would soon make it a reality',[25] and
Paul would go on to be one of the most significant figures in the
technical and entrepreneurial history of early British cinema.

The oneiric quality perceived by contemporary commentators in
both the romance and film offers another way of exploring their common origin. The cinema was early on identified as providing a dreamlike experience (the more lavish cinemas would later be called 'dream
palaces', just as Hollywood would come to be known as the 'dream
factory'). Christie cites an essay by Jules Romains from 1911 describing
the cinema experience: 'A bright circle abruptly illuminates the far wall
. . . The group dream now begins. They sleep; their eyes no longer see.
They are no longer conscious of their bodies. Instead there are only
passing images, a gliding and rustling of dreams.'[26] One obviously
cannot take such descriptions at face value, and it seems rather unlikely
that early audiences were 'no longer conscious of their bodies', no
matter how enthralled they were otherwise. Yet as a contemporary *theory*
of audience reaction Romains's account is significant. The romance, of
course, was also represented as a dreamlike genre, offering fantasies of
escape and self-realization. Anthony Hope, for example, comments
explicitly on the fantasies of figurative mobility offered: 'It shows [the
reader] what they would be if they could, if time and fate and circumstances did not bind, what in a sense they all are, and what their acts
would show them to be if an opportunity offered. So they dream and are
happier, and at least none the worse for their dreams.'[27] R. L. Stevenson
describes the romance as working like a 'daydream' to satisfy the
reader's 'nameless longings'.[28] Like the cinema, then, the romance was
seen to free its readers from the despotism of fact.

Having spent four chapters arguing that the romance contains what
one might one consider popular theory in narrative form, I do not
intend to now about-turn and argue that the romance is pure daydream
fantasy, anymore than is film. But I would suggest that there is a core of
truth to what Hope, Stevenson and Romains are saying: what they
recognize as the oneiric quality of romance and film is that pleasure in
imaginary mobility that characterizes both, and that was most apparent
to contemporary readers and viewers. Early cinema and the romance
were not linked through their both being 'escapist'; rather they both

articulated fantasies of spatio-temporal mobility that could be put to a variety of uses.

The romance itself often thematicizes its own dreamlike (or nightmarish) appeal through those characters who cannot establish whether or not they have dreamt all or part of their adventures (e.g. Lavenham, the hero of *Iras, A Mystery*, Jonathan Harker in *Dracula*). Perhaps the most sustained exploration of the romance as a dreamlike genre, though, is George Du Maurier's *Peter Ibbetson* (1891), which also explicitly links its dream episodes with image technologies. More interestingly still, while remaining firmly on the side of romance, Du Maurier's novel seems to also suggest that the dream romance is the inevitably flawed product of a society that offers no other form of imaginative release to its subjects; it is both a romance and a critique of the culture that produces the romance.

In *Peter Ibbetson*, the eponymous hero is an architect and surveyor, who after an idyllic childhood in France, and an unhappy growth to maturity in England under his uncle's guardianship, is placed in a prison for the criminally insane for the murder of his uncle. Peter's life-sentence does not distress him unduly, however. Through a chance encounter with the lost companion of his French childhood, Mimsey, now the beautiful Duchess of Towers, he learns the secret of 'dreaming true', which enables him, among other useful things, to revisit his lost childhood, preserved in all its detail, and later to visit the periods and scenes in which his ancestors lived. Describing how his first experience of 'dreaming true' differed from ordinary dreams, he compares it to a visit to the camera obscura:

It was something like the camera-obscura on Ramsgate pier: one goes in and finds one's self in total darkness . . . Suddenly there flashes on the sight the moving pictures of the port and all the life therein . . . [N]ot a detail is missed – not a button on a sailor's jacket, not a hair on his face. All the light and color of sea and earth and sky, that serve for many a mile around, are here concentrated within a few square feet. And what color it is! A painter's despair![29]

Unsurprisingly, the imaginary mobility offered by this technicolor dream world comes to gradually replace the real world of the prison as the centre of Peter's life. What the novel offers us, in effect, is a fable of the shift to an image-saturated, modern mass entertainment society, dominated by what Adorno and Horkheimer gloomily, but not entirely inaccurately, termed the 'culture industry'. As I shall show in a moment, this is also a fable of what Rosalind Williams has termed the 'dream world of mass consumption'. The little allegory almost seems parodic: though his life as an architect's assistant had been dreary enough, the novel makes him a literal prisoner, in order to point the contrast between his carceral everyday existence and the free flights of his dream world.[30] In that dream world he lives with the Duchess of Towers and is free to go almost anywhere in the world. Here we have Anthony Hope's reader, set free from the constraints of 'time and fate and circumstances', delivered from the prison-house of everyday life into the fulfilling world of 'true dreams'. All the plenitude of his happy childhood is there, but so are limitless possibilities for travel and for the experience of European cultural treasures.[31] The reader is never, of course, certain whether Peter is mad or not, and he dies in the asylum, writing the diary that is all the proof we have of his story.

If Du Maurier's romance reads society as a prison, there is more than a suggestion that its inmates *belong* in institutions. Read as a romance metanarrative, *Peter Ibbetson* is highly critical of the forms of subjectivity that create a demand for, and are sustained by, romance. Peter himself is imprisoned in his own subjectivity even before he is actually imprisoned; privatized to the point of solipsism, when he is not reading or dreaming, Peter is emotionless. Affect in *Peter Ibbetson* is literally a thing of the past, or of the imaginary.[32] Alienated from his colleagues and his relatives, before his initiation into 'true dreaming' Peter finds solace in contemporary English and French literature (156). It is tempting to recognize in him an early casualty of what Fredric Jameson terms the 'waning of affect' in postmodern, image-saturated society: while being deeply affected to the point of tears by the sight of the (spectral) figures of his long-dead parents, Peter is perfectly happy to club his (real) uncle to death. The only person Peter deeply cares for in the present is the Duchess, and she, it transpires, is really only available in the world of dreams. Du Maurier's version of the modern subject differs substantially from the 'pseudo-individual' theorized by Adorno and Horkheimer, but his cultural diagnosis is in general just as pessimistic as theirs.[33]

Even the escapism promised by 'dreaming true' turns out to be far from perfect. Although Peter's experience seems to be much more intense than that of the spectator of the camera obscura at Ramsgate, insofar as he can walk around and touch things, hear conversations, and effectively re-live the scenes of his past, we discover that he can't really effect anything in the dream world, because just as the characters can't hear him, the objects are unaffected by his touch: they are so many holographs. One of the activities Peter and the Duchess delight in is the garnering of 'dream versions' of their favourite paintings from the galleries of the world. This pleasure soon palls, though:

> Then suddenly, in the midst of all this unparalleled artistic splendour, we felt that a something was wanting. There was a certain hollowness about it; and we discovered that in our case the principal motives for collecting all these beautiful things were absent.
> 1. We were not the sole possessors.
> 2. We had nobody to show them to.
> 3. Therefore we could take no pride in them. (317)

The delightful world of imaginary escape turns out to be severely limited, since the possibility of recapturing the image of the past, or of sampling the visual treasures of the world (at no charge!) only opens up at the cost of the disappearance of the aura of things, and even of people. Here the novel's critique of the romance dream world, which I am arguing prefigures and overlaps with the imaginary pleasures of the cinema, shades into an account of the phantasmagoria of modern consumer culture as theorized by Walter Benjamin. Again, in this respect Du Maurier anticipates later theories of the imaginary of modernity. Anne Friedberg has recently argued that the 'mobile and virtual gaze' that cinema appeals to has a great deal in common with the gaze of the window shopper and other nineteenth-century figures and that 'The same impulse that sent flâneurs through the arcades, traversing the pavement and wearing thin their shoe leather, sent shoppers into the department stores, tourists to exhibitions, spectators into the panorama, diorama, wax museum, and cinema.'[34] And, one might add, sent readers of fiction to buy the romances of Haggard, Stevenson, Stoker, Du Maurier and their peers. Peter's complaint about 'a certain hollowness' would come to be an all too familiar component in accounts of twentieth-century popular culture, modern and postmodern, from jeremiads over the loss of aura, to accounts of how the past itself is only available to us as glossy pastiche. If Peter is an early example of the 'waning of affect', he is also an early sufferer from that 'nostalgia for the real' that comes to haunt a society of the image.

There is a further postmodern anticipation in the dream world of *Peter Ibbetson.* If there is more than a hint of condescension in the descriptions of the romance and film as 'dreamlike', it is a condescension that escapes the realization that experiential reality was undergoing a fundamental mutation, and that the phantasmagorias of modern, global consumer society were closer to the dream than to nineteenth-century realism. The romance was training people for that world just as the cinema would. And yet both, as part of the emergent entertainment industry, were also part of the 'problem', part of the modernizing process as much as theories of it.

ROMANCE AND THE RISE OF NARRATIVE FILM

Discussion of the relations of film and the romance in terms of images and dreams runs the risk of eliding the formal specificity of the two media. Nobody is likely to think that they are reading a novel when they are actually watching a film: the romance is above all a verbal, narrative form while cinema partakes of both narrative and spectacle, the sheer visuality of individual images always threatening to impede the forward motion of plot, or (in sound film) override the dialogue. But this distinction between the two may in turn shed some light on a transitional moment in cinema history. How does one explain the rapid rise to dominance of the narrative feature film? Early cinema is closer to the spectacle of the fair sideshow, or the music hall, both in terms of content and spectatorship.[35] If in its later career film threatened the survival of older forms of popular entertainment, in this period it existed in symbiosis with them, and many early one- and two-reelers were screened at fairs and carnivals, where they shared space with the Borneo man and the fat lady, or indeed with the Somali Village, as we saw in chapter 4. Friedberg argues that the nineteenth-century visual regime inaugurated by such phenomena as the panorama, the arcade, and the exhibition acts as a prologue to the dominance of cinema in the twentieth century. Her account of the emergence of a mobilized and virtual gaze in this period is very convincing, but it is somewhat difficult to explain the emergence of *narrative* cinema in terms of visuality alone. Towards the end of the first decade of the twentieth century – the dates vary from country to country – films with storylines start to displace films centred on spectacle, or the relatively straightforward recording of movement, 'actualities'. This tendency soon became the fixed pattern of development of the cinema industry to the extent that today when most people think of film, they think of the standard ninety-minute fictional narrative feature film, and what Noël Burch terms the Institutional Mode of Representation (IMR), deploying continuity editing, centring of the filmed subject, and a camera-identified implied viewer.[36] Spectacle certainly retains a vital role in popular film (as the work of Laura Mulvey among others has shown), but it rarely replaces narrative as the dominant element in filmic structure, even in the most elaborate of special-effects blockbusters.

I want to suggest now that the plots of popular romance served as an important bridge between the spectacular and the narrative phases of cinema. Noël Burch has argued that after a short period of 'primitive' film making, where various possibilities inherent in the film medium vied for dominance, an illusionist cinema arose that largely shared the representational aims of such nineteenth-century bourgeois forms as the theatre and the novel. I am suggesting, though, that it is the late nineteenth-century romance rather than the mid-century realist novel that anticipates the rise of narrative film. The romance comes from the same cultural nexus that produces commodity spectacles like the various great Exhibitions (London 1851, Paris 1867, 1889, 1900, Chicago 1893, etc.), as well as museums, galleries, arcades and other visual treats; significant connections can be seen to exist among the world-as-exhibition logic of, say, the Paris Exhibition of 1889, with its elaborate reconstruction of a Cairene street, the use of a similar logic in the early department stores, and the fantasies of visual mastery engaged by such map-centred novels as *King Solomon's Mines* (1885). But where the romance differs from these other forms of entertainment is in being strongly *narrative*-driven; the imaginary mobility offered by the romance is predicated on the storyline. It is possible to imagine, then, that the romance could have provided a bridge between a spectacular cinema powered by the pleasures of window shopping for the world, and one which engages the spectator at the level of plot, allowing him or her to enter the window display, as it were. The pleasures of looking could thus combine with those of imaginary agency (through identification with the active romance protagonist). If the first cinema-goers were afraid that the on-screen train of such films as the Lumières' *L'arrivée d'un train en gare de La Ciotat* (1895) would come steaming into the auditorium and crush them, their descendants were more likely to feel themselves to be on the train, moving through the filmic landscape and in a position of visual mastery, as in the early 'phantom rides'.[37] I offer this as a speculation, but what is certain is that when narrative drama displaced documentary and performance as the principal focus of film, the romance, as I have shown, was one of the most important sources for plots. As technology made longer and longer films possible, stories which sutured together spectacle (often imperial spectacle) and strong narrative development clearly possessed considerable attraction. Romance plots could exploit the appeal of imaginary globetrotting while adding narrative interest, as in those African safari films where stock footage of wildlife is intercut with dramatic or romantic scenes among the explorers.

POSTMODERN ROMANCE?

I have argued that the romance is in effect a form of popular modernism, if not the 'modernism in the streets' that Marshall Berman refers to then at least a modernism in the sitting room, and in the railway compartment. I have also shown, though, that a number of romance-revival tropes and plots survive in popular culture, and especially in cinema down to the present, albeit in modified form (rather as high modernism itself survives even in the aftermath of its cultural dominance). I would like to conclude by broaching the question of the connection betweeen the romance and *post*modernism. At the end of chapter 1 I suggested that the professionalized team of men we meet in *Dracula* continues to operate within present-day narratives of popular culture, but what of the other tropes I have described? To what extent do imperial and commodity romances survive into the postmodern? According to one influential theory, postmodernism 'reacts to the austere autonomy of high modernism by impudently embracing the language of commerce and the commodity'.[38] What sort of romance of the commodity would postmodernism create in that case? What would the postmodern version of the mummy story be like? At the same time, if the romance revival and modernism can be thought to exist in complex relation to contemporary imperialism, postmodernism must surely be thought of as existing in some general relation to post World War II decolonization, and to concomitant neocolonialism. What becomes of *King Solomon's Mines* in a postcolonial world? Does the survival of certain romance tropes simply connote a time-lag between historical transition and narrative artifact, or a resistance to historical change and a nostalgia for the past at the level of popular consciousness? Or have those surviving tropes undergone some mutation that enables them to continue to signify in a postmodern and postcolonial cultural economy?

It is possible to track the survival of imperial vision into the high modernist period, as I have shown in chapter 4. The example of Hemingway indicates that the imperial map of the world could also be redeployed in ways that altered its Anglocentrism without fundamentally changing the major divisions of modern/primitive. Nor does this map of the world necessarily disappear with the waning of high modernism; as Marianna Torgovnick argues, primitivist discourse cuts across the modernism/postmodernism divide.³⁹ Similarly, in his recent *Late Imperial Romance* John McClure has argued that the categories of imperial romance live on to underlie the fiction of US writers like Joan Didion, Don de Lillo and Thomas Pynchon. And while it ill behoves me, given the nature of my own study, to interpret thematic similarities as solid evidence for cultural continuities, it is difficult not to discern the persistence of imperial vision in such popular cultural phenomena as the *Indiana Jones* films, *A Passage to India* and *Out of Africa*.⁴⁰ Steven Spielberg was supposedly inspired to make the first of his enormously successful Indiana Jones films, *Raiders of the Lost Ark* (1981) after rereading *King Solomon's Mines*. *Raiders* offers itself as a tongue-in-cheek take on an older sort of adventure film, Saturday serials of the 1930s and 1940s like *Jungle Jim, Lash LaRue, Masked Marvel, Zorro's Fighting Legion* and *Secret Service in Darkest Africa*.⁴¹ This playful postmodern intertextuality may make an ideological reading of the film seem heavy-handed, but the playfulness provides but a thin veneer over the genuine nostalgia the film expresses for a time before decolonization, when the rest of the world provided a colourful backdrop for the adventures of Europeans and Americans. In this nostalgic world there are still blank spaces on the map, lost treasures with auratic powers, and plenty of expendable natives. The colonized know their place, and the real struggle for power is between the forces of good (Indiana, his friends, the USA) and the Nazis.⁴² There would appear to be good reason to believe that the romance of empire has taken quite happily to life in a postcolonial world.

But what of the mummy story? At the beginnning of this Afterword I suggested that the *fin-de-siècle* mummy story is not really the ancestor of the more familiar mummy's curse stories that appear after the Tutankhamen excavations, and that still linger in the imaginary of B-movie horror. Does the mummy story have *any* postmodern equivalent, then? If we want a contemporary heir to the late Victorian commodity romance, I would argue that we have to look not to relatively recent horror film versions of the reanimated mummy (such as *Blood from the Mummy's Tomb* [1971], and *The Mummy Lives* [1992]), but rather to science fiction. The postmodern commodity story replaces the human/commodity relation with the human/android. One of the most influential treatments of this theme in the 1980s was Ridley Scott's visually overwhelming *Blade Runner* (1982),[43] based on Philip K. Dick's *Do Androids Dream of Electric Sheep?*, in which a 'blade runner', a government-employed Los Angeles detective/exterminator, Deckard, has the job of tracking down and destroying four sophisticated androids who have illegally returned to the Earth after fighting their way out of an off-world colony.[44] His mission is made more complicated by the fact that the 'replicants' are identical to humans, and by his emotional involvement with another replicant, Rachael. She is an experimental model whose 'humanity' has been enhanced by equipping her with implanted memories of her childhood; when Deckard meets her she doesn't even know that she is a replicant.

As Donna J. Haraway has written, the story can be understood as a late twentieth-century meditation on the blurring of the lines between the organic and the mechanical, human and not-human. Changing social realities and information and body technologies have made the cyborg, 'a hybrid of machine and organism' the stuff of reality as well as science fiction, and Haraway reads the character of Rachael as an embodiment of the 'fear, love, and confusion' of a cyborg culture.[45] The film also puts in play issues of urban degeneration, the US as a multi-ethnic society, corporate power, and a variety of other concerns that we cannot explore here. However, the film version (more than the book, perhaps) also ponders the relations of humans and commodities in an advanced consumer culture. We are cued to this early on in the film by the sheer omnipresence of advertising images in this future city: giant screens flash ads for a variety of commodities in several languages (Atari, Coca-Cola, TDK, Kyoryoku Wakamoto [sc. a Japanese indigestion remedy][46]); overhead, spacecraft bombard pedestrians with the attractions of off-world colonial life (in a 'golden land of opportunity and adventure').[47] All of this is close enough to the advertising techniques of the present for it to seem even more oppressive, and we are reminded that Ridley Scott himself made a number of innovative and influential ads earlier in his career. It is sometimes difficult to establish just what is going on in particular scenes, not just because of the underlighting and the use of rain, smoke and steam that inspired one critic to describe the film as 'a firework display seen through thick fog', but also because of the visual clutter of the *mise en scène* – this is an object-rich world. The flotsam and jetsam of an advanced consumer society, what Dick's novel terms 'kipple', is strewn everywhere. The underlighting and the smoky interiors and seedy cityscapes graphically link Scott's film to older narratives of urban detection, to the world of 1940s *film noir* – Deckard is a latter-day Philip

Marlowe – but also to the nineteenth-century fiction that presents the detective as an object expert (the two linked, perhaps, by those 'Victorian *noir*' cinema and television versions of the Sherlock Holmes stories that project Conan Doyle's modern detective back into the mid-Victorian era by representing London as a smoky, gaslit sound stage of hansom cabs and pea-soupers). The postmodern detective is at once Philip Marlowe and Sherlock Holmes: the people he must track down are quite literally runaway goods. *Blade Runner* is also a sort of neo-invasion story, not dissimilar to *Iras, A Mystery*, or *Dracula*, in which objects/people are smuggled, or smuggle themselves through national borders. Here Britain is replaced with the Earth itself, though in a familiar Hollywood synecdoche the US (Los Angeles, in fact) stands in for the rest of the world.[48]

The use of earlier visual codes and narrative patterns cannot simply be read as typical 'postmodern pastiche', however. These reanimations of older codes also reflect the fact that some of the older problems represented in those codes – the cognitive mapping of urban space, commodity fetishism – have not gone away. One of the most striking sequences in the film, Deckard's shooting of the replicant, Zhora, also takes us back to the nineteenth-century origins of the commodity problematic. Using decidedly Holmesian methods, Deckard tracks Zhora down to the nightclub where she performs a pornographic floorshow with an artificial snake (the club's owners don't know that she too is 'artificial'). When she realizes who Deckard is, she runs off, and a chase sequence ensues, in which she is pursued through the streets wearing a transparent raincoat over her fairly minimal costume. Deckard shoots her as she plunges through a series of shopping arcade windows (a slow-motion sequence) and we see her slow-run past several series of fashion mannequins before she plunges through a final window and falls. We see her lying dead, gift-wrapped in her plastic macintosh flanked by the 'other' mannequins advertising goods for the Christmas market, while artificial snow falls around her.[49] It is in effect a return to a nineteenth-century 'primal scene' of commodity culture: the arcade with its plate-glass window and eye-catching window display.[50] Zhora, like an animated mannequin who has escaped from the other side of the glass, is reduced to her proper status by the urban detective and commodity-expert, Deckard. W. F. Haug's theory that all commodities become sexualized under capitalism is here literalized: a near-naked dead female on display becomes a grim emblem of the logic of consumer culture, a figure from the necrophile side of commodity fetishism that Walter Benjamin termed the marriage of the 'living body to the inorganic world'.[51] Since her own skin is what is on display (the replicants are interestingly known as 'skin jobs'), it is only appropriate that Zhora's wrapping-turned-shroud is transparent.

But if the detection-plot drive to stabilize people/commodity relations is one tendency of the film, there is a much stronger counter-pull to destabilize them. The detective's relationship to Rachael dramatizes this theme most clearly. Rather like Lavenham in *Iras, A Mystery*, Deckard falls in love with Rachael, even though he knows she is a replicant, with a battery of synthetic memories and emotional responses. He cannot bring himself to 'retire' Rachael, and the film's ending suggests that they pursue a future together.[52] As in the case of the mummy stories, romance partly works to reinscribe subject/object hierarchies (Harrison Ford as Deckard is presented as the hard-edged and masculine complement to Sean Young's doll-like and almost parodically feminine Rachael), but fails to do so completely, the consumer/detective's desire placing him under the spell of the commodity/replicant. However, *Blade Runner*, as a product of the 1980s rather than the 1890s, takes the breakdown of people/commodities relations much further. The mummy-loving protagonists of 'Smith and the Pharaohs' and *She* ran the risk of their own objectification, but in *Blade Runner* we are led to question the possibility of ever distinguishing definitively between people and commodities, in this case between what is born and what is built. The rogue replicants, especially Roy Batty, their leader, seem to be capable of a wide range of 'human' emotions – rather more so than their icy creator, Tyrell. Human/ replicant undecidability is also explored though, through the character Deckard, whose human status is far from certain: the detective, the imaginary stabilizer of nineteenth-century object culture, may after all himself be just another commodity.[53] There seems more than a hint of mockery in the air when a fellow detective, Gaff, comments that by killing Roy Batty, the most fearsome replicant, Deckard has 'done a man's job'. The same Gaff has a habit of leaving little origami figures as his calling card. Deckard finds one of these, a silver-paper unicorn, at his apartment, just before he leaves with Rachael for a new life. Deckard has earlier dreamt of a unicorn, and we are led to wonder whether Gaff shares this (implanted?) dream, or whether he is familiar with Deckard's dreams because he has seen the details of his implanted memories, just as Deckard knows Rachael's childhood memories because he has read her file. Even Zhora's comment to him at the nightclub (where he pretends to be a representative of the 'American

Federation of Variety Artists' investigating the exploitation of per-
formers), 'Are you for real', seems to be double-edged.[54]

The question of Deckard's human/replicant status is inflected by one
of the film's main 'postmodern' themes, the status of truth or history in
an image-saturated society.[55] Here *Blade Runner* explores the same meta-
filmic territory as films like *Total Recall* (also based on a Philip K. Dick
story, *We Can Dream it for You Wholesale*) and the more recent *Strange Days*,
which both touch on film as a 'commodity experience', to use Anne
Friedberg's term, that has hollowed out 'authentic' experience. In *Blade
Runner* this theme is carried by the use of photographs, reminding us of
the nineteenth-century origins of film technology. A number of the
film's characters, including Deckard, display a strong attachment to
photographic images, which appear to offer representations of personal
ties to an older, less kipple-filled world.[56] In the scene at his apartment
after Deckard has killed Zhora, and has in turn been saved from death
by Rachael, she asks him if he has ever taken the Voigt-Kampff test, an
empathy test used to identify replicants (one of the film's many metafil-
mic motifs – film spectatorship is itself a sort of 'empathy test'). He
doesn't reply because he has fallen asleep, but the question echoes in the
viewer's mind. Earlier we learn that the photograph Rachael possesses
of her childhood is falsified – part of the 'emotional cushion' that Tyrell
plans to supply to replicants to make them more manageable – but
Deckard too possesses a number of old family photographs (some of
which look to be from the nineteenth century), and Rachael looks
through them while he sleeps, as if to suggest that his past is just as likely
to be made to order. In Kaja Silverman's words, these photographs 'are
less signifiers of the past than props for Deckard's fantasies, much as
Rachael's and Leon's are'.[57] When Rachael changes her hair-style to
match one of the photographs, she is taking a role for herself in
Deckard's fantasy world, blurring further the distinctions between past/
present, human/replicant, authentic/artificial.

Despite its apparent iconicity, the photograph is a peculiarly fragile
guarantee of the past: the birth of the documentary technologies of
photography and film in the nineteenth century meant also, after all, the
birth of trick photography and special effects. *Blade Runner* thus twins the
infinitely reproducible factory commodity, the replicant, with the mech-
anically reproduced image: both operate according to the logic of the
simulacrum, the copy for which there is no original, or, which is slightly
different, the copy for which the question of the original becomes
irrelevant, and both put human identity in question. Again these are

problematics formed in the nineteenth century, though they had acquired a greater degree of urgency, perhaps, in the US of the early 1980s, the beginning of the Reagan era and the appearance of the 'yuppie', a new breed of conspicuous consumer.[58] When the definition of self grows to increasingly depend on the purchase of 'name-brand' products, how does one escape the conclusion that individuality too is simulacral, that the line between supposedly unique people and supposedly replaceable things is written in pencil? When history and the personal past only appear to us through the mediations of the nostalgia industry, how does one escape the conclusion that memory as the guarantee of identity is fundamentally unreliable? Interestingly, *Blade Runner* seems to partly embrace these conclusions rather than retreating into nostalgia for the real, as Dick's *Do Androids Dream of Electric Sheep?* does.

While it is perhaps unwise to read cultural trends from individual films, this last aspect of Scott's film also indicates that the spell cast by the late nineteenth-century imaginary may be weakening, that the categories that have animated much of twentieth-century culture, popular and high modernist alike, may yield to others. Both *Raiders* and *Blade Runner* can be lumped together as examples of postmodern cinema, then, but their different orientations indicate residual and emergent ideologies of modernity. If *Raiders of the Lost Ark*, and indeed its sequels, *Indiana Jones and the Temple of Doom* (1984) and *Indiana Jones and The Last Crusade* (1989), cling to a version of the modernist primitivist fantasy, the fantasy of a space outside modernity, and of authentic objects secreted away in the blank spaces of the map, *Blade Runner* seems prepared to leave that fantasy behind for good. It is worth noting, of course, that in terms of box-office appeal, Spielberg's imperial nostalgia yarns dramatically out-performed Scott's tale of urban detection, which after a limited cinema release was consigned to the twilight world of cable television, though enjoying a certain cult following. Thus if *Blade Runner* seems to suggest it is time to rethink the categories of the romance, there are plenty of reasons to believe that international popular culture will continue to replicate the imaginary of the *fin de siècle* for some time yet.

Notes

INTRODUCTION

1 See *The Academy: A Weekly Review of Literature and Life*, 6 January 1900, page 3 for a reproduction of the first page of the programme, and R. W. Stallman, *Stephen Crane: A Biography* (New York: George Brazilier, 1968) 491–3, 556–7, for a more detailed account of the play and the party. H. G. Wells also describes the event in his *Experiment in Autobiography: Discoveries and Conclusions of a Very Ordinary Brain (since 1866)* (New York: Macmillan, 1934; repr. Faber and Faber, 1984).

2 Wells, *Experiment in Autobiography* vol. 2, 613.

3 Cited in Stallman, *Stephen Crane* 491.

4 *Experiment in Autobiography* 614.

5 Ibid. 615.

6 In *After the Great Divide: Modernism, Mass Culture, Postmodernism* (Bloomington and Indianapolis: Indiana University Press, 1986) Huyssen discusses the formation of a discourse that distinguishes between 'high' and 'low' culture from the mid nineteenth century on. This discourse appears later in Britain than in the continental literature on which he concentrates.

7 This is the phrase used by Jonathan Harker in *Dracula* when he feels he is being drawn into the Gothic past, but knows that he is firmly anchored in the present.

8 For a complete list of sources on the play see R. W. Stallman, *Stephen Crane: A Critical Bibliography* (Iowa: Iowa State University Press, 1972).

9 Stevenson, of course, died five years before Crane's party, and his critical exchange with Henry James took place in 1884, but as the party itself suggests the same inclusive literary culture certainly survived at least into the 1890s.

10 Leon Edel, *Henry James: A Life* (London: Collins, 1987) 454. As Edel records, James found the romances of H. Rider Haggard less to his taste, but while the violence of H. Rider Haggard's *King Solomon's Mines* and *She* 'unexpectedly depressed' him, he nevertheless read them.

11 Within British cultural studies this polarization has reappeared in a slightly different form as the split between culturalist (reading for popular resistance) and structuralist (emphasizing the extent to which individuals are the

bearers of cultural structures) approaches to the study of popular culture. See Tony Bennett's Introduction to *Popular Culture and Social Relations*, ed. Bennett, Colin Mercer and Janet Woollacott (Milton Keynes and Philadelphia: Open University Press, 1986) and Stuart Hall, 'Notes on Deconstructing the Popular', in John Storey, ed., *Cultural Theory and Popular Culture: A Reader* (New York and London: Harvester, 1994) 455–66, reprinted from R. Samuel, ed, *People's History and Socialist Theory* (London: Routledge, 1981). For Hall, the contents of the term popular culture are always changing, and forms which were once popular may 'become enhanced in cultural value, go up the cultural escalator – and find themselves on the opposite side' (461).

12 To this extent I am following the lead of studies like Michael Denning's *Cover Stories: Narrative and Ideology in the British Spy Thriller* (London: Routledge and Kegan Paul, 1987) and Tony Bennett and Janet Woollacott's *Bond and Beyond: The Political Career of a Popular Hero* (London: Methuen, 1986).

13 Bennett, Introduction, *Popular Culture and Social Relations*.

14 Hall, 'Notes on Deconstructing the Popular', 462.

15 John Frow argues that Hall's approach (which Frow traces to the work of Ernesto Laclau and Chantal Mouffe), by severing the link between culture and class, leads to an unhelpfully narrow definition of class as a purely economic phenomenon, leaving the 'popular' to be defined exclusively in political terms. See John Frow, *Cultural Studies and Cultural Value* (Oxford: Clarendon Press, 1995) 70–80.

16 John Fiske, *Reading the Popular* (Boston: Unwin Hyman, 1989) 2.

17 Quoted in Frow, *Cultural Studies and Cultural Value* 61.

18 Michel de Certeau, *The Practice of Everyday Life*, trans. Steven Rendall (Berkeley, University of California Press, 1988) xiv.

19 While trying to avoid class essentialism, this study employs class as a principal term of analysis for the study of the Victorian period. For a cogent critique of this approach see Patrick Joyce, *Democratic Subjects: The Self and the Social in Nineteenth-Century England* (Cambridge: Cambridge University Press, 1994). Joyce argues that class and 'the social' only come into their own as terms for self-definition at the end of the nineteenth century (on 'the social' see chapter 1 below). On recent debates over class in British historiography see Christopher Kent, 'Victorian Social History: Post-Thompson, Post-Foucault, Postmodern', *Victorian Studies* 40.1 (Autumn 1996) 97–133.

20 See Frow, *Cultural Studies and Cultural Value* 130. On the varying definitions of this 'knowledge class' see 111–30.

21 On the relation of the romance to the domestic novel, see for example Lafcadio Hearn's lecture on the English novel, cited in Harold Orel, *Popular Fiction in England, 1914–1918* (Kentucky: University Press of Kentucky, 1992), ch. 1. Hearn saw George du Maurier, R. L. Stevenson and Rudyard Kipling as the writers who had done most to end the reign of the domestic novel. On the romance revival in general see the essays by R. L. Stevenson, George Saintsbury and Hall Caine collected in John Charles Olmsted's *A*

Victorian Art of Fiction (New York and London: Garland, 1979). For a recent attempt to theorize the shift, see ch. 5 of Elaine Showalter's *Sexual Anarchy: Gender and Culture at the Fin de Siècle* (New York: Penguin, 1990), which analyses the eclipse of the domestic novel and the rise of romance in terms of contemporary gender politics.

22 *Social Text* 1 (1979) 130–48 (141).

23 *The Political Unconscious: Narrative as a Socially Symbolic Act* (Ithaca: Cornell University Press, 1981) 206.

24 Ibid. 207.

25 Ibid. 230.

26 Ibid. 236.

27 Marshall Berman, *All that Is Solid Melts into Air: the Experience of Modernity* (London: Verso, 1983) 5.

28 Ibid. 12, 31.

29 My use of the term 'popular modernism' also owes something to Bill Schwarz's use of the term in 'Englishness and the Paradox of Modernity', *New Formations* 1 (Spring 1987): 147–53. Schwarz associates popular modernism with 'cinema, radio, fashion and beauty contests, mass advertising, airplanes and automobiles, a profusion of daily papers, detective and science fiction, funfairs, Charlie Chaplin, skyscrapers . . .' (152).

30 For a critique of Berman's work and for Berman's response, see Perry Anderson, 'Modernity and Revolution' and Marshall Berman, 'The Signs in the Street: a Response to Perry Anderson', *New Left Review* 144 (1984). Anderson's essay is reprinted in Cary Nelson and Lawrence Grossberg, eds., *Marxism and the Interpretation of Culture* (Urbana and Chicago: University of Illinois Press, 1988) 317–33.

31 *High and Low Moderns* (New York and Oxford: Oxford University Press, 1996) 9. While working within a rather different problematic, Paul Gilroy has recently attempted to complicate our perception of modernity by arguing that 'modernity might itself be thought to begin in the constitutive relationships with outsiders', suggesting that any account of the modern that leaves out the part that the 'black Atlantic', the diasporic history of black Africa, played in its creation must be incomplete. Paul Gilroy, *Black Atlantic: Modernity and Double Consciousness* (London: Verso, 1993) 17. For other recent attempts to reopen the case of modernism and/or modernity see Houston Baker, *Modernism and the Harlem Renaissance* (Chicago and London: University of California Press, 1987), Bonnie Kime Scott, *The Gender of Modernism: A Critical Anthology*, Suzanne Clark, *Sentimental Modernism: Women Writers and the Revolution of the Word* (Bloomington and Indianapolis: Indiana, 1991), Michael North, *The Dialect of Modernism: Race, Language, and Twentieth-Century Literature* (Oxford: Oxford University Press, 1994), and Jon Thompson, *Fiction, Crime and Empire: Clues to Modernity and Postmodernism* (Urbana and Chicago: University of Illinois Press, 1993). For a collection of essays that takes up the work of Berman and Gilroy in relation to British culture, see Mica Nava and Alan O'Shea, eds., *Modern Times: Reflections on a Century of*

English Modernity (London and New York: Routledge, 1996). While not centrally concerned with modernism, David Glover's recent *Vampires, Mummies and Liberals: Bram Stoker and the Politics of Popular Fiction* (Durham and London: Duke University Press, 1996) shows how the positioning of sexuality at the centre of human identity is part of a specifically modern sexual discourse that links a popular writer like Bram Stoker to writers such as D. H. Lawrence and Radclyffe Hall (see esp. 100–35).

32 Benjamin was not, of course, the only pioneer. He himself was partly developing the insights of Georg Simmel's 1903 essay, 'The Metropolis and Mental Life'. Dolf Sternberger, Siegfried Giedion and, more recently, Wolfgang Schivelbusch and Christoph Asendorf have explored different sectors of this same cultural-historical territory. A stream of studies that develop the Benjaminian project in a more literary-critical direction have appeared, such as Rosalind Williams's *Dream Worlds: Mass Consumption in Late Nineteenth-Century France* (Berkeley: University of California Press, 1982), Rachel Bowlby's *Just Looking: Consumer Culture in Dreiser, Gissing and Zola* (New York: Methuen, 1985), Jennifer Wicke's *Advertising Fictions: Literature, Advertising and Social Reading* (New York: Columbia University Press, 1988), and Thomas Richards's *The Commodity Culture of Victorian England: Advertising as Spectacle, 1851–1914* (Stanford: Stanford University Press, 1990).

33 'Notes on Deconstructing the Popular' 457.

34 On the potential usefulness of the term 'structure of feeling' in this connection see *Modern Times* 2.

35 These terms have been recently used by Eve Kosofsky Sedgwick, Patrick Brantlinger and Kathleen Spencer respectively. See *Between Men: English Literature and Homosocial Desire* (New York: Columbia University Press, 1985) 96, *Rule of Darkness: British Literature and Imperialism, 1830–1914* (Ithaca and London: Cornell University Press 1988), and 'Purity and Danger: *Dracula*, the Urban Gothic, and the Late Victorian Degeneracy Crisis', *ELH* 59 (1992) 197–225.

36 By the time of the Villa Diodati party, then, the period of Gothic's ascendancy was almost over. However, on the lingering popularity of Gothic in the early Victorian period see Richard D. Altick, *The English Common Reader: A Social History of the Mass Reading Public 1800–1900* (Chicago: University of Chicago Press, 1957).

37 Terry Lovell, *Consuming Fiction* (London: Verso, 1987).

38 Gary Kelly, *English Fiction of the Romantic Period 1789–1830* (London and New York: Longman, 1989) 42.

39 See her *The Gothic Novel 1790–1830: Plot Summaries and Index to Motifs* (Lexington: University of Kentucky Press, 1981) 10. The critical focus on four or five novels – generally those by Radcliffe, Lewis, Walpole and Godwin – may mislead us as to what most people were actually reading. Tracy's book gives one a good idea of the range of the more 'average' Gothic novel.

40 See Kelly on the readership of the late eighteenth-century novel. On gender and the role of the circulating libraries in shaping the literary

market, see for example the review of recent scholarship in Edward Jacobs, 'Anonymous Signatures: Circulating Libraries, Conventionality, and the Production of Gothic Romances', *ELH* 62 (1995) 603–29.

41 See D. S. Higgins, *Rider Haggard: The Great Storyteller* (London: Cassell, 1981) 187. I would suggest, somewhat tentatively, that both Gothic and the *fin-de-siècle* romance take part in the modernization of British culture, but they belong to very different phases of that modernization.

42 Cited from Bürger's *Theory of the Avant-Garde* in Tony Bennett, *Outside Literature* (London: Routledge, 1990) 80. In formulating my own views on the importance of reception and production I have found Bennett's work, both this text and his earlier work on 'reading formations', invaluable.

43 *The Tale of Terror: A Study of the Gothic Romance* (1921; New York: Russell and Russell, 1963).

44 Montague Summers early noted the surrealists' attempts to annex Gothic, and dismissed it with some hostility in the last chapter of *The Gothic Quest* (1938; New York: Russell and Russell, 1964). Varma, however, in *The Gothic Flame* (London: Barker, 1957) was much more open to the idea of surrealism's Gothic ancestry, though he saw the early nineteenth-century Gothic 'fragments' as more likely predecessors than the Gothic novel (221–3).

45 Vijay Mishra, *The Gothic Sublime* (Albany: SUNY Press, c.1994) 8.

46 Elizabeth MacAndrew, *The Gothic Tradition in Fiction* (New York: Columbia University Press, 1979); William Patrick Day, *In the Circles of Fear and Desire* (Chicago: Chicago University Press, 1985); David Punter, *The Literature of Terror* (London: Longman, 1980). Eve Kosofsky Sedgwick's *Between Men* is not a Gothic survey as such, but it does advance an innovative theory of Gothic fiction which has attracted a good deal of attention.

47 For a good critical account see Jacqueline Howard, *Rereading Gothic: A Bakhtinian Approach.* (Oxford: Clarendon Press, 1994).

48 Edmund Gosse, 'The Tyranny of the Novel', originally published in the *National Review* 19 (April 1892) 163–75, reprinted in John Charles Olmsted, ed., *A Victorian Art of Fiction: Essays on the Novel in British Periodicals 1870–1900* (New York and London: Garland, 1979) 519–33 (522). Gosse is not, he assures us, altogether unhappy under the novel's 'tyranny', but he wishes it to use its power wisely by extending its range past the 'mere record of the billing and cooing of the callow young' (530), something he sees all too much of in the average circulating library novel.

49 The modern writers are designated by school: there is a Realist, a Romancist, an Elsmerian (from Mrs Humphry Ward's popular novel of religious doubt, *Robert Elsmere*), a Stylist, and, a late arrival at the gathering, an American Analyst (who represents the 'school' of Henry James and W. D. Howells). Barrie's descriptions of each of these are far from casual. In fact he puts in their mouths critical pronouncements by recent commentators on the novel, including passages from W. D. Howells (an American Analyst) and Hall Caine (a Romancist).

50 Olmsted, *A Victorian Art of Fiction* 485.

51 George Saintsbury, *The Later Nineteenth Century* (Edinburgh and London: Blackwood, 1907) 392.

52 'The Art of Fiction' (*Longman's Magazine*, September 1884), reprinted in William Veeder and Susan M. Griffin, eds., *The Art of Criticism: Henry James and the Theory and Practice of Fiction* (Chicago and London: Chicago University Press, c.1986) 165–83 (180). See 184–88 for a detailed account of the controversy between Walter Besant, James and Stevenson over the nature of the novel.

53 William Lyon Phelps, *The Advance of the English Novel* (London: John Murray, 1919) 136, 137, 140. Phelps sees 1894–1904 as the golden years of the Romantic Revival, though this late starting point may owe something to his American perspective. The novels that Phelps points to in 1894 include Kipling's *The Jungle Book*, Weyman's *Under the Red Robe* and Hope's *The Prisoner of Zenda*. Interestingly he sees *Trilby* as part of the previous wave of realism. Writing in 1907, George Saintsbury notes the importance of the 'New Romance', as he styles it, but refrains from commenting on the many living authors of the romance. He restricts himself to two romancists who were dead by then: R. L. Stevenson and, rather curiously, William Morris. See *The Later Nineteenth Century* 127–9.

54 R. L. Stevenson, 'A Gossip on Romance', *Longman's Magazine* 1 (November 1882) 69–79 (69). He sounds a similar note in his response to James's 'Art of Fiction', arguing that the 'luxury' of the novel of adventure is 'to lay by our judgement, to be submerged by the tale as by a billow'. See 'A Humble Remonstrance', *Longman's Magazine*, December 1884, reprinted in Claire Harman, ed., *R. L. Stevenson: Essays and Poems* (London: Everyman, 1992) 179–88 (183). Cf. Haggard's defence of romance in the *Contemporary Review* 51 (1887) 172–180, where romance is seen as satisfying the craving of the public 'to be taken out of themselves' (173). The 'weary public' is exhausted from 'the toil and emptiness and vexation of our competitive existence' (174).

55 Stevenson, 'A Gossip on Romance' 73.

56 Ibid. 77.

57 Ibid. 72.

58 On the theory of degeneration see Daniel Pick, *Faces of Degeneration: A European Disorder, c. 1848–1918* (Cambridge: Cambridge University Press, 1993).

59 Andrew Lang, 'Realism and Romance', *Contemporary Review* 52 (1887) 683–93.

60 Ibid. 688.

61 Phelps, *The Advance of the English Novel* 138.

62 'Realism and Romance' 689–90.

63 See Showalter, *Sexual Anarchy* 78–81.

64 On the changes in the publishing industry, see Peter Keating, *The Haunted Study: A Social History of the English Novel 1875–1914* (London: Secker and Warburg, 1989) and his Introduction to the Oxford Popular Fiction edition

of Marie Corelli's *The Sorrows of Satan* (1895; Oxford and New York: Oxford University Press, 1996), Feltes, *Modes of Production of Victorian Novels*, Raymond Williams, *The Long Revolution* (London: Chatto and Windus, 1961) and Michael Denning, *Cover Stories: Narrative and Ideology in the British Spy Thriller* (London and New York: Routledge and Kegan Paul, 1987), ch. 1. See also Altick, *The English Common Reader*, ch. 13, on the triumph of the 'cheap books' movement.

65 I do not wish to repeat here that hoary old version of cultural history that explains the new market for entertainment literature and popular journalism on the basis that Forster's Education Bill of 1870 created a new class of literate but unliterary readers. This legend was effectively put to rest some years ago by Raymond Williams who points out that the substantial readership figures for the popular Sunday newspapers predate the Education Bill. See *The Long Revolution* 173–9.

66 Patricia Anderson, in *The Printed Image and the Transformation of Popular Culture 1790–1860* (Oxford: Clarendon Press, 1991), argues that a modern mass culture begins to take shape rather earlier through illustrated magazines like the *Penny Magazine* and *Reynold's Miscellany*. There are clearly differences of scale between this earlier phase of the mass market and the phase I am talking about, but more importantly, perhaps, the figures it generated by the romance live on, albeit in modified forms, in twentieth-century popular culture, while the 'cult figures' of the earlier literature, like Dick Turpin and Jack Sheppard, fall out of the cultural imaginary before the end of the century.

67 Feltes sees the earlier boom in journalism as simply a 'moment . . . in the whole process culminating in the "new journalism" of the 1880s and 90s' (*Modes of Production* 66).

68 Rudyard Kipling, 'The Three-Decker', in *The Seven Seas* (London: Methuen, 1896) 134–8. Interestingly, Kipling sees Haggard's *She* as continuing the mission of the three-decker: '*She*'s taking tired people to the Islands of the Blest!'

69 Keating, *The Haunted Study* 32.

70 Ibid. 34.

71 Ibid. 56–74.

72 For a useful account of the problems with the term 'mass', see Anderson, *The Printed Image* 7–12.

73 See Cedric Watts, 'Marketing Modernism: How Conrad Prospered', in Ian Willison, Warwick Gould and Warren Cherniak, eds., *Modernist Writers and the Marketplace* (Basingstoke: Macmillan, 1996) 81–8 (83). As Frederick R. Karl notes, Conrad was so appalled at this circumstance that he allowed T. P. O'Connor to re-edit the novel himelf for its serialization, and refused to read proofs. See Karl's *Joseph Conrad: The Three Lives* (New York: Farrar, Straus and Giroux, 1979) 555.

74 Feltes, *Modes of Production* 63.

75 Keating, *The Haunted Study* 43.

76 Ibid. 16.

77 In *Sexual Anarchy* Showalter represents the romance trend as a reaction against the domination of the market by domestic realism, and by that of George Eliot in particular. The 'boys club' of Kipling, Stevenson and Haggard is thus an aggressive attempt to deny Eliot's influence. While this is an engaging explanation, it underestimates the extent to which the writers of romance were affected by large-scale changes in the market.

78 Lang, 'Realism and Romance' 690.

79 See W. Hamish Fraser, *The Coming of the Mass Market, 1850–1914* (Hamden, CT: Archon, 1981).

80 There are, of course, older ways of dividing high and low literary culture. As Patricia Anderson shows, there was evident middle-class hostility to the 'penny dreadfuls' and other forms of popular literature. But the clear division of *middle-class* literature into high and low categories only appears in the period I am discussing, and the theorization of 'mass culture' in the work of T. S. Eliot, F. R. Leavis, Theodor Adorno and others belongs to the era of high modernism.

81 See Thomas Strychacz, *Modernism, Mass Culture and Professionalism* (Cambridge: Cambridge University Press, 1993).

82 Huyssen, *After the Great Divide* 46.

83 Suzanne Clark, *Sentimental Modernism: Women Writers and the Revolution of the Word* (Bloomington and Indianapolis: Indiana University Press, 1991) 9.

84 Marianna Torgovnick, *Gone Primitive: Savage Intellects, Modern Lives* (Chicago: Chicago UP, 1990).

85 David Harvey, *The Condition of Postmodernity: An Enquiry into the Origins of Cultural Change* (Cambridge, MA, and Oxford: Blackwell, 1990) 23.

86 On modernism and professionalism see Strychacz, *Modernism, Mass Culture and Professionalism*; on modernism and imperialism see Edward Said, *Culture and Imperialism* (New York: Knopf, 1993); on modernism and consumer culture see, for example, Jennifer Wicke, '*Mrs Dalloway* Goes to Market: Woolf, Keynes, and Modern Markets', *Novel* 28.1 (1994) 5–23.

87 See Louis Althusser, 'Ideology and the Ideological State Apparatuses' in *Lenin and Philosophy and other Essays* (New York: Monthly Review Press, 1971).

88 e.g. Barthes and Levi-Strauss. For an excellent discussion of the use of the concept of myth in analyses of popular fiction – notably *Dracula* in both Bram Stoker's and Francis Ford Coppola's versions – see David Glover, 'Travels in Romania: Myths of Origin, Myths of Blood' *Discourse* 16.1 (1993) 126–44.

89 Gianni Vattimo, *The Transparent Society*, trans. David Webb (Cambridge: Polity Press, 1992), ch. 3, 'Myth Rediscovered', especially 35–6. On Althusser, fiction and ideology, see Lennard Davis, *Factual Fictions: the Origins of the English Novel* (New York: Columbia, 1983), ch. 12.

90 See Gordon Martel, 'The Meaning of Power: Rethinking the Decline and Fall of Great Britain', *International History Review* 13.4 (November 1991)

661–880 (667, 663).

91 Martin Wiener, *English Culture and the Decline of the Industrial Spirit, 1850–1980* (Cambridge: Cambridge University Press, 1981).

92 W. D. Rubinstein, *Capitalism, Culture, and Decline in Britain, 1750–1990* (London: Routledge, 1993). See especially Martel's 'The Meaning of Power', Keith Nelson's ' "Greatly Exaggerated": The Myth of the Decline of Great Britain before 1914', and John R. Ferris, ' "The Greatest Power on Earth": Great Britain in the 1920s', *International History Review* 13.4 (November 1991) 695–725, and 726–50. On the survival of imperial ideologies in Britain until the 1950s see John M. MacKenzie, *Propaganda and Empire* (Manchester: Manchester University Press, 1984).

93 For a more complete list of those historical processes that might be seen to constitute the modern see Berman, *All that is Solid Melts into Air* 16.

94 Chris Marker's filmic meditation on representation and history, *Sans Soleil* (France: Argos Films, 1983) explores vertigo as a metaphor for the relation to the past.

1 INCORPORATED BODIES: *DRACULA* AND PROFESSIONALISM

1 By male homosocial I mean those ties between men which, while fostering close and even highly charged bonds between them, proscribe homoerotic contact. See Eve Kosofsky Sedgwick, *Between Men: English Literature and Homosocial Desire* (New York: Columbia University Press, 1985) ch. 1 *et passim.*

2 *The Rise of Professional Society: England since 1880* (London and New York: Routledge, 1989).

3 *Fiction, Crime and Empire: Clues to Modernity and Postmodernism* (Urbana and Chicago: University of Illinois Press, 1993) 28.

4 Patrick Brantlinger, *Rule of Darkness: British Literature and Imperialism, 1830–1914* (Ithaca and London: Cornell University Press, 1988) 230.

5 *Degeneration* (London: Heinemann, 1895) vii. Nordau did not, however, assume that degeneration was linked to the end of the century. Rather, the root cause of degeneration was modernity itself: people were being poisoned with bad foodstuffs, tobacco, opium, urban pollution and, more importantly, they were suffering from hysterical fatigue because of the accelerated pace of nineteenth-century life. The first generation who felt the full force of nineteenth-century modernization suffered from 'acquired' hysteria, a form of organic damage to the nerves, which they passed on genetically to their children. See *Degeneration* 39–40.

6 Quoted in Daniel Pick, *Faces of Degeneration: A European Disorder, c.1848–1918* (Cambridge: Cambridge University Press, 1993) 24 and 24n.

7 Bram Dijkstra, *Idols of Perversity: Fantasies of Feminine Evil in Fin-de-Siècle Culture* (Oxford: Oxford University Press, 1986) ch. 7. On the impact of Nordau see Pick, *Faces of Degeneration*, ch. 6; and William Greenslade, *Degeneration, Culture and the Novel 1880–1940* (Cambridge: Cambridge University Press,

1994), ch. 6. On degeneration and the novel see also Stephen Arata, *Fictions of Loss in the Victorian Fin de Siècle* (Cambridge: Cambridge University Press, 1996).

8 *The Picture of Dorian Gray* (1891; New York: Airmont, 1964) 178.

9 These figures are taken from Walter A. Arnstein's *Britain Yesterday and Today: 1830 to the Present* (1966; Lexington: D. C. Heath, 1988) 164. Britain, of course, wasn't alone in this scramble for new territory: between 1876 and 1915 France added some 3.5 million square miles, Germany, France and Italy approximately 1 million each, and the USA approximately 100,000. See Eric Hobsbawm, *The Age of Empire, 1875–1914* (New York: Vintage, 1989) 59.

10 See David Glover, *Vampires, Mummies and Liberals: Bram Stoker and the Politics of Popular Fiction* (Durham and London: Duke University Press, 1996) 11–13 (12). Glover argues that Bram Stoker's fiction can be read as an attempt to reconcile the values of liberalism with the various new scientific ideologies that threatened liberalism's conception of the subject.

11 On the appearance of these 'organic state intellectuals' see Stuart Hall and Bill Schwarz, 'State and Society, 1880–1930', in Mary Langan and Bill Schwarz eds., *Crises in the British State 1880–1930* (London: Hutchinson, 1985) 7–32 (19–20).

12 W. D. Rubinstein, *Capitalism, Culture, and Decline in Britain, 1750–1990* (London and New York: Routledge, 1993) 24. Rubinstein casts a decidedly cold eye on the account of Britain's decline given by Martin Wiener in his much-cited *English Culture and Decline of the Industrial Spirit, 1850–1980* (Cambridge: Cambridge University Press, 1981).

13 See Perkin, *The Rise of Professional Society* 56.

14 Ibid. 59.

15 For an account of a similar transformation in French society see Jacques Donzelot, *The Policing of Families*, trans. Robert Hurley (London: Hutchinson, 1979).

16 Quoted in Devendra P. Varma, *The Gothic Flame* (London: Barker, 1957) 217.

17 David Punter, *The Literature of Terror* (London: Longman, 1980).

18 Both criticism and crisis have their origins in the Greek verb *krino*, to decide.

19 The resonances between these two nineteenth-century fictional monsters have been remarked on before now. Franco Moretti treats the two together in his fine essay 'The Dialectic of Fear' in *Signs Taken for Wonders: Essays in the Sociology of Literary Forms* (London: Verso, 1988). William Veeder notes in his foreword to an anthology solely devoted to *Dracula* criticism, Margaret Carter, ed., *Dracula: the Vampire and the Critics* (Ann Arbor: UMI Research Press, 1988), that *Frankenstein* had earlier achieved this same mark of critical attention with George Levine and U. C. Knoepflmacher's *The Endurance of Frankenstein* (Berkeley: University of California Press, 1979).

20 Richard Wasson, 'The Politics of Dracula', reprinted in Carter, *Dracula* 19–23.

21 Phyllis A. Roth, 'Suddenly Sexual Women in Bram Stoker's *Dracula*', reprinted in Carter, *Dracula* 57–67; Judith Weissman, 'Women and Vam-

pires: *Dracula* as a Victorian Novel', reprinted in Carter, *Dracula* 69–77.

22 Christopher Craft, ' "Kiss me with those Red Lips": Gender and Inversion in Bram Stoker's *Dracula*', reprinted in Carter, *Dracula* 167–90 (190).

23 Stephen D. Arata, 'The Occidental Tourist: *Dracula* and the Anxiety of Reverse Colonization', *Victorian Studies* 33 (1990) 621–45.

24 Ibid. 623.

25 Jennifer Wicke, 'Vampiric Typewriting: *Dracula* and its Media', *ELH* 59 (1992) 467–93.

26 Ibid. 469.

27 See Ann Cvetkovich, *Mixed Feelings: Feminism, Mass Culture, and Victorian Sensationalism* (New Brunswick, NJ: Rutgers University Press, 1992). For an exemplary account of the way in which the British novel has anticipated and participated in historical change rather than reflected it see Nancy Armstrong's *Desire and Domestic Fiction: A Political History of the Novel* (New York and Oxford: Oxford University Press, 1987).

28 For an exemplary recent treatment of *Dracula* that avoids the allegorical imperative, and that reads the novel in the context of Stoker's largely ignored other work as well as in terms of its broader cultural context, see David Glover's *Vampires, Mummies and Liberals*. For a recent approach to the novel that pays attention to the figurative power of the vampire see Judith Halberstam, 'Technologies of Monstrosity: Bram Stoker's *Dracula*', *Victorian Studies* 36 (Spring 1993) 333–52.

29 On the connections between modernism and the new prominence of the imperial metropolis see Raymond Williams, *The Politics of Modernism: Against the New Conformists* (London: Verso, 1989) 37–48. On modernism and imperialism see, for example, Edward Said, *Culture and Imperialism* (New York: Knopf, 1993) 186–90. On the complexity of the relations of professionalism, literary criticism and modernism see Bruce Robbins, *Secular Vocations: Intellectuals, Professionalism, Culture* (London and New York: Verso, 1993) ch. 2.

30 Thomas Strychacz, *Modernism, Mass Culture and Professionalism* (Cambridge: Cambridge University Press, 1993) 27.

31 *Dracula* (1897; Harmondsworth: Penguin, 1985) 449. Subsequent references in the text.

32 We are never given little Quincey's full name, but we can assume it is something like Quincey Jonathan Arthur John Abraham (or Van Helsing) Harker. The name Abraham, of course, also links him to another professional family: that of Bram (Abraham) Stoker himself, a lawyer, and brother of two doctors.

33 Wicke and Craft also comment on the question of little Quincey's origins: for Wicke his multiple parentage suggests the simulacra that are (almost) all that remain of the adventure's record; Craft sees Quincey as the displaced product of the symbolic gang-rape of Lucy in the tomb.

34 As Ann Cvetkovich has described, this narrative in which a particular construction of the woman enables certain strategies of professionalized male intervention is produced earlier in the century in the sensation novel.

See *Mixed Feelings*, ch. 3. The emergent scientific/medical discourse that appears toward the end of *Lady Audley's Secret* to justify Lady Audley's incarceration operates as the master-discourse of *Dracula* almost from the beginning.

35 The English aristocracy was certainly lending its prestige to the world of business in the 1890s. In 1896 167 English noblemen, one quarter of the active peerage, were company directors. See Perkin, *The Rise of Professional Society* 366.

36 As Jeffrey Richards notes, a similar team appears in *The Jewel of Seven Stars*, this time made up of a barrister (the hero, Malcolm Ross), a doctor, an archeologist and two policemen. See his essay 'Gender, Race and Sexuality in Bram Stoker's Other Novels', in Christopher Parker, ed., *Gender Roles and Sexuality in Victorian Literature* (Aldershot: Scolar Press, c.1995) 143–71 (150).

37 In this respect *Dracula* should be compared with R. L. Stevenson's *The Strange Case of Dr Jekyll and Mr Hyde* (1886), which also pits a team of professional men against a degenerate criminal individualist. For a nuanced reading of Stevenson's text in terms of professionalism see Arata, *Fictions of Loss in the Victorian Fin de Siècle*, chapter 2.

38 The original manuscript list of characters is reproduced in David J. Skal, *Hollywood Gothic: The Tangled Web of Dracula from Novel to Stage to Screen* (London: André Deutsch, 1992) 11.

39 Glover, *Vampires, Mummies and Liberals* 45.

40 David Glover suggests that Mina is not just a representative of women who entered the workforce in these para-professional roles. Citing the example of the successful journalist Flora Shaw, he notes that Mina also recalls 'the exceptional cases of upwardly mobile ladies whose contradictory response to the suffrage movement gave them a strategic position in late Victorian society' (*Vampire, Mummies Liberals* 96).

41 Glover, *Vampires, Mummies and Liberals* 96. Glover points out that Stoker was himself on friendly terms with a number of New Woman novelists in later years, while seeing them as his 'moral and ideological competitors' (106–7).

42 On Stoker's deployment of the codes of chivalry see Richards, 'Gender, Race and Sexuality' 154–5.

43 Glover argues that the hysterical dimension to Stoker's male characters is part of the latter's attempts to combine competing versions of masculinity: older notions of the 'man of feeling' and high Victorian ideas of masculine self-control. Glover links this in turn to Stoker's wish to valorize the emotionalism that nineteenth-century commentators such as Renan and Arnold had associated with the Irish 'national character' (*Vampires, Mummies and Liberals* 79–80). Another way of reading the textual excess around male-male relations is suggested by Talia Schaffer's in ' "A Wilde Desire Took Me": The Homoerotic History of *Dracula*', *ELH* 61.2 (1994): 381–425, where she argues that *Dracula* 'explores Stoker's fear and anxiety as a closeted homosexual man during Oscar Wilde's trial' (381).

44 Quoted in R. K. R. Thornton, *The Decadent Dilemma* (London: Edward

Arnold, 1983) 39 from an Ellis essay of 1889. As Thornton remarks, the italics and the explanatory nature of the passage in which it occurs suggest that this may be the first use of the word in this sense in English.

45 On ego-mania see Nordau, *Degeneration* 243.

46 See *The Making of the English Working Class* (New York: Random House, 1966). On the subsequent history of the figure of combination see Nancy Armstrong, *Desire and Domestic Fiction*, ch, 4.

47 Patrick Joyce, *Democratic Subjects: The Self and the Social in Nineteenth-Century England* (Cambridge: Cambridge University Press, 1994) 17.

48 Moretti, *Signs Taken for Wonders* 83–108.

49 Jani Scandura, 'Deadly Professions: *Dracula*, Undertakers, and the Embalmed Corpse', *Victorian Studies* 40.1 (Autumn 1996): 1–30.

50 For the discussion which follows I have relied mostly on Magali Sarfatti Larson's *The Rise of Professionalism: A Sociological Analysis* (Berleley: University of California Press, 1977) and Harold Perkin's *The Rise of Professional Society*. Larson offers a more analytical account of the ideology of professionalism as well as useful historical material on nineteenth-century English professionalism. Perkin's account is more historically dense, but he is less clear about the specific characteristics of professionalism, tending to treat most of the non-owning section of the middle class as professional. Annie Witz's *Professions of Patriarchy* (London: Routledge, 1992) treats the connections between professionalism and gender, something largely ignored by Larson and Perkin.

51 Larson, *The Rise of Professionalism* xvii.

52 Even after these acts, what is striking about the traditional professions in Britain is the amount of independence they retain from state control. See Keith M. Macdonald, *The Sociology of the Professions* (London: Sage, 1995) 72–9.

53 Perkin, *The Rise of Professional Society* 85.

54 Hobsbawm, *Age of Empire* 44.

55 Perkin, *The Rise of Professional Society* 85–6.

56 Larson argues that because of the universal need it serves medicine became 'one of the principal diffusors of the stereotyped image of profession among the public' (*The Rise of Professionalism* 39). The tendency to see medicine as the exemplary profession has continued to operate in sociological approaches to professions.

57 *Thrillers: Genesis and Structure of a Popular Genre* (London: Edward Arnold, 1978).

58 Until very recently the novel has attracted very little in the way of critical attention, though see David Glover's ' "Dark enough fur any man": Bram Stoker's Sexual Ethnology and the Question of Irish Nationalism', in *Late Imperial Culture*, eds. Roman de la Campa, E. Ann Kaplan and Michael Sprinker (London: Verso, 1995) 53–71, as well as the expanded version of this essay in *Vampires, Mummies and Liberals*, for a lucid account of the politics of *The Snake's Pass* and its relation to Stoker's other texts. I am grateful to

David Glover for allowing me to read an earlier draft of this essay.

59 *The Snake's Pass* (1890; Dingle, Ireland: Brandon Press, 1990) 59. Further references in the text.

60 On professionalism and job security see Rubinstein, *Capitalism, Culture, and Decline in Britain* 124–5.

61 cf. Van Helsing's convincing Lord Godalming of the necessity of Lucy's staking by describing his own attachment to her: 'I gave what you gave: the blood of my veins; I gave it, I, who was not, like you, her lover, but only her physician and her friend. I gave her my nights and days – before death, after death; and if my death can do her good even now, when she is the dead Un-Dead, she shall have it freely'(248).

62 Nikolas Rose, *Governing the Soul: The Shaping of the Private Self* (London: Routledge, 1990) 8.

63 Seward's asylum seems to lie half-way between the two models of the asylum which Elaine Showalter describes as dominating Victorian England. In the period between 1830 and the rise of Darwinist thought, the prevalent model was that of the asylum as home, with a regime of paternal therapy. The paternal model was replaced by what Showalter, after Foucault, calls psychiatric policing. See Showalter, *The Female Malady: Women, Madness and English Culture* (New York: Pantheon, 1985), especially chs. 3, 4 and 5. The policing model, with its possibilites for intervention within and outside the asylum, seems to be in the ascendant in *Dracula*.

64 In their concern with controlling the physical and human environment the eugenicists found common ground with the new liberals. See Glover, *Vampires, Mummies and Liberals* 93.

65 On professionalism and patriarchy see Witz, *Professions of Patriarchy* and Macdonald, *The Sociology of the Professions* 124–56.

66 See Witz, *Professions of Patriarchy* ch. 3.

67 As Scandura puts it, citing Burton Bledstein's *The Culture of Professionalism* (1976): 'as a product of modernity, the professional was himself parasitic, cultivating what Bledstein calls "an atmosphere of constant crisis"'. See Scandura, 'Deadly Professions' 21.

68 See for example Bruce Robbins's reading of the 1966 western, *The Professionals* in *Secular Vocations* (London: Verso, 1993) 29–56.

2 THE IMPERIAL TREASURE HUNT: *THE SNAKE'S PASS*
AND THE LIMITS OF ROMANCE

1 The novels are, of course, fantasies of control rather than evidence of it. I would agree with the view advanced by Thomas Richards that the modern strategies of social and political control documented in the work of Michel Foucault were rarely successfully exported to Britain's overseas territories, in part due to the fact that Britain's colonial possessions grew too quickly. See Richards, *The Imperial Archive: Knowledge and the Fantasy of Empire* (London and New York: Verso, 1993) 2–3.

2 In the case of R. L. Stevenson's *Treasure Island*, the map preceded the novel. See Stevenson, 'My First Book: Treasure Island', in Claire Tomalin ed., *R. L. Stevenson, Essays and Poems* (London: Everyman, 1992) 209–16.

3 David Glover provides a nuanced and detailed account of Stoker's conflicted relation to Irish nationalism in *Vampires, Mummies and Liberals: Bram Stoker and the Politics of Popular Fiction* (Durham and London: Duke University Press, 1996), esp. 28–9 and 50–1. His nationalist acquaintance included Sir William and Lady Wilde in his student days, and later the Home Rule MP, William O'Brien. Chris Morash notes that letters written by Stoker's wife, Florence Stoker, née Balcombe, suggest that John Dillon, a militant Irish nationalist and an orginator of the 'Plan of Campaign' was a family friend. See ' "Ever Under Some Unnatural Condition": Bram Stoker and the Colonial Fantastic', in Brian Cosgrove, ed., *Literature and the Supernatural: Essays for the Maynooth Bicentenary* (Dublin: Columba Press, 1995) 95–119 (112).

4 There are significant resemblances between Stoker's position as a writer and that of the present-day Anglophone postcolonial writer, who is often both writing for an implied international, Euro-American reader and addressing an implied 'local' reader. Chantal Zabus has recently explored the way this dual address situation has left its effects on the linguistic structures of the African Anglophone novel in *The African Palimpsest: Indigenization of Language in the West African Europhone Novel* (Amsterdam: Rodopi, 1991). Cf. Paul Gilroy's *The Black Atlantic: Modernity and Double Consciousness* (Cambridge: Harvard University Press, 1993), where he refers to 'the stereophonic, bilingual, or bifocal cultural forms' (3) evolved by a diasporic black culture.

5 Homi K. Bhabha, *The Location of Culture* (London and New York: Routledge, 1994) 5.

6 Tony Bennett develops a theory of 'reading formations', the interpretive frames through which texts are 'produced' by readers in 'Texts, Readers, Reading Formations', in Philip Rice and Patricia Waugh, eds., *Modern Literary Theory* (London: Routledge, 1989). *Bond and Beyond: The Political Career of a Popular Hero* (London: Methuen, 1986), co-written with Janet Woollacott, uses the idea of 'reading formations' to discuss the cultural effects of the James Bond novels, films, etc. Bennett's more recent *Outside Literature* (London: Routledge, 1990) continues along similar lines, arguing for the development of a criticism that can give an adequate account of the institutional frameworks (e.g. schools) within which texts have their readerly effects.

7 See Stoker's *Personal Reminiscences of Henry Irving* vol. 1 (New York: Macmillan, 1906) 27–8. Robert H. MacDonald remarks in this connection that 'two sides of imperialism, the acquisition of territory and a campaign of propaganda, physical conquest and making imperialism "popular", went hand in hand'. See *The Language of Empire: Myths and Metaphors of Popular Imperialism, 1880–1918* (Manchester: Manchester University Press, 1994) 2.

8 Martin Green, in his *Dreams of Adventure, Deeds of Empire* (New York: Basic Books, 1979) draws up a useful list of adventure motifs, but he is interested in identifying the connections between all adventure fiction from *Robinson Crusoe* on, while I am more concerned with isolating those features which were important in the late nineteenth and early twentieth-century romances. See also MacDonald, *The Language of Empire* 210–11.

9 On the opposition between individually experienced space and 'official' place see Michel de Certeau, *The Practice of Everyday Life*, trans. Steven Rendall (Berkeley: University of California Press, 1988) 117.

10 On the gendering of the African landscape in Haggard see Nancy Armstrong, 'The Occidental Alice', *differences* 2. 2 (1990): 2–39 (30–1); Anne McClintock, 'Maidens, Maps and Mines: *King Solomon's Mines* and the Reinvention of Patriarchy in Colonial South Africa', in Cherryl Walker, ed., *Women and Gender in Southern Africa to 1845* (London: James Currey, 1990) 97–124 and her more recent *Imperial Leather: Race, Gender and Sexuality in the Colonial Contest* (New York and London: Routledge, 1995), 1–5 and 241–4; William J. Scheick, 'Adolescent Pornography and Imperialism in Haggard's *King Solomon's Mines*', *ELT* 34.1 1991): 18–30.

11 *The Language of Empire* 30. On T. E. Lawrence as a specifically modernist figure who oscillates between the ethos of imperial adventure and a more disenchanted relation to the idea of heroism see Graham Dawson, *Soldier Heroes: British Adventure, Empire and the Imagining of Masculinities* (London and New York: Routledge, 1994) 167–207.

12 Dawson, *Soldier Heroes* 80–1.

13 See John M. MacKenzie, *Propaganda and Empire: The Manipulation of British Public Opinion, 1880–1960* (Manchester: Manchester University Press, 1984), ch. 1, John M. MacKenzie, ed., *Imperialism and Popular Culture* (Manchester: Manchester University Press, 1986), McClintock, *Imperial Leather*, and MacDonald, *The Language of Empire*, ch. 3, on the multiple ways in which the empire entered popular consciousness.

14 Tony Bennett, 'The Exhibitionary Complex', in Nicholas B. Dirks et al. eds., *Culture/Power/History: A Reader in Contemporary Social Theory* (Princeton: Princeton University Press, 1994) 123–54.

15 As described by Michel Foucault, a heterotopia is 'a kind of effectively enacted utopia in which the real sites, all the other real sites that can be found within the culture, are simultaneously represented, contested, and inverted'. Unlike utopias, that is, heterotopias overlap with actual physical space. See 'Of Other Spaces', trans. Jay Miskowiev, *Diacritics* 16.1 (1986): 22–7, and see ch. 4 below.

16 *The Snake's Pass* (1890; Dingle: Brandon Press, 1990) 8, 9. Subsequent references will be given in the text.

17 Jefferson Hunter argues that after the turn-of-the-century romance writers become increasingly self-conscious about such fantasies of a place beyond modernity. See his *Edwardian Fiction* (Camdridge, MA, and London: Harvard University Press, 1982) 77–98. But see chapter 4 below on the persist-

ence of the idea of 'blank spaces' on the map.

18 The 'primitive' aspect of romance is discussed by Andrew Lang in his contribution to the debate on romance fiction, 'Realism and Romance', *Contemporary Review* 52 (1887): 683–93. See also the Introduction above.

19 On the 'monarch-of-all-I-survey' trope in imperial discourse see Mary Louise Pratt, *Imperial Eyes: Travel Writing and Transculturation* (Routledge: London and New York, 1992) 201–8.

20 H. Rider Haggard, *King Solomon's Mines* (1885; Airmont, New York 1967) 77–8. Subsequent references will be given in the text.

21 On fantasies of imperial knowledge see Richards, *The Imperial Archive*.

22 The use of the map to produce the spaces of empire as desirable is almost parodic in *King Solomon's Mines*, where the map is explicitly 'feminized'. For example, the explorers pass through the mountain pass between 'Sheba's Breasts' to reach Kukuanaland. See Armstrong, 'Occidental Alice', McClintock, *Imperial Leather* and Scheick, 'Adolescent Pornography and Imperialism'. For McClintock, the sexualized map in Haggard's novel is 'a technology of possession, operating under the guise of scientific exactitude' (*Imperial Leather* 115). For a response that suggests a less Foucauldian reading of this map, see Laura Chrisman, 'Gendering Imperial Culture: *King Solomon's Mines* and Feminist Criticism', in Keith Ansell-Pearson, Benita Parry and Judith Squires, eds., *Edward Said and the Gravity of History* (London: Lawrence and Wishart, 1997).

23 That this wealth more or less falls into the hands of the adventurers without it being their primary objective suggests that one of the functions of the imperial romance is to dissimulate the financial stakes of empire. As Peter Hulme observes in *Colonial Encounters: Europe and the Caribbean 1497–1797* (1986; London and New York: Routledge, 1992), 'the "pure" adventure story . . . reached its apogee as the tentacles of European colonialism were at their greatest reach in the late nineteenth century. The larger the degree of financial involvement in the non-European world, the more determinedly non-financial European adventure stories became' (182–3).

24 A similar motif reappears in *Dracula* (1897), where the Count digs for the hoards of gold secreted in Transylvanian soil during its violent past. On *Dracula*'s Irish resonances see Glover, *Vampires, Mummies and Liberals*.

25 Kevin McLaughlin, in 'The Financial Imp: Ethics and Finance in Nineteenth-Century Fiction', *Novel* 29.2 (1996): 165–83, notes that an 'emphasis on the peculiar financial character of adventure separates Stevenson from many of his British contemporaries' (173). Stevenson, of course, resembles Stoker in his rather oblique insertion into British culture.

26 See McClintock, *Imperial Leather*, 238–40.

27 On Havelock's role in endowing the Victorian hero with a definitive shape see Dawson, *Soldier Heroes* 79–154, especially 144–51. The Viking seems to function as the common ideal of manhood for both Stoker and Haggard. Stoker uses 'Viking' as a term of approbation in his *Personal Reminiscences of Henry Irving* as well as in his novels (Quincey Morris, for example, is a 'moral

Viking'). This usage may owe something to the earlier adventure novels of Charles Kingsley, though perhaps also to the growing interest in Anglo-Saxon culture. Arthur and Norah's wedding takes place in the 'grand old church' at Hythe, 'where the bones of so many brave old Norsemen rest after a thousand years' (247). On Stoker's Nordic motifs see Richards, 'Gender, Race and Sexuality in Bram Stoker's Other Novels', in Christopher Parker, ed., *Gender Roles and Sexuality in Victorian Literature* (Aldershot: Scolar Press, c.1995) 143–71 (167).

28 See Louis James, 'Tom Brown's Imperialist Sons', *Victorian Studies* 17 (1973) 89–99. Henty shows more clearly than most the line of this development. Consider the comments of Guy Arnold on the Hentian hero: 'He early established the type – manly, straightforward, could give and take punishment (taking it without complaint although more usually he seemed to be giving it), fearless, never lying, resourceful . . . His youthful heroes almost always develop strong physiques: they usually learn to box and this enables them to defeat bigger and older opponents'. Guy Arnold, *Held Fast for England: G. A. Henty, Imperialist Boys' Writer* (London: Hamish Hamilton, 1980) 31.

29 *Under Two Flags* (1867; Oxford and New York: Oxford University Press, 1995) 137. Ouida's novel pre-dates the romance revival, and belongs to a rather different structure of feeling, but it nonetheless anticipates some later romance trends, and clearly influences later works like A. E. W. Mason's *The Four Feathers*. On 'playing the game', see MacDonald, *The Language of Empire* 21–5.

30 Michael Denning, *Cover Stories: Narrative and Ideology in the British Spy Thriller* (London and New York: Routledge and Kegan Paul, 1987) 33–6. As Tony Bennett and Janet Woollacott have pointed out, Bond's physical prowess differs from that of his spy novel predecessors in an important respect: Bond works at being in top physical shape; it is not just a side-effect of his being a well-bred Englishman. Bond, that is, is a real professional, not a gentleman adventurer. See *Bond and Beyond* 111, and see the discussion of professionalism in chapter 1.

31 Harold Perkin, *The Rise of Professional Society: England Since 1880* (Routledge: London and New York, 1989) 159.

32 Stoker's novel of 1909, *The Lady of the Shroud*, may be a partial exception. See Glover, *Vampires, Mummies and Liberals* 13. Stoker himself had an early interest in the connections between professionalism, efficiency and empire. As Chris Morash notes, Stoker's first book, written while he was still a civil servant working at Dublin Castle, *The Duties of Clerks of Petty Sessions in Ireland* (1879), aims to provide a set of effective procedures for use throughout the empire (Morash, ' "Ever Under Some Unnatural Condition" ' 106).

33 An exception is Haggard's *Allan Quatermain* (1887), where Sir Henry Curtis does marry an African woman – but she is white, the queen of a mysterious white African nation.

34 On Lawrence of Arabia in relation to Victorian heroic masculinity see

Dawson, *Soldier Heroes* 186.

35　See Glover, *Vampires, Mummies and Liberals* 21–57 for an excellent account of Stoker's attitude to Victorian theories of race.

36　See David Cairns and Shaun Richards, *Writing Ireland: Colonialism, Nationalism and Culture* (Manchester: Manchester University Press, 1988) ch. 3.

37　Cf. David Lloyd's *Anomalous States: Irish Writing and the Postcolonial Moment* (Durham: Duke University Press, 1993) 150–5 on the novel as silencing heteroglossia, and on the imagined community of the novel as an exclusive structure.

38　As Eric Hobsbawm points out, 'There were peasant revolts, or agitations treated as such, between 1879 and 1894 in Ireland, Spain, Sicily and Rumania.' See *The Age of Empire 1875–1914* (New York: Vintage Books, 1989) 36.

39　He wrote that 'a writer being murdered would . . . throw a bull's eye light upon this cowardly business'. The death of his father seems to have put a stop to this bizarre plan. See Frank McLynn, *Robert Louis Stevenson, A Biography* (London: Hutchinson, 1993) 274–6. The Land War also features prominently in Anthony Trollope's *The Landleaguers* (1883).

40　I have drawn mostly on F. S. L. Lyons's *Ireland Since the Famine* (New York: Scribners, 1971) and R. F. Foster's *Modern Ireland 1600–1972* (London: Penguin, 1989) 373–428 for this summary of the Land War and Parnellite politics. Michael Davitt's *The Fall of Feudalism in Ireland* (London and New York: Harper, 1904) provides an interesting account by one of the leaders of the Land League. For a detailed description of Mayo's place in the Land War see Donald E. Jordan's *Land and Popular Politics in Ireland: County Mayo from the Plantation to the Land War* (Cambridge: Cambridge University Press, 1994).

41　Glover, *Vampires, Mummies and Liberals* 30.

42　Foster, *Modern Ireland* 403.

43　The benign paternalism involved here recalls the somewhat different political fantasy of J. A. Froude's historical romance *The Two Chiefs of Dunboy* (1889), where Colonel Goring establishes a model estate which, like Arthur Severn's, depends on mineral resources. Goring's estate is made possible through a copper-mine on the property, which he has worked by Cornish settlers he brings over.

44　When Murdock and Phelim Joyce fight in chapter 3 the priest, Father Ryan, is able to quell Murdock. He urges calm on Joyce too, but notes that 'ye're not one of my people' (36).

45　*The Times*, 19 August 1882, 5.

46　In addition to the *The Times*, *The Mysteries of Ireland* (Printed for the Booksellers, London [1883?]) provides a useful, if somewhat sensational, contemporary account of the murders. For a recent account see Jarlath Waldron, *Maamtrasna: The Murders and the Mystery* (Dublin: Edmund Burke, 1992). Anthony Trollope fictionalized the incident in his unfinished novel of the Land War, *The Landleaguers*, substituting the Kelly family of Kerrycullion for the Joyces of the Joyce country. See *The Landleaguers* (1883; London: The Trollope Society, 1995) ch. 47. I am grateful to Mary Jean Corbett for drawing my attention to this.

47 Patrick Brantlinger and Richard Boyle suggest that Hyde's murder of Sir Danvers Carew, MP, in Stevenson's novel would have recalled for contemporary readers the Phoenix Park murders and the general threat of Fenianism. See their 'The Education of Edward Hyde: Stevenson's "Gothic Gnome" and the Mass Readership of Late-Victorian England', in William Veeder and Gordon Hirsch, eds., *Dr Jekyll and Mr Hyde after 100 Years* (Chicago and London: University of Chicago Press, c.1988) 265–82 (274).

48 *The Times*, 21 August 1882, 5.

49 Note how this use of journey-as-transition recalls Jonathan Harker's passage through the Burgo Pass to Dracula's castle. See Glover, *Vampires, Mummies and Liberals* 32–4.

50 *The Times*, 21 August 1882, 5.

51 Andy's subsequent tale of capturing, skinning and eating a deer who escapes from 'me Lard's demesne beyant at Wisport' (sc. Westport) also hints at veiled hostility. Andy's jokes about the deer's 'bankrupt' status likewise suggest the Land War.

52 It is interesting to see this imagery of insubstantiality return in the account of postcolonial Irish identity given by Daniel Corkery, one of the most dogmatic proponents of a vision of Irish identity as Catholic and Gaelic: 'Everywhere in the mentality of Irish people are flux and uncertainty. Our national consciousness may be described, in a native phrase, as a quaking sod. It gives no footing. It is not English, nor Irish, nor Anglo-Irish . . .' Quoted in Lloyd, *Anomalous States* 43.

53 Perhaps the following passage from Spenser is the one Sutherland has in mind: 'Then the Irishe whom before they banished into the mountaines where they lived onelye uppon white meates as it is recorded seinge now the landes so dispeopled and wekened came down into all the plaines adioyninge and thence expellinge those fewe Englishe that remayned repossessed them againe . . . This is one of the occasions by which all those Countries which lyinge neare unto anye mountaines or Irishe desertes [viz. bogs] had been planted with Englishe weare shortely displanted and loste; as namely in Mounster all the landes adioyninge unto Slewlogher, Arlo and the bog of Allon . . .' *A View of the Present State of Ireland* in *Spenser's Prose Works* (Baltimore: Johns Hopkins University Press, 1966) 56–7. On Spenser, Ireland and landscape see Patricia Coughlan, 'Ireland and Incivility in Spenser', in Patricia Coughlan, ed., *Spenser and Ireland* (Cork: Cork University Press, 1989) esp. 53, 54.

54 Luke Gibbons, ' "Some Hysterical Hatred": History, Hysteria and the Literary Revival', *Irish University Review* 27.1 (1997): 7–23 (14).

55 More recently, of course, Seamus Heaney has explored the bog as a preserver of history. See in particular the bog poems in *North* (1975).

56 Luke Gibbons, ' "Some Hysterical Hatred" '.

57 See John Wilson Foster, *Fictions of the Irish Literary Revival: A Changeling Art* (Syracuse: Syracuse University Press, 1987) 32–44, and Cairns and Richards, *Writing Ireland* 51–7. See also Terry Eagleton, *Heathcliff and the Great Hunger: Studies in Irish Culture* (London and New York: Verso, 1995) 101–3.

58 Gibbons, '"Some Hysterical Hatred"' 14. It might be argued, of course, that British modernity has also been distinguished by the existence of a thoroughly commercially minded aristocracy. See Ellen Meiksins Wood, *The Pristine Culture of Capitalism: A Historical Essay on Old Regimes and Modern States* (London and New York: Verso, 1991).

59 *Vampires, Mummies and Liberals* 50.

60 Quoted in David Greene and Edward Stephens, *J. M. Synge: 1871–1909*, revised edition (New York and London: New York University Press, 1989) 283, and see below, chapter 4.

61 Morash, '"Ever Under Some Unnatural Condition"' 113.

62 Luke Gibbons argues that the hysterical figure of the bog also has its equivalent in the later work of Yeats, where in 'Meditations in Time of Civil War' the 'levelled lawns and gravelled ways' of the Big House conceal the layered history of colonial violence. See '"Some Hysterical Hatred"' 16–23.

63 David Lloyd, among others, argues that imperialism and nationalism are homologous ideologies. See *Anomalous States: Irish Writing and the Post-Colonial Moment* (Durham: Duke University Press, 1993) 46, and his earlier *Nationalism and Minor Literature: James Clarence Mangan and the Emergence of Irish Cultural Nationalism* (Berkeley: University of California Press, 1987).

64 On the strain of anti-modernism of British imperialism, see Martin Green, *Dreams of Adventure, Deeds of Empire* (New York: Basic Books, 1979) 115. The anti-modernism of the Revival is well expressed in AE's essay 'Nationality and Imperialism', reprinted in Mark Storey, ed., *Poetry in Ireland Since 1800: A Sourcebook* (London: Routledge, 1988). Of course the recovery of a national past and the conception of a national culture was an important project in England too, notably in the rise of the university English department as we now know it. As Terry Eagleton succinctly puts it: 'Hitching the study of modern English to the rude manly vigour of the Anglo-Saxon was one way of laying claim to a . . . suitably authorizing heritage. 'The Crisis of Contemporary Culture', *New Left Review* 196 (1992) 29–41(31).

65 Phyllis A. Roth, *Bram Stoker* (Boston: Twayne Publishers, 1982) 27.

66 The latter phrase is used by a contemporary reviewer of the novel. See *Harper's Monthly*, February 1891, 488.

3 'MUMMIE IS BECOME MERCHANDISE': THE MUMMY STORY
AS COMMODITY THEORY

1 Sir Wiliam Foster, ed, *The Travels of John Sanderson in the Levant 1584–1602*. Works Issued by the Hakluyt Society, Second Series, No. 67 (London: Hakluyt Society, 1931) 44–5.

2 Warren R. Dawson, 'Pettigrew's Demonstrations Upon Mummies. A Chapter in the History of Egyptology', *Journal of Egyptian Archeology* 20 (1934) 170–82 (178).

3 Discussion of the different parts that mummies played in British culture in the early modern period and in the early nineteenth century – two bizarre instances of what Arjun Appadurai has called the 'social life of things' – is unfortunately outside the ambit of this chapter. The resemblance of the bituminous substance used in mummification to an established remedy, pissasphalt, may have been the basis for the widespread use of mummy flesh in materia medica. This use led to Sir Thomas Browne's well-known observation in *Urne Burial* that 'Mummie is become Merchandise, Mizraim cures wounds, and Pharaoh is sold for Balsoms.' Mummy's familiarity as a remedy in Britain is suggested by passing references in Shakespeare, Beaumont and Fletcher and John Donne, but also by more detailed remarks in the writings of Browne, Francis Bacon and Sir Robert Boyle. For an overview see Karl H. Dannenfeldt, 'Egypt and Egyptian Antiquities in the Renaissance', *Studies in the Renaissance* 6 (1959) 7–27; John David Wortham, *The Genesis of British Egyptology 1549–1906* (Norman: University of Oklahoma Press, 1971); and Brian M. Fagan, *The Rape of the Nile: Tomb Robbers, Tourists and Archeologists in Egypt* (New York: Scribner's, 1975). On the vogue for unrollings in the 1830s and 1840s see Dawson, E. Reginald Taylor, 'The Humours of Archeology, or the Canterbury Congress of 1844 and the Early Days of the Association', *Journal of the British Archeological Association* 38 (1932) 183–234, and Bob Brier's recent *Egyptian Mummies: Unraveling the Secrets of an Ancient Art* (New York: William Morrow and Company, c.1994).

4 This is not to say that there were *no* literary mummies before the 1880s. In Jane Webb Loudon's *The Mummy! A Tale of the Twenty-Second Century* (London: Henry Colburn, 1827) one of the characters revives a mummy, who then occasionally appears to play Mephistopheles to the novel's various political schemers. The futuristic trappings thinly veil the novel's didactic aims, and Loudon's tale has little in common with later mummy fiction. In the end the mummy reveals that it was really God who revived him, and spells out the novel's moral programme: 'that knowledge above the sphere of man's capacity produces only wretchedness, and that to be contented with our station, and to make ourselves useful to our fellow-creatures, is the only true path to happiness' (302). In France, the mummy as love object is developed as early as Théophile Gautier's *Le Roman de la Momie* (1858). Bulwer Lytton's *The Ring of Amasis* (1863), while not a mummy story of the later sort, offers an earlier example of the theme of Egyptiana in the English home.

5 Richards, *The Commodity Culture of Victorian England: Advertising and Spectacle, 1851–1914* (Stanford: Stanford University Press, 1991) 123.

6 Ibid. 19.

7 The first accounts of unrollings as scientific spectacle begin to appear in the second half of the eighteenth century, though they don't seem to have

enjoyed any great popularity until the early nineteenth century. See for example, 'Of a Mummy, inspected at London, 1763 by John Hadley M.D' and 'Observations on some Egyptian Mummies opened in London by John Frederick Blumenbach, M.D. F.R.S.' in the *Philosophical Transactions of the Royal Society of London.*

8 Dawson, 'Pettigrew's Demonstrations' 174.

9 See Christine El Mahdy, *Mummies, Myth and Magic in Ancient Egypt* (London: Thames, 1989) 176.

10 Taylor, 'The Humours of Archeology' 212–13.

11 Timothy Mitchell, *Colonising Egypt* (Cambridge: Cambridge University Press, 1988).

12 Thus while what Michel Foucault terms the birth of the clinic effectively meant the end of the anatomy theatre as public spectacle, that spectacle did not altogether disappear from European culture. Rather, in a new form of ritual that combined anatomy and Orientalism, the place of the European body, now confined within the modern hospital, was taken by the foreign body.

13 To this extent mummy unwrapping recalls the Balinese cockfight as Clifford Geertz explicates it. Just as there is no final unwrapping, there is no definitive cockfight: 'once a match is ended the crowd's attention turns totally to the next, with no looking back'. *The Interpretation of Cultures* (New York: Basic Books, 1973) 445.

14 Dawson, 'Pettigrew's Demonstrations' 176–7.

15 Ibid. 176–7.

16 This topos also looks back to older representations of mysterious Egypt. In Shakespeare's *Antony and Cleopatra*, Cleopatra is Egypt by conventional appellation; but metaphorically, her 'infinite variety' also connotes that of the country she rules: 'Age cannot wither her, nor custom stale / Her infinite variety: other women cloy / The appetites they feed; but she makes hungry / Where most she satisfies . . .' (Act II, scene ii, lines 240–3). I am grateful to Garrett Sullivan for bringing this connection to my attention.

17 'Hysteria and the End of Carnival; Festivity and Bourgeois Neurosis', in *The Violence of Representation*, ed. Nancy Armstrong and Leonard Tennenhouse (New York: Routledge, 1989) 155–70 (170).

18 See for example W. Hamish Fraser's *The Coming of the Mass Market 1850–1914* (Hamden, CT: Archon, 1981). The literary and cultural implications of this shift have been discussed by a number of critics in the last fifteen years or so. Among the landmarks one might count Rachel Bowlby's exploration of the effects of the new phenomenology of the commodity in *Just Looking: Consumer Culture in Dreiser, Gissing and Zola* (New York: Methuen, 1985), Nancy Armstrong's description of the role of this new object culture in the definition of the Victorian subject of desire in 'The Occidental Alice', *differences* 2. 2 (1990) 2–39; and Thomas Richards's account of the representational strategies of Victorian commodity culture in *The Commodity Culture of Victorian England* (Stanford: Stanford University Press, 1990). See also Law-

rence Birken, *Consuming Desire: Sexual Science and the Emergence of a Culture of Abundance, 1871–1914* (Ithaca: Cornell University Press, 1988) ch. 1. For an argument that a consumer society is already discernible in the previous century see Neil McKendrick, John Brewer and J. H. Plumb, *The Birth of a Consumer Society: The Commercialization of 18th-Century England* (Bloomington: Indiana University Press, 1982).

19 *Reflections*, ed. Peter Demetz, trans. Edmund Jephcott (New York: Schocken Books, 1978) 153.

20 See Birken, *Consuming Desire*, ch. 1. Attempts to historicize the marginalist trend in economic theory are by no means new. Nikolai Bukharin undertook to do just that in *Economic Theory of the Leisure Class* (1927). Bukharin saw marginalism as the typical expression of the point of view of a rentier class, outside of the process of production. See Mark Blaug, *Economic Theory in Retrospect* (Cambridge: Cambridge University Press, 1978) 316.

21 In *Capital* vol. 1, trans. Ben Fowkes (Harmondsworth: Penguin, 1982). Subsequent references are given in the text.

22 In *The Great Keinplatz Experiment and Other Tales of the Unseen* (New York: Doran, 1919) 179–224. Subsequent references are given in the text.

23 Marx is not, of course, oblivious to the role that consumers play in the economy, for the first thing he tells us about the commodity is that it 'satisfies human needs of whatever kind' (125). Nor are these needs necessarily objective or physical: 'whether they arise . . . from the stomach or the imagination makes no difference' (125). For an object to be of value, it must be an object of utility for someone (131); there must be a market for the commodity produced. Nevertheless, Marx clearly makes value depend on production, and on intention. From the point of view of exchange, commodities are valuable because 'human labour-power has been expended to produce them . . . As crystals of this social substance . . . they are values – commodity values' (128). Moreover, the commodity form only appears when 'exchange has already acquired a sufficient extension and importance to allow useful things to be produced *for the purpose* of being exchanged, so that their character as values has already to be *taken into consideration* during production' (166, my emphasis).

24 See William Pietz, 'Fetishism and Materialism: The Limits of Theory in Marx', in Emily Apter and William Pietz, eds., *Fetishism as Cultural Discourse* (Ithaca: Cornell University Press, 1993) 132.

25 Tylor's anthropological interests were shared by one of the most enthusiastic advocates of (and as H. Rider Haggard's collaborator participant in) the 'romance revival', Andrew Lang, who became Gifford Lecturer at St Andrews University on Natural Religion in 1888, the same year that Tylor was appointed to a similar post at the University of Aberdeen.

26 Rémy G. Saisselin, while he is more concerned with the American home, gives a useful account of the middle-class drive to collect objects from other cultures, as well as from the past of their own in *The Bourgeois and the Bibelot* (New Brunswick: Rutgers University Press, 1984. See also Armstrong, 'The

Occidental Alice' 26. On the specific interest in Egyptiana, and on Egyptian motifs in European design see James S. Curl's *The Egyptian Revival: An Introductory Study of a Recurring Theme in the History of Taste* (London: Allen, 1982). By the turn of the century there existed a flourishing market in fake Egyptiana, as the supply of the genuine article lagged behind demand. See T. G. Wakeling, *Forged Egyptian Antiquities* (London: Black, 1912).

27 *Colonising Egypt* 13.

28 Susan Stewart, *On Longing* (Baltimore: Johns Hopkins University Press, 1984) 158.

29 On the cultural significance of collections in general see Walter Benjamin's 'Unpacking my Library', in *Illuminations* ed., Hannah Arendt, trans. Harry Zohn (New York: Schocken, 1978), Stewart, *On Longing*, and James Clifford 'Objects and Selves – an Afterword' in George W. Stocking Jr, ed., *Objects and Selves: Essays in Museums and Material Culture* (Madison: University of Wisconsin Press, 1985) 236–46. On the role of collectibles in nineteenth-century American and European middle-class culture see Rémy G. Saisselin's *The Bourgeois and the Bibelot*.

30 Stewart, *On Longing* 159.

31 *Illuminations* 67.

32 *The Imperial Archive: Knowledge and the Fantasy of Empire* (London and New York: Verso, 1993) ch. 1.

33 For a detailed account of the functioning of the British Museum in relation to Empire in the late nineteenth and early twentieth century, see Annie Coombes, *Reinventing Africa: Museums, Material Culture and popular Imagination in Late Victorian and Edwardian England* (New Haven and London: Yale University Press, 1994). Museums, of course, continue to function as sites for the construction of national identity and for the articulation of the relations of the nation and the global system. For an example of how ancient Egypt has been recently put to work within this symbolic system see Melani McAlister, ' "The Common Heritage of Mankind": Race, Nation, and Masculinity in the King Tut Exhibit', *Representations* 54 (Spring 1996) 80–103.

34 *House of Commons Sessional Papers* vol. 6 (London, 1870).

35 Ibid. 172.

36 See David K. Van Keuren, 'Museums and Ideology: Augustus Pitt-Rivers, Anthropological Museums and Social Change in Later Victorian Britain', in Patrick Brantlinger, ed., *Energy and Entropy: Science and Culture in Victorian Britain: Essays from Victorian Studies* (Bloomington: Indiana University Press, 1989) 271.

37 See Van Keuren, 'Museums and Ideology' 287. While the tag *natura non facit* [not *facet*] *saltum* is pre-Darwinian, it is significant that Darwin gives it new currency by citing it with approval on several occasions in *The Origin of Species* (1859; New York: Collier, 1962), especially in ch. 6. He sees it as an old canon 'which every fresh addition to our knowledge tends to confirm' (Darwin, *The Origin of Species* 468, and ch. 6 *passim*). On the Pitt-Rivers and other ethnographic collections see Coombes, *Reinventing Africa*, ch. 7.

38 Janet Adam Smith, ed., *Robert Louis Stevenson, Collected Poems* (London: Rupert Hart-Davis, 1971) 271–3. This version of the poem was enclosed in a letter to Colvin dated 2 December 1889, from the schooner *Equator*. A manuscript with minor variations exists dated October 1889, Apemama. The poem and poem xxxvi, 'The tropics vanish, and meseems that I', (which also refers to the British Museum), from *Songs of Travel*, were published as one poem in *Longman's Magazine* vol. 25, no. 147 (1895) 262–3.

39 Quoted in *Collected Poems* 512.

40 Ian Fletcher, ed., *British Poetry and Prose 1870–1905* (Oxford: Oxford University Press, 1987) 157.

41 Frank McLynn, *Robert Louis Stevenson, A Biography* (London: Hutchinson, 1993) 357. Stevenson's poem may well have been inspired by the sight of this collection. He describes the king as being 'possessed by the seven devils of the collector. He hears a thing spoken of, and a shadow comes on his face. "I think I no got him," he will say; and the treasures he has seem worthless in comparison' (357). Not the least interesting aspect of Stevenson's encounter with Tembinok is that, notwithstanding his mournful depiction of the Easter Island statues, he himself purchased a local 'fetish', 'the devil-box of Apemama', a totem shell in a wooden box, to give to Andrew Lang, who studied 'natural religion' (362–3, and see note 25 above). Tembinok's collection is echoed in the description of the 'multiplicity and disorder of romantic things', the 'whole curiosity-shop of sea curios' in Attwater's store-rooms in *The Ebb Tide* (1894; London: Everyman, 1994) 89.

42 Max Nordau, *Degeneration* (London: Heinemann, 1895) 27.

43 See Saisselin, *The Bourgeois and the Bibelot* 53–74. Nancy Armstrong argues that the handling of these new commodities became the province of the middle-class woman, and she suggests that this had consequences for the way women were perceived as appetitive: 'Englishwomen were responsible for putting the objects that flooded in from the colonies in place. To do so, women had to want such objects, and once they did, women became dangerous' ('The Occidental Alice' 34).

44 Cited in Asa Briggs, *Victorian Things* (London: Batsford, 1988) 220.

45 Ibid. 220.

46 Ibid. 246.

47 Bram Stoker, *The Jewel of Seven Stars* (1904; London: Arrow, 1980) 37.

48 'The Ring of Thoth', in *The Great Keinplatz Experiment* 139–62 (161).

49 'Smith and the Pharaohs', in *The Best Short Stories of Rider Haggard*, ed. Peter Haining (London: Joseph, 1981) 148–91 (173). Subsequent references are given in the text.

50 Dorothy Van Ghent, *The English Novel; Form and Function* (New York: Holt, 1961) 125–38.

51 For a very different interpretation of the collector, which presents him as a model for the writer of modern life see Ackbar Abbas, 'Walter Benjamin's Collector: The Fate of Modern Experience', *New Literary History* 20.1 (1988) 217–37.

52 *Reflections* 65.
53 'To live means to leave traces. In the interior these are emphasized. An abundance of covers and protectors, liners and cases is devised, on which the traces of objects of everday use are imprinted. The traces of the occupant also leave their impression on the interior. The detective story that follows these traces comes into being.' See Benjamin, *Illuminations* 29.
54 See Briggs, *Victorian Things* 215.
55 The *OED* reveals that mummies also entered the commercial imagination in quite a different way in the early twentieth century: 'mummies' became a stock exchange slang term for Egyptian securities.
56 Translated as 'The Mummy's Foot' in Lafcadio Hearn, trans., *Stories By Gautier* (New York: Dutton, 1908) 52–70. Subsequent references are given in the text. The resistance of the mummy to collection features prominently in non-literary museum stories too. During Budge's tenure as Keeper of Egyptian antiquities, one of the museum's coffin lids (no. 22542), that of a chantress of Amen-Ra, became a rich source of urban myth. The tortured expression of the face depicted on the lid led to proposals to put the soul to rest through a séance. As Marjorie Caygill recounts, 'Publicity about the séance merged with other wild tales and then became transmuted into a legend that, following considerable death and destruction in the British Museum, the Keeper of Egyptian Antiquities sold the coffin lid to an American who transported his new purchase on the *Titanic* thereby occasioning that vessel's collision with an iceberg. Although a large proportion of the passengers perished, the coffin lid was said to have obtained a place in a lifeboat and gone on to spread calamities in the United States and Canada before sinking the *Empress of Ireland* and ending up in the St. Lawrence River.' See Marjorie Caygill, *The Story of the British Museum* (London: British Museum Publications, 1981) 51, and E. A. Wallis Budge, *By Nile and Tigris* (London: Murray, 1920) vol. 2, 392–3.
57 As one of the characters points out, the name suggests the French *ma mie*, my darling, though the more colloquial pun on 'mammy'' (mother) is also possible.
58 They are in fact discussing the violation of their tombs by the living. It is interesting to collate 'Smith and the Pharaohs' with Rider Haggard's criticism of the destruction of mummies in a newspaper article he contributed to the *Daily Mail* on 'The Trade in the Dead'. See *The Best Short Stories of H. Rider Haggard* 141–7.
59 Shortly after their discovery at the end of the nineteenth century, x-rays were used in studying mummies, obviating the need to unroll them.
60 *She* (1887; New York; Pyramid Books, 1966) 137. Subsequent references are given in the text.
61 Mark Twain, *The Innocents Abroad, or The New Pilgrim's Progress* (New York: Harper, 1911) 386.
62 *The Yellow God, An Idol of Africa* (New York: Cupples, 1908) 186. One is also reminded here of the preservation of the bodies of the dead kings in *King*

Solomon's Mines, who are, in effect, fossilized in their cave through stalactite formation – a sort of natural mummification.

63 H. D. Everett, *Iras, A Mystery* (New York: Harper, 1906) 75. Subsequent references are given in the text.

64 The Carter/Carnarvon discovery of Tutankhamen's tomb in 1923 sparked a revival of interest in mummies, and may have been in part responsible for the popularity of narratives that dwelt on the mummy's curse, displacing the mummy stories that had appealed to the previous generation. The Hollywood films actually start in the 1930s with *The Mummy* (1932), which had a partial sequel in the 1940 *The Mummy's Hand*. The sequel in turn spawned *The Mummy's Tomb* (1942), *The Mummy's Ghost* (1944) and *The Mummy's Curse* (1944). The British series was launched with Terence Fisher's *The Mummy* (1959), and continued with *Curse of the Mummy's Tomb* (1964), *The Mummy's Shroud* (1966) and *Blood from the Mummy's Tomb* (1971). The latter film, like the 1980 *The Awakening*, was based on Stoker's *The Jewel of Seven Stars*. On film mummies see Brier's *Egyptian Mummies*, ch. 11.

65 In most editions of the novel the ending has actually been changed, allowing Margaret to survive the revival, but there is some doubt as to whether Stoker himself supplied this more upbeat resolution. See David Glover, *Vampires, Mummies and Liberals* 91–2.

66 Grant Allen, 'New Year's Eve Among the Mummies', *Strange Stories* (London: Chatto, 1884) 130.

67 The story also resembles in many respects Julian Hawthorne's mummy tale, 'The Unseen Man's Story', in *Six Cent Sam's* (1893).

68 See for example Nancy Armstrong's *Desire and Domestic Fiction* (1987). Fredric Jameson's *The Political Unconscious* (1981) also provides an influential account of the way nineteenth-century fiction encodes the political at the level of character, though gender is not an important category for Jameson's analysis.

69 *Reflections* 153.

70 W. F. Haug, *Critique of Commodity Aesthetics: Appearance, Sexuality and Advertising in Capitalist Society*, trans. Robert Bock (Minneapolis: University of Minnesota Press, 1986) 55.

71 Ibid. 24.

72 Ibid. 56.

73 See Fraser, *The Coming of the Mass Market* 136–7.

74 I am thinking of Jean Baudrillard's claim that 'Disneyland is presented as imaginary in order to make us believe that the rest is real.' See *Jean Baudrillard: Selected Writings*, ed. Mark Poster (Cambridge: Polity Press, 1988) 172.

4 ACROSS THE GREAT DIVIDE: MODERNISM, POPULAR FICTION AND THE PRIMITIVE

1 This is not to say that it was the most important vehicle for middle-class ideology *tout court*. To theorize what might have played that part, we would

have to take account of the public schools with their culture of games, classics and 'fagging', the continuing role of organized religion (despite widespread religious scepticism among intellectuals), and a host of other ideological formations. Cf. C. L. R James's provocative claim that 'cricket and football were the greatest cultural influences in nineteenth-century Britain, leaving far behind Tennyson's poems, Beardsley's drawings and concerts of the Philharmonic Society. These filled space in print but not in minds.' See *Beyond A Boundary* (New York: Pantheon Books, 1983) 70.

2 T. S. Eliot, *Selected Essays*, 3rd enlarged edition (London: Faber and Faber, 1951) 460.

3 Suzanne Clark, *Sentimental Modernism: Women Writers and the Revolution of the Word* (Bloomington and Indianapolis: Indiana University Press, 1991) 9.

4 Clark suggests that this doesn't happen until the 1920s and 1930s, when modernism began to secure more cultural authority, and when the New Critics carried their version of modernist values into the universities (ibid. 35–6). In Britain the same process was carried forward by T. S. Eliot, I. A. Richards and by the *Scrutiny* group. See Francis Mulhern, *The Moment of Scrutiny* (London: NLB, 1979) 3–41.

5 Clark, *Sentimental Modernism* 8.

6 Andreas Huyssen, *After the Great Divide: Modernism, Mass Culture, Postmodernism* (Bloomington and Indianapolis: Indiana University Press, c.1986) vii, 47.

7 Ibid. 53.

8 See Peter Keating, *The Haunted Study: A Social History of the English Novel, 1875–1914* (London: Secker and Warburg, 1989) 38, and on Joyce see also Richard Ellmann, *James Joyce* (Oxford: Oxford University Press, 1983) 50. As Ellmann notes, Joyce later pokes fun at this venture, and the story becomes 'Matcham's Masterstroke' in *Ulysses*.

9 See Robert Crawford, *The Savage and the City in the Works of T. S. Eliot* (Oxford: Clarendon Press, 1987) 10–12, 15–25, 172 *et passim* on Eliot's interest in Arthur Conan Doyle, Mayne Reid and R. L. Stevenson, *inter alia*.

10 See his appreciation of Marie Lloyd, originally published in the *Dial* in 1922, reprinted with some changes as 'Marie Lloyd' in *Selected Essays* 456–9 (458). For his use of vaudeville material see for example the 'Tambo and Bones' songs in *Sweeney Agonistes*.

11 Letter to Walter Benjamin, 18 March 1936, cited in Huyssen, *After the Great Divide* 58.

12 Theodor Adorno, *Prisms*, trans. Samuel and Shierry Weber (Cambridge, MA: MIT Press, 1990) 154.

13 *Culture and Imperialism* (New York: Knopf, 1993) 188.

14 Ibid. 188.

15 On James's appropriation for the modernist canon see Michael Anesko, *'Friction with the Market': Henry James and the Profession of Authorship* (New York and Oxford: Oxford University Press, 1986) 6. On Conrad's conflicted relationship to the market, see for example Mark Wollager, 'Killing Stevie: Modernity, Modernism, and Mastery in Conrad and Hitchcock', *Modern*

Language Quarterly 58.3 (1997) 323–50.

16 'Modernism and Cultural Theory' in Raymond Williams, *The Politics of Modernism*, edited and introduced by Tony Pinkney (London: Verso, 1989) 1–29 (20). Pinkney is describing the British academy, but his remarks have, I believe, a more general application.

17 Jon Thompson, *Fiction, Crime and Empire: Clues to Modernity and Postmodernism* (Urbana and Chicago: University of Illinois Press, 1993) 114.

18 Thomas Strychacz, *Modernism, Mass Culture and Professionalism* (Cambridge: Cambridge University Press, 1993).

19 Marianna Torgovnick, *Gone Primitive: Savage Intellects, Modern Lives* (Chicago: Chicago University Press, 1990) 8.

20 Torgovnick's *Gone Primitive* provides a good introduction to the different strands of modernist primitivism. See especially sections 2 and 3. On Eliot's use of primitivism see also Crawford, *The Savage and the City*.

21 See Michael Bell, *Primitivism* (London: Methuen, 1972) 32–55 and Torgovnick, *Gone Primitive* 159–74 on Lawrence. Bell points out that Lawrence's use of primitivism is quite different to the more self-conscious and distanced use of primitive motifs in, for example, T. S. Eliot. Eliot quite evidently does not wish for a return to prerational mode of thinking like Lawrence's 'blood-consciousness'.

22 See Michel Foucault, 'Of Other Spaces', trans. Jay Miskowiev, *Diacritics* 16.1 (1986) 22–7.

23 Ibid. 24.

24 William F. Dennehy, *Record: The Irish International Exhibition, 1907* (Dublin: Hely's, 1909) 34. For a description of the opening and an outline of the attractions, see the *Irish Times* for 4 May and 6 May 1907.

25 'The Great White Fair in Dublin: How there has arisen on the Site of the Old Donnybrook Fair a Great Exhibition as Typical of the New Ireland as the Former Festival as of the Ireland of the Past', *The World's Work* vol. 9 (May 1907) 570–6 (570–1). A similar reverence for modernization informs Stoker's essay in the same volume on the Harland and Wolff ship-building yard in Belfast, where he sees natural disadvantages of location overcome by 'the perfection of business organization'.

26 Ibid. 573.

27 'Pioneering on the West Coast', by 'Pat', *The World's Work* vol. 9 (May 1907) 630–3.

28 *Irish Times*, 9 May 1907, 6.

29 Ann Saddlemyer, ed., *Letters to Molly: John Millington Synge to Máire O'Neill 1906–1909* (Cambridge, MA: Belknap Press of Harvard University Press, 1971) 132–3.

30 According to Synge, in the keen 'the inner consciousness of the people seems to lay itself bare for an instant, and to reveal the mood of beings who feel their isolation in the face of a universe that wars on them with winds and seas'. See *The Aran Islands*, in *Collected Works* vol. 2, *Prose*, ed. Alan Price (London: Oxford University Press, 1966) 75. That the keen could be a

personal form rather than, or as well as, an expression of popular consciousness is evident from Eibhlín Dhubh Ní Chonaill's famous lament for her
husband, *Caoineadh Airt Uí Laoghaire* (1773).

31 John Wilson Foster offers a nuanced introduction to the issue of the
relations between international modernism and the Irish Literary Revival
in *Colonial Consequences: Essays in Irish Literature and Culture* (Dublin: Lilliput,
1991) 44–59. See also Terry Eagleton, *Heathcliff and the Great Hunger: Studies in
Irish Culture* (London and New York: Verso, 1995) ch. 7.

32 In their hostility to the influx of foreign 'garbage' into Ireland the Gaelic
League were considerably more vocal than the Irish Literary Theatre
group. See, for example, Douglas Hyde's animadversions against 'penny
dreadfuls, shilling shockers, and still more the garbage of vulgar English
weeklies like *Bow Bells* and the *Police Intelligence*' in his essay, 'The Necessity
of De-Anglicizing Ireland' in Mark Storey, ed., *Poetry and Ireland Since 1800: A
Sourcebook* (London: Routledge, 1988).

33 Quoted in David H. Greene and Edward M. Stephens, *J. M. Synge:
1871–1909*, revised edition (New York and London: New York University
Press, 1989) 200. I have drawn heavily on this work for the biographical
materials that follow.

34 Quoted in Greene and Stephens, *J. M. Synge* 283.

35 Cf. Eagleton, *Heathcliff and the Great Hunger* 302–3 and ch. 7 *passim*.

36 David Cairns and Shaun Richards, *Writing Ireland: Colonialism, Nationalism
and Culture* (Manchester: Manchester University Press, 1985) 72–3.

37 On the figure of the peasant in the culture wars of the late nineteenth and
early twentieth century, see Edward Hirsch, 'The Imaginary Irish Peasant',
PMLA 106 (October 1991) 1116–33. 'Because the Protestant intellectuals did
not see the peasant as a figure out of their own immediate or historical past,
they had no trouble preserving the rural archetype as pagan and primitive
rather than as fundamentally Catholic' (1122). This is not to say that the
peasant figures they invoked were in all respects identical. Hirsch notes that
the spirituality of Yeats's peasants is quite different to the earthiness of
Synge's. Although Joyce tried to leave behind the romanticized vision of the
peasant of the Revival *and* of the Irish nationalist camp both, he himself
represents the west of Ireland as a more 'primitive' place in 'The Dead'
(1127).

38 See Greene and Stephens, *J. M. Synge* 5.

39 Ibid. 66.

40 David M. Kiely, *John Millington Synge: A Biography* (Dublin: Gill and Macmillan, 1994) 17. Yeats's reference to a 'life that had never found expression'
should also be taken with a grain of salt. Even if we ignore the islanders'
own storytelling tradition Emily Lawless had written a novel set in the
islands, *Grania: The Story of an Island* (1892). Synge read the novel before
visiting the islands, and enjoyed it while feeling that it did not capture 'the
real Aran spirit'. See Greene and Stephens, *J. M. Synge* 95.

41 On the question of the influence of Le Braz and Loti on Synge see Nicholas

Grene, *Synge: A Critical Study of the Plays*, revised edition (Basingstoke: Macmillan, 1985) 21–2.

42 An irony not lost upon his staunchly unionist mother, who decided that she would support him at home, but would give him no more money 'to go and live in Paris idle'. Quoted in Greene and Stephens, *J. M. Synge* 68.

43 Quoted in ibid. 68.

44 David Greene suggests that Synge possibly exaggerated the primitive aspects of island life while downplaying aspects that did not interest him – the role of religion, for example. See *J. M. Synge* 94.

45 *The Aran Islands*, in *Collected Works* vol. 2, 53. Subsequent references are given in the text.

46 It is interesting to note that at this moment World Standard Time was close to becoming a reality, though still several years away at the time of Synge's gift. France, for example, still had numerous unstandardized local times up to 1891. Local times did not really get their death-blow until 1913. In that year World Standard Time became a real possibility when time signals were broadcast around the world by radio from the Eiffel Tower. See Kern, *The Culture of Time and Space 1880–1918* (Cambridge, MA: Harvard University Press, 1983) 12, 13.

47 On the question of the accuracy of this description see Grene, *Synge* 30.

48 Synge doesn't seem to notice that the islands have a clearly defined sexual division of labour. In part because of this, very few of the island women could speak English. As we shall see below, though, it is an island woman whom he presents as a sort of natural artist in *Riders to the Sea*.

49 Interestingly, *Riders* was a favourite of quite a different Irish modernist, James Joyce, not otherwise known for his love of the Literary Revival, and it was one of the plays which Joyce put on with the English Players in Zurich during the First World War, Nora taking one of the smaller parts. Joyce had earlier translated the play into Italian, and had even memorized some of Maurya's speeches. He was himself to rework Synge's thematics of death and return in the west of Ireland in 'The Dead'. See Richard Ellmann, *James Joyce, New and Revised Edition* (New York: Oxford University Press, 1983) 440–1, 124.

50 *The Complete Plays of John M. Synge* (New York: Vintage Books, n.d.) 93. Subsequent references are given in the text.

51 On Synge's use of his island materials for the purposes of tragedy see Grene, *Synge* 41–59.

52 Greene and Stephens, *J. M. Synge* 151.

53 *Capital*, trans. Ben Fowkes (Harmondsworth: Penguin, 1982) vol. 1, 163–4. See above, chapter 3.

54 Ann Saddleymer, ed., *The Collected Letters of John Millington Synge* vol. 1 *1971–1907* (Oxford: Clarendon Press, 1983) 78n.

55 Quoted in Saddlemyer, ed., *Collected Letters* 79n.

56 The topos of the weaver, or sempstress, or knitter as writer is of course as old as the *Odyssey*. Nineteenth-century reinventions of the motif appear in

texts as different as *The Scarlet Letter* and *The Lady of Shalott*. More recently, Salman Rushdie has revived it in *Shame*.

57 *The Condition of Postmodernity: An Inquiry into the Origin of Cultural Change* (Cambridge, MA, and London: Blackwell, 1990) 22. Of course in some cases the road to uniqueness lay through the extinction of idiosyncratic authorial traces on the work rather than through any more obvious foster-ing of authorial style. Thus despite the 'poetics of impersonality' of Eliot, his poetry everywhere announces itself as distinctly Eliotic.

58 cf. Eagleton's comment that the 'loneliness of the disinherited intellectual finds its echo in the collective isolation of peasant life, but discovers there too a community which might compensate for it' (*Heathcliff and the Great Hunger* 312).

59 For a view critical of the tendency to see Christy purely as an artist figure see Grene, *Synge* 135–6.

60 cf. Eagleton, *Heathcliff and the Great Hunger* 269–70 on the modernist fantasy of language as an alternative homeland.

61 James R. Mellow, *Hemingway: A Life Without Consequences* (London: Hodder and Stoughton, 1993) 283.

62 James Fenton, ed., *Ernest Hemingway: The Collected Stories* (London: Every-man, 1995) 770–771. See Mellow, *Hemingway* 92–3 on the early attempts to write for the *Saturday Evening Post* and *Red Book*.

63 cf. Jeffrey Meyers in his Introduction to *Hemingway: the Critical Heritage* (London: Routledge, 1982), claims that 'the stylistic influence of Ring Lardner, [Sherwood] Anderson and Stein has been much discussed and vastly over-rated' (5).

64 See Thomas Strychacz, '*In Our Time*, Out of Season', in Scott Donaldson, ed., *The Cambridge Companion to Ernest Hemingway* (Cambridge: Cambridge University Press, 1996) 55–86 (58).

65 For a nuanced account of the various ways in which modernist art drew on African and Oceanic artifacts, as well as on more local 'primitive' materials, see Charles Harrison, Francis Frascina and Gill Perry, *Primitivism, Cubism, Abstraction: The Early Twentieth Century* (New Haven and London: Yale University Press, 1993).

66 Quoted in Phyllis Rose, *Jazz Cleopatra: Josephine Baker in her Time* (London: Chatto and Windus, 1990).

67 See Anne Chisholm, *Nancy Cunard* (London: Sidgwick and Jackson, 1979) 101, 104.

68 Cunard was by no means the only promulgator of black culture in Europe in the 1920s of course; rather she is a well-known example of a more general process. For example, in July 1922 readers of the avant-garde *Broom* would have found reviews of *The Book of American Negro Poetry* and Claude Mackay's *Harlem Shadows* alongside contributions by Fernand Leger, e.e. cummings, Pablo Picasso, Paul Eluard and Pirandello.

69 See Greil Marcus, *Lipstick Traces: A Secret History of the Twentieth Century* (London: Secker and Warburg, 1990) 218–21.

70 While Lewis and Hemingway were united in their dislike of Anderson's primitivism, Lewis would later turn on Hemingway's own writing, accusing him in 'Ernest Hemingway: The "Dumb Ox"' in *Men Without Art* (1934) of deriving his style from Gertrude Stein's 'baby talk', and of creating protagonists who were as passive as oxen. Hemingway would retaliate in *A Moveable Feast* (1936) by describing Lewis as having the eyes of an 'unsuccessful rapist'.

71 Review published in *The New Republic* (November 1925), reproduced in *Hemingway, the Critical Heritage* 67–9.

72 *The Torrents of Spring* (1926: London: Arrow, 1994) 57.

73 Manuscript cited in Mellow, *Hemingway* 172. Nick Adams is equally dismissive of 'skyscraper primitives' in the original version of 'Big Two-Hearted River'.

74 *Broom* 1.1 (November 1921) 76.

75 *Broom* 2.2 (December 1921) 192.

76 *The Short Stories of Ernest Hemingway* (New York: Scribner's, 1966) 215.

77 Eliot, of course, had his own version of primitivism, in which the city appears as jungle as well as wasteland, for example in his Sweeney poems. In Eliot's unpublished 'King Bolo and his Big Black Queen' poems, Bolo is a rakish man about town, but also ruler over a tribe of ' "some primitive people called the Bolovians" '. See Crawford, *The Savage and the City in the Works of T. S. Eliot* 83 *et passim*.

78 As Jeffrey Meyers notes with disapproval, 'On his second African safari in 1954 Hemingway moved from primitivism to primitive. Though going native was especially frowned upon during the Mau-Mau emergency, he shaved his head, hunted with a spear, dyed his clothes the rusty Masai color, and began an elaborate courtship of his African "fiancée" '. See Jeffrey Meyers, *Hemingway: A Biography* (New York: Harper and Row, 1985) 502. See also Mellow, *Hemingway* 585. Mellow notes that Hemingway's nick-name in *The Green Hills of Africa*, B'wana M'Kumba, is close enough to Macomber (446). cf. Graham Dawson, *Soldier Heroes: British Adventure, Empire and the Imagining of Masculinities* (London and New York: Routledge, 1994) 172–3, and 184 on modernism and the attractions of otherness.

79 Richards, *The Commodity Culture of Victorian England: Advertising and Spectacle, 1851–1914* (Stanford: Stanford University Press, 1991) 126.

80 See Arjun Appadurai, ed., *The Social Life of Things* (Cambridge: Cambridge University Press, 1986) 73–7.

81 *Fiesta* (1927; London: Grafton, 1988) 104–5.

82 On the modernist equation of mass culture and the feminine see Huyssen, *After the Great Divide* 44–62.

83 In his biography of Hemingway Mellow identifies the model for Mrs Macomber as Jane Mason, a wealthy friend of the Hemingways, who had endorsed cosmetic products.

84 Kipling makes this same equation between female sexuality and advertising

culture in 'Wireless', where the consumptive pharmacist's assistant is in love with a well-fed young woman who closely resembles a figure from an advertisement in the shop's window display. Fritz Leiber's 'The Girl with the Hungry Eyes' (1949) is an interesting example of a later and more explicit treatment of the same theme.

85 For a reproduction of this 1952 advertisement see Robert Scholes and Nancy R. Comley, *The Practice of Reading*, 2nd edition (New York: St Martin's, 1985) 80. Under the heading, 'How would you put a glass of Ballantine Ale into words?' there is a Hemingway testimonial to the pleasures of the product which contains echoes of Jake's account of the fishing at Burguete: 'Bob Benchley first introduced me to Ballantine Ale. It has been a good companion ever since. You have to work hard to deserve to drink it. But I would rather have a bottle of Ballantine Ale than any other drink after fighting a really big fish . . . And you ought to taste it on a hot day when you have worked a big marlin fast because there were sharks after him. You are tired all the way through . . .'

86 *The Collected Stories* 629–70.
87 James Fenton, Introduction to *Collected Stories* xx.
88 See David Simpson's *Fetishism and Imagination: Dickens, Melville, Conrad* (Baltimore and London: Johns Hopkins University Press, 1982) on the history of the term fetishism in literary theory from the Romantics on.
89 See *Selected Poems and Prefaces by William Wordsworth*, Jack Stillinger ed. (Boston: Houghton Mifflin, 1965) 447.
90 Hugh Kenner, *The Mechanic Muse* (New York and Oxford: Oxford University Press, 1987) 115–31 (117).
91 *Mythologies* (New York: Hill and Wang, 1972) 145.
92 Ibid. 146.
93 Fredric Jameson, *Marxism and Form* (Princeton: Princeton University Press, 1971) 409.
94 Ibid. 412.

AFTERWORD: THE LONG GOODBYE

1 It is possible to overstate the lack of continuity between the *fin-de-siècle* mummy and the later versions. After all, there *are* vengeful mummy narratives from the period 1880–1914, as in Conan Doyle's 'Lot 249' (1892), Guy Boothby's *Pharos the Egyptian* (1899), and Ambrose Pratt's *The Living Mummy* (1910). It is not until 1971 that film returns to *fin-de-siècle* fiction for inspiration, in the Hammer horror film, *Blood from the Mummy's Tomb*, based on Bram Stoker's *The Jewel of Seven Stars*.
2 W. T. Stead published *She* in 1903 as the first volume in his Penny Novels series, and before long sold half a million copies. See D. S. Higgins, *Rider Haggard: The Great Storyteller* (London: Cassell, 1981) 187. But even much later cheap editions continued to sell well, if less dramatically. According to Higgins 52,886 copies of Haggard's books sold in cheap editions between

October 1921 and the end of March 1922 (*The Great Storyteller* 238). On the Sanders stories see Robert H. MacDonald, *The Language of Empire: Myths and Metaphors of Popular Imperialism, 1880–1918* (Manchester: Manchester University Press, 1994) ch. 7.

3 Kipling's *Toomai of the Elephants* only reached the screen the year after Kipling's death as *Elephant Boy* (1937). Hollywood paid handsomely for the film rights to Conrad's *Victory*, *Lord Jim* and *Nostromo*. See Cedric Watts, 'Marketing Modernism: How Conrad Prospered', in Ian Willison, Warwick Gould and Warren Cherniak, eds., *Modernist Writers and the Marketplace* (Basingstoke: Macmillan, 1996) 81–8 (86).

4 See for example John MacKenzie, *Propaganda and Empire: The Manipulation of British Public Opinion, 1880–1960* (Manchester: Manchester University Press, 1984) ch. 3. The early film industry also contributed to empire through geographical films as well as through adapted adventure romances. As a French critic noted in 1912, 'One indisputable advantage of the geographical film, is that it helps link the colonies to the mother country. It shows us all the outlets offered to French enterprise by our vast overseas possessions . . . The cinema will be the best emigration agency of the future.' Quoted in Noël Burch, *Life to Those Shadows* (London: British Film Institute, 1990) 53. For a wide-ranging survey of the role of the cinema in fostering an imperial imaginary, see Ella Shohat, 'Gender and the Culture of Empire: Toward a Feminist Ethnography of the Cinema', *Quarterly Review of Film and Video* 13.1–3 (1991) 45–84.

5 Higgins, *Rider Haggard* 224.

6 Ibid. 239. Theda Bara (1890–1955) was the original screen 'vamp', and appeared in quite a few adaptations of Victorian novels, including *Lady Audley's Secret*, *East Lynne* and *Under Two Flags*.

7 *Halliwell's Filmgoer's Companion*, 8th edition (London: Paladin, 1987) 928. Among the other Haggard works taken up by the nascent film industry were *The World's Desire*, co-written with Andrew Lang, filmed in 1915, and *Dawn*, filmed in 1917.

8 David J. Skal, *Hollywood Gothic: The Tangled Web of Dracula from Novel to Stage to Screen* (London: André Deutsch, 1992) 99.

9 Ibid. 191.

10 *Bond and Beyond: The Political Career of a Popular Hero* (London: Methuen, 1986) 14.

11 A full discussion of the cinematic adventures of romance tropes is outside the scope of this study. David Skal has recently charted the new meanings that accreted around the more morbid strains of Victorian romance in *The Monster Show: A Cultural History of Horror* (New York and London: Penguin, 1994).

12 See Richard Hardin, 'The Man who wrote *The Blue Lagoon*: Stacpoole's Pastoral Center', *ELT* 39.2 (1996) 204–20 on the novel's links to the contemporary vogue of anthropology associated with Andrew Lang and E. B. Tylor, *inter alia*.

13 Perhaps more surprisingly, Du Maurier's largely forgotten *Peter Ibbetson* has been adapted twice, as *Forever* (1921), which deals with the events of the protagonist's childhood, and *Peter Ibbetson* (1935) with Gary Cooper.

14 Sources consulted in compiling this list of novels-to-screen adaptations included Halliwell's *Filmgoer's Companion* and *Film Guide* (London: Paladin, 1986), Rachael Low and Roger Manvell's *History of the British Cinema* vol. 1, 1896–1906, vol. 2, 1906–1914 and vol. 3, 1914–18 (London: Allen and Unwin, 1973), and Rachael Low's vol. 4, 1918–29 (London: Allen and Unwin, 1971), as well as the extremely useful International Movie Database Web Site.

15 Both novels, of course, owe a good deal to Ouida's earlier desert melodrama, *Under Two Flags*.

16 On Lawrence as a modern 'star' see Dawson, *Soldier Heroes* 194–5.

17 Ibid. 189–90. Kipling's *Kim*, of course, is another source for this narrative strain.

18 Since Buchan's novel appeared in 1915 it is very much on the borderline of the period under consideration. Certainly Michael Denning in *Cover Stories: Narrative and Ideology in the British Spy Thriller* (London and New York: Routledge and Kegan Paul, 1987) makes a case for it as a forerunner of a new subgenre, the spy novel. He also points out, though, that this new genre maintains a high degree of continuity with the popular adventure novels that preceded it. Dawson (*Soldier Heroes* 189) notes that Buchan's *Greenmantle* (1917) and its successors are closely tied to Lawrence's career.

19 See his introduction to the Oxford University Press edition of Ouida's *Under Two Flags*.

20 See Raymond Williams, 'The Technology and the Society', in Tony Bennett, ed., *Popular Fiction: Technology, Ideology, Production, Fiction* (London and New York: Routledge, 1990) 9–22.

21 Siegfried Giedion, *Mechanization Takes Command: A Contribution to Anonymous History* (New York and London: Norton, c. 1975) 3. Jonathan Crary in *Techniques of the Observer: On Vision and Modernity in the Nineteenth Century* (Cambridge, MA, and London: MIT Press, 1991) makes a similar point to Giedion's: 'technology is always a concomitant or subordinate part of other forces. For Gilles Deleuze, 'A society is defined by its amalgamations, not by its tools . . . tools exist only in relation to the interminglings they make possible' (8). For Donna Haraway, 'Machines are time slices into the social organism that made them.' See Nicholas Dirks, Geoff Eley and Sherry B. Ortner, eds., *Culture/Power/History: A Reader in Contemporary Social History* (Princeton: Princeton University Press, 1994) 82.

22 *The Last Machine: Early Cinema and the Birth of the Modern World* (London: BFI, 1994) 27. Cf. Anne Friedberg, *Window Shopping: Cinema and the Postmodern* (Berkeley and Los Angeles: University of California Press, c.1993) on the development of a 'mobile and virtual gaze' in the nineteenth century before the advent of cinema linked to the consumer culture and new transporta-

tion technologies.

23 Christie, *The Last Machine* 30; see also Friedberg, *Window Shopping* 90–4, 104–6.

24 Friedberg, *Window Shopping* 94.

25 Christie, *The Last Machine* 31.

26 Ibid. 132. On the cinema as a dream-like experience see Michael Chanan, *The Dream that Kicks: The Prehistory and Early Years of Cinema in Britain*, 2nd edition (London and New York: Routledge, 1996) 41–2, and 265–72.

27 Cited in Kathleen L. Spencer, 'Purity and Danger: *Dracula*, the Urban Gothic, and the Late Victorian Degeneracy Crisis', *ELH* 59 (1992) 197–225 (202).

28 R. L. Stevenson, 'A Gossip on Romance', *Longman's Magazine* 1 (November 1882) 69–79 (72).

29 George Du Maurier, *Peter Ibbetson* (1892; New York: Harper and Bros., 1919) 215–16. Subsequent references are given in the text.

30 D. A. Miller remarks in *The Novel and the Police* (Berkeley: University of California Press, 1988) that 'the liberal/carceral opposition is the foundation of the liberal subject as well as the basis of the novel's own role in producing him' (220). The romances of the *fin de siècle* seem to place that liberal subject squarely in the domain of fantasy.

31 There are interesting resemblances between du Maurier's novel and Jules Verne's *Castle in the Carpathians* (1893), where the technology element is more to the fore, and in which 'a man shuts himself up in a lonely castle in order, night after night, to "project" for himself the perfect simulacrum of a loved woman singer who had died young but whose image and voice he had managed to capture with a marvellous machine while she was still alive.' See Burch, *Life to Those Shadows* 41n.

32 For the role of the novel in shaping privatized forms of subjectivity in the nineteenth century see Miller's *The Novel and the Police* and Lennard Davis, *Resisting Novels: Ideology and Fiction* (New York and London: Methuen, 1987).

33 On 'pseudo individuality' see John Cumming, trans., *Dialectic of Enlightenment* (New York: Continuum, 1991) 154–6.

34 Friedberg, *Window Shopping* 94.

35 On the spectacular aspect of early cinema see Tom Gunning, 'The Cinema of Attraction(s): Early Film, Its Spectator and the Avant-Garde', in Thomas Elsaesser, ed., *Early Cinema: Space, Frame, Narrative* (Bloomington: Indiana University Press, 1991) 56–62.

36 Burch, *Life to those Shadows*.

37 The 'phantom rides' appeared as soon as film makers realized the panoramic possibilities of mounting a camera on a moving vehicle, the train being the natural choice. Possibly the earliest of these films is the Lumières' *Leaving Jerusalem by Railway* (1896). As Christie records, '[W]ithin a few years, almost every exotic railway journey, from the Alps to the American West, had yielded its share of phantom rides' (*The Last Machine* 18). On the

shift in audience reaction see Burch, *Life to those Shadows* 39. Burch 35 and Chanan, *The Dream that Kicks* 238–9 point to the importance of travelogue films in the development of film.

38 Terry Eagleton, cited in Harvey, *The Condition of Postmodernity* 7.

39 See Marianna Torgovnick, *Gone Primitive: Savage Intellects, Modern Lives* (Chicago: Chicago University Press, 1990).

40 See Salman Rushdie's essay, 'Outside the Whale' in his *Imaginary Homelands: Essays and Criticism, 1981–1991* (London: Granta, 1991) for an acute commentary on the lingering imperial nostalgia for the Raj in British film and television.

41 For a full list of possible sources see Andrew Gordon, '*Raiders of the Lost Ark*: Totem and Taboo', *Extrapolation* 32.3 (1991) 256–67 (266n). *Raiders* and its first sequel, *Indiana Jones and the Temple of Doom* (1984), also rehearse motifs from a whole array of earlier imperial narratives, from *The Moonstone* to *The Yellow God*.

42 In this respect *Indiana Jones and the Temple of Doom* (1984) is an interesting departure, since it can at least imagine a powerful non-European enemy. With its references to Thugee and the Indian Mutiny this sequel offers a rather more anxious view of the blank spaces of the map.

43 The film has a rather tangled production and release history, which is discussed in detail by Rick Instrell in '*Blade Runner*: the Economic Shaping of the Film', in John Orr and Colin Nicholson, eds., *Cinema and Fiction: New Modes of Adapting, 1950–1990* (Edinburgh: Edinburgh University Press, 1992) 160–70. The analysis that follows is based on the 'director's cut' of the film, which differs in a number of respects from that originally released in cinemas.

44 These androids are not strictly speaking commodities on the open market: they appear to have been built by the Tyrell corporation for sale to the government for use as slave-labour in its off-world colonies. Some of the ads we hear in the film advertise other replicants for personal use by colonists: 'a loyal trouble-free companion given to you upon your arrival absolutely free. Use your new friend as a personal body-servant or a tireless field hand – the custom tailored genetically engineered humanoid replicant designed especially for your needs.' Quoted by William Kolb in '*Blade Runner* Film Notes', in Judith Kerman, ed., *Retrofitting 'Blade Runner': Issues in Ridley Scott's 'Blade Runner' and Philip K. Dick's 'Do Androids Dream of Electric Sheep?'* (Bowling Green, Ohio: Bowling Green University Popular Press, c.1991) 154–77 (155). There were originally six replicants, and one is supposed to have been killed entering the Tyrell building, so there should actually be five. The numerical error crept in as a result of last-minute script-changes during filming. See William Kolb, 'Script to Screen: *Blade Runner* in Perspective', in Kerman 132–53 (140).

45 See *Simians, Cyborgs, and Women: The Reinvention of Nature* (London: Free Association Press, 1990) 178, 149. See also David Harvey's reading of the film as a representation of the fragmented postmodern experience of time and space in *The Condition of Postmodernity* 308–23.

46 The last is identified by William M. Kolb (Kerman 155).

47 The off-planet origins (secondary origins anyway) of the replicants scarcely hide the fact that the economy described is essentially that of late capitalism. For the late twentieth-century US, off-planet may be taken to mean the 'invisible' third-world manufacturing bases of multi-national companies, as well as the equally invisible domestic sweat-shops of New York or Los Angeles.

48 That all the replicants are white, while the film's Los Angeles appears to be largely Asian, suggests that the film translates racial difference as well as people/commodities into the people/replicant opposition. On the replicants as signifiers of 'blackness' see Kaja Silverman, 'Back to the Future', *Camera Obscura* 27 (September 1991) 109–32 (114–15).

49 In a subsequent scene Deckard's superior, Bryant, mentions a replicant dead on the sidewalk rather than in a window display. This was originally Leon, not Zhora. See Kolb's 'Film Notes' (Kerman 164). We are reminded that the replicants returned to Earth because they wish to extend their shelf-life, the four-year life-span that the Tyrell corporation gives them as a failsafe device. The display contains Christmas goods because the action takes place in November 2019. The run-up to Christmas, a religious festival that has become a commercial feast is, of course, an appropriate setting for a film that deals with commodification.

50 For Anne Friedberg, '[F]rom the middle of the nineteenth century, as if in a historical relay of looks, the shop window succeeded the mirror as a site of identity construction, and then – gradually – the shop window was displaced and incorporated by the cinema screen.' *Window Shopping* 66.

51 Benjamin, *Reflections*, ed., Peter Demetz, trans. Edmund Jephcott (New York: Schocken, 1978) 153.

52 The ending of the director's cut of the film, in which we see a lift-door close on Rachael, just after Deckard has picked up Gaff's origami unicorn (see below) differs significantly from the cinema-release version, in which Deckard and Rachael appear to leave the rain and smog of Los Angeles for the clear air of the mountains – a sequence reputedly assembled from out-takes of Stanley Kubrick's *The Shining*. See Kolb, 'Script to Screen', Kerman 141 and Instrell, '*Blade Runner*' 164.

53 If Deckard is a replicant, he must be an earlier, punier version than the replicants he pursues, since they all appear to be more than his physical match.

54 This scene presumably derives from one in *The Big Sleep*, where Philip Marlowe pretends to be a rather effete collector of rare books to gain access to the Geiger bookstore, which is being used as a front for a pornography and blackmail business. On *Blade Runner*'s ties to the hard-boiled detective film see Leonard G. Heldreth, 'The Cutting Edges of *Blade Runner*', in Kerman 40–52.

55 Kaja Silverman claims that the film encourages us to view the difference between humans and replicants as purely ideological. See 'Back to the

Future' 111.

56 C. Michael Fisher, 'Of Living Machines and Living-Machines: *Blade Runner* and the Terminal Genre', *New Literary History* 20.1 (1988) 187–98 (196).

57 Silverman, 'Back to the Future' 125. On the film's use of still photographs see Elissa Marder, '*Blade Runner*'s Moving Still', *Camera Obscura* 27 (September 1991) 77–87.

58 See Thomas B. Byers, 'Commodity Futures: Corporate State and Personal Style in Three Recent Science-Fiction Movies', *Science Fiction Studies* 14 (1987) 326–39 (326).

Index